THE ONE AND ONLY

Peter Perrett - Homme Fatale

by

Nina Antonia

SAF Publishing Ltd

SAF Publishing Ltd

First published in 1996 by SAF Publishing Ltd.

SAF Publishing Ltd.
12 Conway Gardens,
Wembley, Middx. HA9 8TR
ENGLAND
TEL: 0181 904 6263
FAX: 0181 930 8565

ISBN 0 946719 160

Text copyright © Nina Antonia 1996

The right of Nina Antonia to be identified as the author of this work has been asserted by her in accordance with the Copyright, Design and Patents Act, 1988.

All rights reserved. No part of this publication may be reproduced, stored in a retrieval system, or transmitted in any form, or by any means, electronic, photocopying, recording or otherwise, without the prior permission of the publisher.

All lyrics © Complete Music Ltd., reprinted by kind permission.

A CIP catalogue record for this book is available from the British Library

Printed in England by Redwood Books, Trowbridge, Wiltshire.

Wholesale and Book Trade Distribution:
UK & Europe: Airlift Book Co, 8 The Arena, Mollison Ave, Enfield, Middx. EN3 7NJ Tel: 0181-804 0400   Fax: 0181-804 0044
USA: Last Gasp, 777 Florida Street, San Francisco, CA 94110. USA.
Tel: 415 824 6636 Fax: 415 824 1836
Canada: Marginal Distribution, Unit 103, 277 George Street North, Peterborough, Ontario, Canada K9J 3G9. Tel/Fax: 705 745 2326

The stars rise, the moon bends her arc,
Each glow-worm winks her spark,
Let us get home before the night grows dark:
For clouds may gather
Tho' this is summer weather,
Put out the lights and drench us thro';
Then if we lost our way what should we do?

(Extract from *The Goblin Market* by Christina Rossetti)

ACKNOWLEDGEMENTS

This book is dedicated to Peter and Zena Perrett. A large thank you to them for their time, patience and honesty. Also to the next generation — Peter Jnr and Jamie.

I am also greatly indebted to the other former members of The Only Ones:
John Perry for his concise appraisals and belief in the project.
Mike Kellie for the guidance and philosophy.
Alan Mair for his straight talk.

Many thanks to all the other interviewees who contributed their time and perished memories (in alphabetical order): Mick Atkins, David Clarke, Giovanni Dadamo, Koulla Kakoulli, Nick Kent, Adrian Maddox, Pete Makowski, Malcolm McLaren, Miyuki, Jon Newey, Jay Price, John Roberts, David Sandison, Judy Totton, Steven Ward, Henry Williams.

For their help in many different shapes and formats from the obscure to the obvious (in alphabetical order): David Arnoff, Andy from *On The Beat*, Rocking Bobby Benjamin, Steve Brickle, EDAS, Mick Fish, Scott Free, Dave Hallbery, Kanita, Dave Kusworth, Freddie Lynx, Dee Malone, Kumi Noro, Paul Du Noyer, Patti Palladin, Malcolm Sinclair, John and Bob Whitfield.

In a league of their own: My dear daughter Severina and Maria McCormack for her unstinting support and encouragement throughout the project.

In retrospect: To Johnny Thunders for making the introductions, a long, long time ago.

Photographic Acknowledgements

The Perretts' collection: 9, 11, 23 (both), 32, 45, 48, 59 (bottom), 152, 168, 184 (both)
David Arnoff: 171, 173 (both), 177, 180, 221
CBS: back cover, 104, 125, 138, Anton Corbijn/CBS: 161
Goodacre: 219 (bottom)
Alan Mair collection: 135, 149, 157
Jon Newey collection: 35, 38
Kumi Noro: front cover, 3, 6, 219 (top), 222
Patti Palladin collection: 111
John Whitfield: 59 (top), 63, 75, 87, 118

In the case of some photographs it has not proved possible to ascertain or trace original copyright holders, if the photographers concerned wish to contact the publisher a credit will be included in any future editions.

CONTENTS

Chapter 1 - Pale Sister Of The Night 7

Chapter 2 - Shapes In The Fire 19

Chapter 3 - Death Or Glory 29

Chapter 4 - The Turner Prize 43

Chapter 5 - The Sporting Life 57

Chapter 6 - Around & Around 71

Chapter 7 - The Wraith's Progress 83

Chapter 8 - The Late Show 101

Chapter 9 - Out Of Eden 115

Chapter 10 - Serpent's Kiss 131

Chapter 11 - Castle Built On Sand 147

Chapter 12 - Mourning Glory 165

Chapter 13- The Fall Of The House Of Perrett 183

Chapter 14 - Orpheus Ascending 195

Chapter 15 - Sticky Endings 211

CHAPTER 1 – Pale Sister of the Night

The rest of the world looked to the stars on that sultry July night in 1969, wrapped in the euphoria of science fiction becoming fact as Neil Armstrong bobbed about on the moon's pitted surface in an ungainly rumba. The young couple however, were rapt in the sweep of first love, oblivious to anything outside their romantic realm, especially President Nixon's overheated declaration that this was, 'The greatest week since the creation of the world'. It was only later in the afterglow, when the two ex-virgins disengaged — untangling legs, hair, lips — that the boy sat up in bed and whispered to his girl, 'Do you realise the Americans have just landed on the moon?' It had been one giant step for mankind and a giant leap into the unknown for Peter Perrett and Xenoulla Kakoulli.

For the moment they felt safe, unaware that Xenoulla's father Dimitris had not only alerted the entire Greek community to be on the look-out for the runaways, but was conducting his own door-to-door search. From congested Catford to the leafier glades of Forest Hill, Dimitris roared as he roamed, armed with a shotgun and a short-fuse temper.

It wasn't as though Peter's parents weren't equally distraught, just less dramatic. Greek tragedy clashing with polite English angst. University and hushed days spent in scholarly pursuit should have beckoned their only child, not the seductive embrace of a strange girl.

The boy's parents, Albert and Amelia, paced their neat, second-floor flat in the large Victorian house where the family had lived since moving from Brockley to Forest Hill in 1956. It had seemed like the right kind of area to bring up a child. To the Perretts, Forest Hill was a haven of hilly avenues free from the inner city claustrophobia that had begun to close in on the outskirts of their neighbourhood. Its fading gentility had appealed to Amelia, conjuring up phantom traces of a rose-tinted past where fine ladies sipped Earl Grey tea from bone china. Even if prosperity's dreams were on the decline, it still seemed a place for aspirations, and young Peter would wear the heavy crown of their expectations.

The investiture of baby Peter Albert Neil Perrett took place on April 8th, 1952 at King's College Hospital, Camberwell. After a difficult pregnancy, Peter's safe arrival was an answered prayer. The child that Albert and Amelia had waited for had finally made the mortal starting line — all his disembodied ghost brothers and sisters had fallen before him in a mournful progression of miscarriages. A black ribbon of misfortune threaded through the maternal lineage, stretching back to the gas chambers of World War II where most of Amelia's relatives met their tragic end. Amelia Leopoldina Fischer escaped to Vienna only to be incarcerated for the dubious crime of socialism. On release, the young woman and her first husband fled on a boat down the Danube, out of the Austrian Empire and bound for occupied Palestine. There Amelia met her second husband who was a terrorist, and though this marriage was also short-lived it produced one daughter, Edith.

It was against the harsh backdrop of the two thousand year old Middle East conflict that Amelia encountered Albert Perrett. Albert was an Englishman who, having joined the Palestine police force, had risen to become a chief prosecution officer. One of the last cases he tried before returning to London with Amelia was that of Tommy 'Just Like That' Cooper and the Opium Jukebox Case as it became known. The fez-wearing funny man and his wife (who turned King's evidence) were members of a troupe of travelling players who had been caught smuggling opium and hashish inside a jukebox.

The Britain where Mr and Mrs Perrett began their new life had also entered the jukebox age, although its use was not quite as nefarious as Tommy Cooper's Palestinian playlist. By the mid-50's no self-respecting coffee bar was without a Wurlitzer. Most of the sounds were black hits bleached for the white market, or the milkshake froth of Doris Day and Perry Como. Like a cleansing storm, the clouds of rock 'n' roll were gathering. It would be some time before the implications struck the insular Perrett residence, where a refined way of life had been cultivated by a mother who erred toward the snobbish and an upright and principled father. Albert Perrett was an idealistic man, like so many of his generation possessed of an almost utopian belief in the power of education. Knowledge was the golden gift he would give to his son. His own ambitions had been foiled by economic necessity. Unable to continue legal training in England, where he hoped to practise, Albert and his brother set up a firm of building contractors, Elf & Sons. The rest of Mr

Right: Albert and Amelia Perrett on holiday, just after the birth of Peter.

Perrett's time was dedicated to nurturing his prodigious child. While other boys mangled toys and grazed their knees, Peter Perrett enjoyed a quiet game of chess. Peter:

> "My father came from South London, from a working class family. He wasn't allowed to read books, if his father caught him, he would beat him. At the age of 13 he was supporting his parents and six brothers and sisters. He had about four jobs. He was self-educated and because of that, education was very important to him. My father educated me up until the age of five when I went to Holy Trinity primary school. At the age of four I knew all my times tables, I could do simple algebra and I could play chess.

My father took me to a psychologist to have an IQ test. Later he told me that it was immeasurable, close to 200. I was really into maths, I found it fun at that age, then I went to Holy Trinity. I was put a year ahead so I was with older kids, which meant that I had to repeat the last year of primary school because I wasn't old enough to go to secondary school. I stayed and did the year again and that's when I started being naughty. I used to correct the teachers when they got things wrong. I was bored by it."

Just a bus ride away, young Xenoulla was too exhausted to have made the acquaintance of monotony. Zena:

"I come from a large Greek Cypriot immigrant family. I came to England when I was three, we settled in South East London and eventually moved to a house in Catford. I was the oldest of a family of eight children including myself. Most of my childhood was spent being like a mother. I didn't really have a childhood, it was mainly bringing up kids and doing housework. By the time I was eight, I was earning money from making clothes for dolls. I missed quite a lot of my primary school years 'cos I was staying at home looking after babies to help my mother, Loulla. She used to work in the day and she had an evening job as well."

Xenoulla and Peter may have seemed as dissimilar as a tower block to an ivory tower but they would meet in the middle on a bridge marked escape. For all the apparent niceties of Peter Perrett's background, a cotton-wool neurosis took the place of clear affection between mother and son. Albert was ready to cut the apron strings once Peter had taken his eleven plus.

Peter's excellent results were rewarded by a scholarship. Mr Perrett's decision to send his son to Bancroft's boarding school in Woodford Green, Essex, was intended to be a privilege and not the punishment Peter took it as. The English myth of character building via the public school system was laid on already insecure foundations. Thin-skinned and supernaturally attractive for a boy, Peter suffered under a bully's regime where brutality was the team badge and sensitivity the bait, until he learned to run with the pack. Peter:

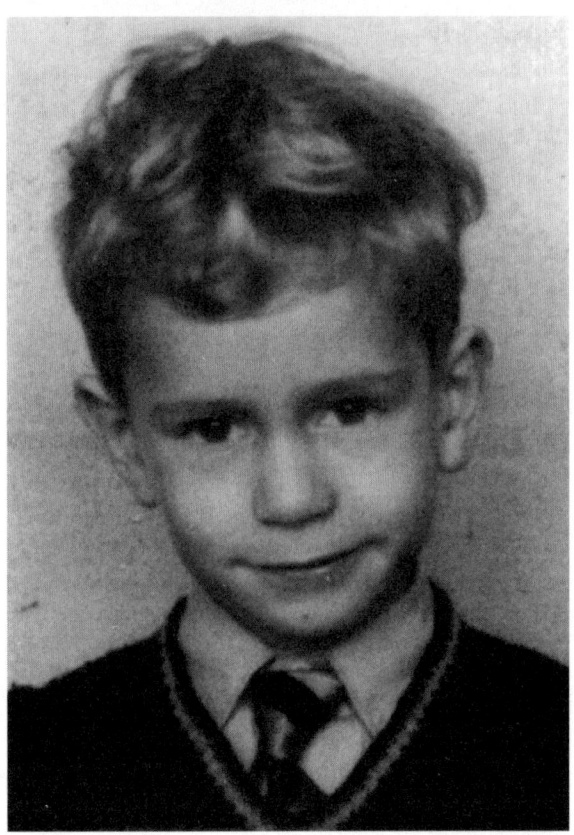

Right: Portrait of a budding disruptive influence. Peter Perrett, aged 7.

"I was really unhappy there, I couldn't understand why they'd sent me away and that's when I started getting into lots of trouble. The first year I got beaten up every single day. The prefects were allowed to cane you and the older boys would beat you up. As soon as I entered the second year, I started beating up the younger boys. Once I got into the third year I realised I wasn't into that."

With the milky tenderness of the child who tries, Peter fuelled his father's dreams with a feigned interest in becoming a scientist, when in truth the only goal he aspired to was on a football field. By the time he reached his early teens, the pout turned into a scowl and Peter was ready to drop a personal H-bomb — not only on his parents' hopes but on everyone representing authority. While he grew his hazel locks over his collar, the allure of music and its associated rebel tendencies displaced sport as his abiding passion. He carried his 45's like a fledgling pop

THE ONE AND ONLY: Peter Perrett - Homme Fatale

assassin with a vinyl armoury of The Beatles, Yardbirds, Kinks and Stones.

In common with those other pretty boys Marc Bolan and David Bowie, who would also go on to wrap 'Sarf London' identities around their vocal chords, Peter began the flowering of his style in the narcissistic threads of Mod. By 15, learning to smoke and ride a scooter were the only subjects Peter studied. The academic halo had not just slipped, it was deliberately thrown away. After resoundingly poor examination results, Bancroft's saw fit to expel Master Perrett, marking his file "Disruptive Influence". Peter:

> "In a way I'd lost my childhood. Going to public school was a total void. I only took six 'O' levels because I was stopped from taking chemistry, physics, history and maths. I'd been barred from those subjects. I wasn't allowed into the physics class because I'd get up on the desk and start singing Small Faces' songs in the middle of a lesson. I lit a fire in a desk during maths and was banned from history as punishment for refusing to take part in a rugby match. I was a very angry young man. I had a lot of violence inside of me. I thought learning was a total waste of time."

The shimmering summer of '67 was a fine time to face expulsion. Peter, whose hair was even longer now, progressed from Mod to hippy to greet the psychedelic dawn. Wandering into Covent Garden, he joined the glittering stream of flower children in their diaphanous attire of Indian silks and Portobello Market make-believe, searching for the Electric Garden before it blossomed into Middle Earth. Peter spent the summer months in a swirling dayglo pageant of events, his large green eyes flickering like strobes, set off against nightclub light shows. He blotted out parental warnings with the full throttle of Pink Floyd's "Interstellar Overdrive". Peter:

> "Out of the English groups that there were around to see in '67, Pink Floyd were the best. Sometimes the whole set would just be two half-hour instrumentals and quite often Syd wouldn't show up. I went specifically to see them at the Windsor National Jazz and Blues Festival and they announced that he hadn't turned up. It was such a fucking let down."

For Peter, Pink Floyd without Syd Barrett was akin to a dark mine without diamonds. When the audience were told that Floyd were unable to appear and in their place — 'Would you please give a big welcome to former Manfred Mann frontman Paul Jones!' — there wasn't the sound of even one hand clapping.

However, Peter did attend the Freak Community's coming out ball — the 14-hour Technicolour Dream — held in Alexandra Palace. Between 7,000 and 10,000 crazy daisies and dandies traipsed into the vast glass pavilion, paying one guinea per person in aid of the financially beleaguered underground paper *International Times* (IT). As records of attendance vary, it is reasonable to assume that any serious attempt at a head count was a stoned affair. Brian Jones was rumoured to be there, slumped in Moroccan robes. John Lennon arrived in an Afghan coat and granny glasses. A rainbow of lights and music turned Ally Pally into a throbbing kaleidoscopic bauble. As the moon made way for the sun, Pink Floyd took to the stage but Barrett was out of orbit — even the white Stratocaster hanging limply around his neck failed to anchor him. Poor beautiful Syd. The psychedelic conjurer and co-founder of Floyd was permanently out to acid lunch and very soon he would be out of the band. Syd Barrett's sanity had faded along with the summer.

Autumn term began with Peter enrolled in the quaintly titled Haberdashers' Askes school in Hatcham. The former guild-funded independent day school with its prestigious reputation had no idea they had taken on such a totally unearthed live wire. Ex-pupil Steve Nice (later to become Steve Harley of Cockney Rebel) recalls Peter as being "moody". It is doubtful if the staff remember Perrett quite so fondly after he flagrantly violated the school motto — 'Serve and Obey'. Peter:

> "I was there for four terms. At the end of each term, the headmaster brought me and my dad in and said unless I changed I would be expelled. I was very juvenile for my age, I'd make stupid noises in class and sing songs like Arthur Brown's "I am the God of Hell Fire!" I started thinking of myself as a communist and an anarchist. I didn't know what either of them were but I thought they sounded good.
>
> There was this thing called an UCCA form which you filled in to apply for University, but they didn't want me to put in for it because they wanted me to do an 'S' level, which is an exam for going on to

Oxford or Cambridge. But after the fourth term, I attacked a teacher with an umbrella. It was a stupid thing to do because he was really nice. I could never understand why I did things. I was expelled in the Christmas term. I was meant to go on to Norwood Technical College to finish my 'A' levels."

In every neighbourhood, kids select their peers with psychic antennae and dress code clues. In '69 the division between hippy and straight was obvious on sight, but connecting with a clique that shared your own musical wavelength took fine tuning. With January's icy breath at his back, Peter infiltrated the South East London scene; it would prove to be a most pivotal move in his early creative development. Peter had recently found a personal catalyst in the form of Bob Dylan. Ardently seeking further information on the American singer, Perrett caught whispers of a Dylan bootleg that was circulating amongst local hipsters and he set out to trace the source. Peter:

"Eventually someone told me who the guy was that had the bootleg, his name was John Whitfield and he played piano in a school band. I saw him in the street one day, went up to him and asked him about it. Zena was with him, that was the first time I ever met her. I was 16 and she was 18."

Zena:

"One day when John and I were walking up the the hill, this young guy came along. He had long straight hair and these full lips, he just looked like a skinny Jim Morrison. He totally ignored me 'cos I looked like a school girl, and came up to John Whitfield and asked him if he had any Bob Dylan bootlegs. That's how I met Peter Perrett. He ended up walking back with us to John's flat, where John played keyboards and I'd sing. Peter and I got talking 'cos I was the first girl he'd met who was into Dylan."

Peter may have been the one responsible for pruning Xenoulla's rolling name into a more streamlined form, but it was Zena who altered the course of their destiny. While the tight reins of family duty still bound Zena, over the years she had learned to manouevre within them. A series of twists in the Kakoulli's story had also allowed a little slack.

The first and most dramatic occurred just days before Mrs Kakoulli gave birth to her last child. When a severe headache was diagnosed as a tumour, Loulla Kakoulli was rushed to hospital where she had a healthy baby girl called Koulla, before slipping into a coma. Loulla was discharged nine months later following successful surgery. A casual observer might have thought the household reverted to normal on her return. Under closer scrutiny the emotional landscape between Mr and Mrs Kakoulli had improved greatly. Realising that he had nearly lost his wife, Dimitris dropped his latest mistress, a teenage cousin, and repented of his roving ways. His temper was still hotter than August in Athens but he began to treat Loulla with affection and respect, much to the pleased astonishment of his offspring.

Life would never become a Mediterranean version of The Waltons but the unexpected arrival of two previously unknown teenage brothers, Kallis and Dino, from their mother's first marriage considerably enlarged Zena's horizons. Although Kallis went back to Cyprus once his mother was on the mend, 16 year old Dino stayed. Zena:

> "My brother moved in. He was really into music and playing bass guitar. I was very influenced by him. I bought an acoustic guitar just before I went to secondary school. The first music I'd heard was Elvis which didn't do anything for me, but at the age of 11 I came across Dylan and that totally changed my life. That became my escape. I also liked the blues and would listen to Bessie Smith, I could relate to it. I used to sing along and play the guitar to myself. I was fanatical about it. My mother would call out, 'Xenoulla stop that singing, have you done the house work yet?' Then my younger brother Harry started to get into it and I taught him to play the guitar as well. Dino moved out after two years but he left behind the seeds of his music."

Even the furthest corners of suburbia had felt the impact of pop and protest culture from swinging London, and all of it lay just beyond Zena's front door. Her break came when Mrs Kakoulli took a late shift in a biscuit factory. In the gap between her mother leaving and Dimitris returning from work, Zena suddenly found a couple of hours grace. In these precious hours she met with others sharing a similar climate of mind. Zena was introduced to an enclave of Dylan devotees by a school

THE ONE AND ONLY: Peter Perrett - Homme Fatale

friend who was dating one of the local kingpins Bob Whitfield, whose brother John was already a popular fixture on the neighbourhood group scene. Taking inspiration from The Band's *Music From Big Pink* and Dylan's *John Wesley Harding*, John Whitfield and a few of his playing pals including drummer Jon Newey invited Zena to join their ranks.

Like Peter, Jon Newey had gone to the 14-hour Technicolour baptism of hippy and come away blinded by enlightenment — "instead of studying for 'O' levels I was drawing psychedelic designs and reading *International Times*". He finished school in '67 with the primary aim of playing drums. Jon Newey:

"I started to rehearse with John Whitfield, he played piano and harmonium. His parents had a house on the corner of Hornimans Drive in Forest Hill and they had a basement where John and I would play covers of Dylan numbers. Zena came down and was doing folk songs. She was passionate about music and had a good voice. We ended up playing a couple of songs with her. John and I backed her at a school gig which Peter came down to because by that time he'd started going out with her. Peter and I got on pretty well from the off because we both shared interests. I'd asked him what he was into and he said Dylan and The Velvet Underground."

In one swoop, the strands of Peter Perrett's future were presented to him — in uniting with Zena, he was not only embarking on a lasting relationship but was also aligning himself with the cornerstones of his first band, England's Glory. Peter:

"Zena was the first girl I could ever talk to, up until that time most of the girls I'd been out with I didn't have anything in common with, apart from the fact I fancied them. Zena was as fanatical about Bob Dylan as I was. Instead of going to college, we used to meet in school time. She had to be home early otherwise her parents would kill her. It was just a friendship to begin with, from January until I actually kissed her in May."

The developing romance would have far-reaching effects — hastening the course of Zena and her brother Harry's escape plot. With the looming threat of an arranged marriage and a parade of suitors being welcomed in by her parents, Zena was seized by panic. Her dream of running away to become a singer might yet be frog-marched down the aisle and evicted from her life. The added complication of a boyfriend quickened the pace of the break out. After their first kiss, when Peter proclaimed his love, Zena alerted him to her plight:

> "I tried to tell Peter as best I could about my family. He was just stunned, he was a total rebel and couldn't believe it was for real until my brother spoke to him."

In the lull, Zena began to encourage and nurture a talent that innocently eclipsed her own. Zena:

> "I'd started going round to Peter's parents' house to spend time with him instead of going to school. I remember him showing me all these lyrics that he'd been writing since he was 12. I used to write songs but to me it was difficult, a chore. I said to him, 'Why don't you play an instrument?'. 'I can't play guitar', he said. 'It's easy, I'll teach you'. I started singing and playing to him, he thought my voice was amazing.
>
> He started playing and within months he was better than me and I'd been playing since I was 11. Whenever he's interested in something, he gets blinkers on and totally devours it, but he never really wanted to be a guitarist, it was more a vehicle for his lyrics. When I started hearing Peter putting words to music, I stopped singing. I know it sounds crazy, it's almost like how his father felt about him, living his life through his son made his dreams."

Zena became the protector of Peter's flame, while he in turn liberated the self-effacing girl who had hidden from the attention of boys inside her oversized duffle coat. Fortunately for Miss Kakoulli, all that sewing for dolls meant that she had grown into a fine and inventive seamstress who could recreate and customise second-hand clothes picked up in charity shops. Stashed away in her bedroom was a secret vampy trampy wardrobe waiting to be worn. Zena:

> "I really had a thing about my appearance and Peter had only ever seen me in my school uniform but I'd made all these outrageous outfits. When you're restricted you go the other way. I had long black see-through chiffon dresses, miniskirts with matching pants that were

shorter than anything else that was around. I had all these clothes that I was making for the time when I finally left home."

She made her debut after slipping out at midnight to join Peter at a party. Cinders was transformed into the belle of the ball in transparent peach chiffon. Peter was captivated. All the taboo activity had seeped into her spirit, and unable to suppress the rebellious streak Zena almost stood up to Dimitris. Zena:

"My father had started talking about Dylan, he had begun to hate him because I was changing. That was the last time my father hit me, he almost killed me. Harry and I left a few days later. Something was on television and my views weren't the same as his — just where did I get my ideas from? — he started hitting me and my mother started screaming."

In a carefully co-ordinated campaign, Zena and her brother picked up their last wage packets from summer jobs and scooted off to a girlfriend's house where they had been storing clothes in readiness for the great adventure. Waiting with Peter, John Whitfield and Jon Newey had set up a runaway HQ in the makeshift crash pad.

When the evening cast darkening shadows over the front room, Peter and Zena retired for their first night together, leaving the other two to spliff up and tune into the moon landing. As the high-tech Michelin man stumbled around dead rocks in silent space, the earth hung suspended above the young couple, another planet bathed in a beautiful bloom of light.

CHAPTER 2 – Shapes In The Fire

Ever since the Beat Generation and the publication in the late '50s of Jack Kerouac's adventures in *On The Road*, nomadic hoards of young bohemians have cut loose and hitched a ride to experience. The free spirits found favoured ports of cool, exploring shady territories and veiled mysteries from Paris to San Francisco or Marrakech to Katmandu. Peter, Zena and Harry may only have got as far as Colchester in Essex but they would return feeling as if they'd seen the world, bringing back with them a mosaic of reminiscences. At first, the trio of waifs had been content to crash with pals in London until Dimitris caught the scent of their trail after paying John Whitfield a shotgun visit. Fearing capture at best and GBH at worst, they made their way to Essex where an old schoolfriend of Zena's promised temporary refuge. Zena:

> "I can't believe it when I think about us — three kids on the road, sleeping out; a naive 18 year old girl that had never, ever been this far from home before, Peter who was street-wise but only 16 and Harry even younger than him. One night before we got to Essex, we were in Colchester on the beach, absolutely starving and these bums who lived rough took us under their wing and showed us how to eat, they taught us a bit about surviving on the road."

Peter:

"We were hitching, sleeping in fields, bus shelters, telephone kiosks, which were really uncomfortable. Launderettes were warm when they opened in the morning. We had to beg for tuppence to buy a packet of skins then get the dog-ends off the street. We used to go into cafés and order one cup of tea between the three of us and wait until people had finished their meals then we'd dive on the left-over chips. That's the way we survived. After a while it got a bit hard, not having baths was difficult, so we came back to London where Zena had the bright idea of contacting the National Council for Civil Liberties."

The address and phone number of the NCCL at 4 Camden High Street, NW1, had been widely circulated around the underground in a hippy handbook entitled *Project Free London*. Helpful sections provided a laid-back guide to the drop-out zone, covering all points of necessity from scrounging free food to dealing with bum trips: '*As a last resort you should call in a doctor who can administer a tranquilizer, generally Largactil. Mental hospitalisation should be considered a very bad trip indeed!*' If one came through the psychedelic maelstrom with the strength to flick to the Social Services section, the NCCL promised to right the wrongs of injustice. Well, nearly. While they were prepared to offer shelter to Zena and Harry in a flat near a rather happening venue called The Roundhouse, Peter was told to sling his hook. A liberal outlook seemed to have eluded the Civil Liberties agenda as far as Peter and Zena's unmarried status was concerned. With no particular place to go, the elfish urchin ambled off to Regent's Park. Peter:

> "I used to sleep in the park on a bench. Luckily it was the summer, although it was cold when I woke up, it was just about bearable. You'd come around with a squirrel sitting on you. Then Zena got a job in a patisserie as a pastry cook. I used to spend the days walking around the outside of Regent's Park Zoo trying to see what animals I could, 'cos I didn't have enough money to pay to get in. I'd get up in the morning and go to the public toilets to clean my teeth, all the tramps used to go there for their morning wash. Occasionally, at night Zena would sneak me into the flat where she was staying."

After six weeks, the fugitive threesome moved into their first undesirable residence after a local landlord had offered Zena a low rent room in a derelict house he was in the process of renovating. Zena:

> "You've never seen anything like it, there were holes in the windows and no doors. The landlord had made it sound amazing when he told me about it. I didn't realise at the time that he was a pimp, and by getting me in there he thought he'd get around me. He didn't know that I had a boyfriend. The first time I realised he was pimping was when this naked woman came into the room, she'd been raped and drugged by him."

Despite the young couple's housing predicament, they continued their renegade honeymoon with Zena carefully budgeting her wages and picking fruit and vegetables from the end of day spoils that had fallen to the ground in Camden Market. Although they could rarely afford to go out, Peter and Zena went to the Rolling Stones' Hyde Park concert and made the pilgrimage to see Bob Dylan and The Band top the bill at the penultimate Isle of Wight Festival on August 31st, 1969.

As dusk fell and Dylan and company were already several hours late on stage, a couple of enterprising drug dealers worked the site, advertising business by twirling red and green electric yo-yos — cheery beams of light in the cheese-cloth crush. Close to midnight Dylan finally slipped through the smoky veil of hash clouds. Amazingly Peter bumped into Jon Newey who had signed up for art school, while maintaining a series of semi-pro bands. Vague promises were uttered about keeping in touch before they separated into the vast crowd.

Peter and Zena attended the odd freak gathering but they were more nocturnal by nature than the sunshine flower children. Peter had cut off all style association with any tribe except his own. Zena flitted by his side, a peroxide blonde satin vampire. Unfortunately, brutality and reality began to seep through the damp walls of their love nest. The sorry cries of the landlord's ruined women didn't help the ambience, nor did Harry's developing animosity toward Peter for taking up his sister's attention. A further additive to the unhappy brew was Peter's snappy temper. Peter:

"I had a lot of aggression, I used to beat Zena up occasionally, I don't know whether it was the violence at boarding school that made me think it was normal but I always used to regret it. I got really crazy until I was 22 or 23. I'd always been very self-centred. I thought everybody existed just for my purpose."

The final revelation that brought the cauldron to the boil was Zena's unplanned pregnancy. In search of sanity, the teenagers graduated to a bedsit in Tulse Hill, Zena's diminutive 18-inch waist thickening with each passing day. Zena:

"I was devastated, I didn't want the baby. It was everything that my parents said would happen. I'd wanted to leave home and show that I could be a success, I wanted to prove my father wrong. I was petrified that he would find us. Peter didn't quite know how to take the pregnancy. I mean he loved me but he was very young and rebellious. I was working, supporting him. He wasn't very good at working. I wanted him to carry on studying, to finish his 'A' levels. I didn't want to be blamed for spoiling his education."

With plucky determination she soldiered on through autumn, acting as den mother, lover and provider, holding down a supermarket job as her distended belly pushed through the nylon checkout uniform. There was no poetry in the situation, except for the development of Peter's songwriting skills. Wrapped up in a tumble of bedclothes, he practiced regularly, spurred on by boredom and the need to avoid hypothermia. Peter:

"Because it was so cold, I used to spend all day in bed. Zena would come home at lunch time, we'd make love, then I'd still lay in bed. She'd come home after work and we'd make love again. That's when I started playing the guitar quite a lot, I was at home with nothing to do. Eventually Zena became ill, we realised that she couldn't work forever. There was no way I could look after her, I'd never had a job. Because she started to get sick, she decided to contact her parents."

In December, Peter, Zena and Harry came in from the cold and gave themselves up to their respective parents. Loulla and Dimitris were quick to sweep up the emotional rubble, offering a series of tidy options to their wayward daughter. It was too late for a termination, but a new life in Cyprus complete with an arranged marriage was on offer, if the baby was put up for adoption. A second and more palatable choice was to marry the long-haired English boy who'd led her astray in the first place. With a conclusion drawn, Dimitris relaxed his slaughterhouse shoulders, laid down his gun and tenderly embraced his headstrong Xenoulla. A cease-fire was declared. When the dust began to settle, so did the parental ulcers as both sides met to discuss arrangements for the wedding.

Peter's forthcoming betrothal to *that Greek girl* irrevocably widened the gulf between mother and son. Little Princes were expected to pair off with Princesses, not foreign Cinderellas. Albert on the other hand was all for doing the decent thing. Lewisham registry office was booked for January 10th with a Greek ceremony the following day.

While the junior insubordinates underwent enforced separation and supervision, their parents began to groom them for the big days; attempting to iron out the kinks in their personalities. First Peter's luscious locks had to go — preferring to be his own Delilah, he hacked his hair into

Shapes In The Fire

Above: The confetti convicts outside the Registry Office.

Right: Peter on his wedding day. 'Til death do us part.

a vicious pre-punk electric shock feather cut and practiced fastening his tie like a noose. Zena meanwhile was ceremoniously stripped of her dolly bird rags and forced into a matronly colourblind twin set. Peter:

> "The last thing I wanted to do was get married at the age of 17 but I didn't want to stop seeing Zena either. My parents were against it, they hated Zena for ages for taking their little boy away and mucking up my education. The day before the wedding I was trying to get a couple of my friends to come to Scotland with me, I was going to run away but I didn't.
>
> The next time I saw Zena was at the registry office. I didn't recognise her, they'd put her in a horrible lime green suit and done her hair up in a bun. I went crazy with her. Then the registrar started losing his temper. 'Are you going to get married or not? We've got people waiting'. So we went through with it but I was in a real mood. At the end the registrar said, 'You may kiss the bride', and I said, 'You're joking', and walked out. I'd got over it by the next day. When I was young I thought you should do whatever you wanted and fuck everybody else."

In her vulnerable state, Zena had allowed her parents to take over, not least because she believed that married status would be the key to release from family domination. After the registry office disaster, the beleaguered bride sobbed a river of muddy mascara, convinced that Peter wouldn't make it to the final leg of the event. Peter:

> "The Greek ceremony was the next day, that was really weird. It lasted about three hours and it was all ritual which I didn't understand. Nobody had told me what I was meant to do, I just had to follow. We had crowns on our heads and we walked around a table three times and kissed the bible. Then the priest held out his hand, I was meant to kiss it but I shook it instead. I didn't know what was going on at all. Finally we did this money dance, when you dance and they pin money on you but Zena's dad took it all."

Chuck Berry would have wept for them. Unlike the story of the joyful teenage couple in his classic confetti rocker "You Never Can Tell", the chapel bells didn't chime out. They tolled for oncoming hardship. Mr and Mrs Perrett began their married life in the Kakoulli family residence with little privacy or romance.

The baby of the clan, Koulla, summarises herself as, "being the youngest, I've always tried to be the loudest. I was the last to get anything. If there was a box of chocolates, I'd get the soft centres!" While there is a similarity in appearance to her eldest sister, Koulla's open heart-shaped face and full mouth indicate a more extrovert character than Zena's slightly austere, feline features. Given her strict upbringing, in a house where male visitors meant the girls were packed off upstairs to protect their mental chastity, the introduction of Peter as a 'safe' figure aroused Koulla's youthful curiosity. Koulla:

"Peter's got such a weird personality. Without trying he's the weirdest person that I know. Most of the people who are like Peter try hard to be reclusive. Mysterious. Popstarish. Peter just is. I'm sure he was like that when he was born. He came to live with my mum and dad. He was really quiet. I think he's very shy, especially at family things. I think he feels awkward. He went from being an only child to going into a really crazy family. My dad was a larger-than-life character. He used to have shotguns and he'd talk about violent things he'd done in Cyprus. If anyone would come and visit, he'd show off his gun collection. He'd do that to Peter."

Peter:

"They treated me with civility I suppose. They just made the best of a bad job. I know that I wasn't their ideal son-in-law."

Everyday living was pervaded by Zena's worsening condition. Owing to bureaucracy, she could not be admitted to hospital without a doctor's letter. The fact that they had been "on the road" excommunicated them from any GP's services until Peter stormed a local surgery, singeing the doctor's sideburns with his fervent plea. Zena was finally allowed into a maternity unit where staff diagnosed toxemia, a serious poisoning of the blood and possibly life-threatening if left untreated. Her ordeal had only just begun. On March 6th, the teenage parents wrapped their severely premature baby daughter, Nicola, in a pastel pink shawl. Two days later, a nurse laid out a handkerchief sized shroud. The hospital then prepared to take court action against the Perretts who lacked the funds to pay for a funeral until a charity stepped in. Peter:

"I was upset and angry when the baby died, but I'd always been angry at society. Nothing surprised me really."

During convalescence, with Peter's encouragement, Zena befriended an unmarried mother in the next bed. Kathy Barrett was to become Peter's first mistress. Peter:

"I hadn't lived yet. I didn't want to get married, although Zena was my best friend. To begin with I thought I loved her, but as I met other people I felt this excitement inside me and thought that maybe I didn't love her. It wasn't until about 1980 that I discovered that real love is being best friends with someone. I've treated Zena really terribly but I was a child then. I just felt I ought to get lots of experience."

The new decade saw Peter's increasing rejection of society's constraints and his first steps into the subterranean domain of drug dealing. The disposition of the corrupt angel who would come to front The Only Ones was still a novice in subversive gestures, but learning fast.

Peter made ready to infiltrate the world of sex, drugs and music with a rather meek entrance fee which he was quick to put to ill use — buying up quantities of hash. In the summer of 1970, he and his wife enrolled at North London Polytechnic. While Zena was genuinely keen to pursue a sociology degree, Peter's general arts degree grant was used in down payment on his apprenticeship in iniquity.

He started dealing hash like many a struggling artist, using the returns to finance his musical evolution. Perish the thought of a straight job in the square world. There was something offbeat and faintly gentrified to such low level selling.

According to the pharmaceutical prophet Timothy Leary there were, "three groups who are bringing about the great evolution of the new age that we are going through now. They are the dope dealers, the rock musicians and the Underground artists and writers". In Peter's case it was two for the price of one.

With the first proceeds, Peter treated himself to a 1963 Stratocaster and a shiny set of weighing scales. Peter:

"I'd started smoking hash and going into the Poly on the first day of each term to get the grant cheque. I'd realised that you could make money buying large bits and cutting them up into small bits. I thought it was a good way of making money and it was better than going to work. I started doing that in a small way while we were still living at Zena's parents. There weren't any criminals involved. It was a friendly thing to do, without any bad vibes attached to it."

Peter's songs were still in the realms of curtains drawn, bedroom strumming — the fledgling lyricist playing guitar. Peter:

"I never practiced guitar at all. The only time I played was when I wanted to write a song. I never really wanted to be a guitarist but I did start to think that the songs were good and I wanted to play them with a group."

He filled the hourglass with ruby ditties cloaked in dark Velvet Underground tones, refining his compositions until he breathed life into his first complete song, a forlorn contemplation called "Flowers Die". It was during this period that Peter and Zena set off on their torrid waltz of betrayal, reunion and almost continual shape-shifting of the boundaries of their relationship. Stepping in and out of time with one another while remaining ever constant, the first rip in the marriage vows came whilst on a trip to Wales with Kathy Barrett in tow. Initially, Zena was unaware of Peter and Kathy's lingering looks and deepening friendship, until one blazing afternoon when she caught two sun-drenched silhouettes merging into one black shadow in the corner of her vision. Zena:

"At first I was devastated when I saw him kissing her. I didn't want to go and confront him, I felt that if I cared about him I should let him do what he wanted to do. I just got on the next coach back to London and had a moment of realisation that all my life had been what other people wanted. My parents had ruled me and I'd given myself totally to Peter. I decided that when I got home I wasn't going to ask for a divorce but I would see Peter and ask him to pretend to get a flat with me so I could leave my parents and carry on with my life. I felt so empty on that journey and so alone for the first time in my life."

The Perretts didn't realise that they were initiating a cycle of part-time separation when they got their shared flat together in Forest Hill. Peter may have drifted but he always came back. In the months that followed

Zena took up a fashion course while Peter expanded his hashish empire and lyrical repertoire.

Finally he was ready to take his latest compositions beyond the bedroom. After Zena, the first recipient of a preview was old pal Jon Newey. Whether or not Peter was aware of it, approaching Newey was a wise move. Of all the Forest Hill contenders, Jon had travelled furthest down the rock 'n' roll highway. He had gone from dabbling in a succession of will o' the wisp bands that were born in the afternoon, peaked at midnight and faded into hangover by the morning. He then progressed to semi-pro status with Plasma which included guitarist David Clarke, a band which evolved into support slot perennials They Bite, again with Clarke and singer Menna Davies. When he re-connected with Peter, Jon was playing congas in a professional psychedelic funk combo, Crew, and kicking his platform boots against the threat of a commercial direction and satin stage suits. Jon Newey:

> "During all this time, I'd seen Pete on an occasional basis. He'd come to one or two of the gigs, and visited various flats that I'd had, but I hadn't had the time to see a lot of my old friends. I remember that he'd been around and played a couple of songs once before, which I thought were quite interesting but I didn't really think a lot more of it because I was so busy. Then in the spring of '72 he came over to my place and played me a bunch of stuff that he'd been writing and to put it very simply, I was floored. They were absolutely excellent songs."

Peter remained cross-legged on the floor clutching his guitar:

> "I suppose it was my arrogance, I thought I was special. I thought I was the best songwriter in England, even though I wasn't back then."

He even had a name for the prospective band, taken from the humble box of household matches used to light up a spliff that sparked off Peter Perrett's radiant imagination. England's Glory glowed in the warm fire of his pipe dreams.

Chapter 3 – Death Or Glory

The musical slipstream into which England's Glory would propel themselves was filled with all the dark energies that would eventually culminate in punk. Navigating the territory, where the perverse aristocracy of the bitter new season were limbering up, took an innate kinship.

On the stadium side strode the supergroups such as Led Zeppelin and The Who, while the progressive rock division epitomised by Yes and Emerson, Lake and Palmer, also played to vast audiences. In the middle, the charts were lit by The Osmonds' Cheshire cat grins and lined with the tartan scarves of the Bay City Rollers. The glam contingent, namely Slade, Sweet and Gary Glitter, sweated to a quaking beat. Marc Bolan presided over all on his glitter and papier-mâché throne.

Pub rock lurked in the margins; a down-home alehouse alternative, centred around the Hope and Anchor in Islington. Up above, the Martians circled — David Bowie was off on his Starman trip, while Roxy Music were Teddy Boy lounge lizard aliens. Earthbound relatives included Mott The Hoople and Cockney Rebel. If England's Glory belonged in any category, it was with the sickly aesthetes who sucked up society's ills and breathed them out like fire.

In 1972, America's premier subversives seeped over to England on a tide of excess. The New York Dolls were amongst the first of the lower empire libertines to make an entrance — the cross-dressing delinquents crash-landed in London after playing Wembley Pool in aid of the Spastics Society. The distraught Dolls had to cut short a proposed tour when their 18 year old drummer, Billy Murcia, got mashed on pills and booze at a party and failed to regain consciousness. The band staggered back to the States with one of their own in a body bag and an ever-deepening mythology. To both their admirers and detractors, the New York Dolls were the outriders of an intensified period of rock degeneracy.

In the hierarchy of rock 'n' roll delirium, Detroit demon Iggy Pop and his cohorts, The Stooges, were one long exorcism of modern life. Holed up in a studio, the lank-haired gang sharpened their guitars for a gig at the

Scala in King's Cross. It would be more of an onslaught than a UK debut, as crazed 'acrobrat' Iggy vent his fury on an unsuspecting audience.

Less bombastic but equally dangerous, the co-founder of the Velvet Underground, Lou Reed, was just about to tour with a former Long Island bar band, The Tots. Reed was the most sophisticated of all the US reprobates.

Although Peter Perrett dipped into a gentler palette of themes and his youthful experiences still had a suburban feel, there was an unwholesome tinge to his lyrics coupled with an impulse towards the darker side of human nature that became apparent with England's Glory. By turning negative subjects into creativity, Peter began to draw blood from the same wound as the American ambassadors, and in one context or another would connect with them all.

In the meantime, Jon Newey had dispensed with his former band, Crew, and was scouting around for potential members of England's Glory. In his quest, Newey spent a fair amount of time with the Perretts. He had already noted Peter's metamorphosis from the 'unconfident tag-along individual' that he had first met several years earlier, to the more self-assured character who had thrown away his dealer's 'L' plates and now had a considerable clientele. Peter's alternative trading not only helped to fund England's Glory, it also began to shade his aura of mystique. Jon Newey:

> "I'd seen Peter over the years, I'd noticed a change happening. He was getting older and growing a lot more confident. By then he and Zena were living in a flat in Waldram Park Road, dealing dope. You can't deal dope unless you are confident. He had developed a certain cool which came through the dealing. People are always ringing you up for things. You are in a controlling situation.
>
> Peter and Zena would get up around lunch time, have something to eat, smoke a joint, sit and play cards or chess during the afternoon, listen to records. People would start turning up to score at about 6 o'clock. Later on in the evening, Peter would go out on a run in the car, sometimes I'd make deliveries with him. They weren't dealing in major amounts of hash — a weight a week maybe — which had its advantages because we could pay for rehearsal time and a roadie to pick the gear up."

When not rushing on a run, Peter concentrated on his songs while Jon organised the line-up. Harry Kakoulli had always been a sure thing from the start. Although he was the baby of the band, Harry had a natural flair for playing bass and developed a musical rapport with Peter from sitting in on countless casual strum sessions. They had already made an inauspicious debut together at Catford Polytechnic, led by Peter on a three string guitar, accompanied by two of Harry's long forgotten pals.

England's Glory's first guitarist was Alistair Kinnear, an underground face who had run the light show at The Roundhouse and had been an acquaintance of Newey's on the psychedelic circuit. With Kinnear in tow, the nascent unit checked into Underhill rehearsal studios in Blackheath. Throughout the summer of '72, England's Glory became Underhill regulars, practicing for up to three nights a week. The small studio was a hive of activity. In another room, Lou Reed was putting The Tots through their paces, while further down the corridor Iggy and the Stooges droned in preparation for their King's Cross gig. Even though England's Glory had their own voice to add to the clamour, Alistair Kinnear was proving to be off-key in more ways than one. Jon Newey:

> "We cut a demo tape which was done on a Revox, with Alistair playing guitar and electric violin, which was rough but quite interesting. It became quite obvious that Alistair wasn't together and wouldn't make certain rehearsals. He was a very lovely, gentle bloke but for want of a better word, he was a bit of an acid casualty and pretty spaced out most of the time. It was very sad to see but we couldn't really continue with him. We then had a Japanese guitarist called Kazoo for a little while, but he had work permit problems. Then I said, 'Well, I know a guitarist who I think could make this happen', which was David Clarke."

Having abandoned groups in favour of a lucrative busking career, Clarke had hooked up romantically and musically with former They Bite singer, Menna Davies. He had withdrawn from the band scene after too many big time promises had burst into little bubbles. He became bored with the prevailing progressive rock climate which was at odds with his cut-and-thrust riffing. When Newey called, Clarke offered his services, though only as a temporary hired hand. David Clarke:

Above: Old schoolfriend Bob Jope and Peter at John Whitfield's 21st birthday party.

"Jon phoned and said he'd met this guy who was a great singer, writing great songs. I said I didn't want to know, but he persuaded me to go along. I joined the band with a bad attitude really 'cos I said I wasn't going to stay but I'd help out if they needed a guitarist. They said they were going to record an album and I said I would do that, but when it was finished I would leave. I said I would join as long as it cost me nothing. Peter paid for everything. I didn't pay towards the rehearsals or the recording. I was just a jobbing musician. I liked Peter, although I didn't get to know him terribly well. I thought he wrote great lyrics and he looked and sounded good but I wasn't particularly into it, I'm more of a hard rocker and he was poetically bedsit."

In keeping with the wistful image David Clarke had of Peter, the latest line-up of England's Glory trooped into Jon Newey's bedroom in Streatham, where they rigged up a cassette player and a single microphone. While Newey beat time on a biscuit box and Harry slapped bass, Clarke eased himself into the somewhat Autumnal ambience of the session. Hunched over the mike, Peter tested his world-weary vocals before leading the band through a sweetly maudlin set of some 12 provisionally titled numbers including, "What You're Doing To Me", "Going Back To January", "Sweet Morning", "Good Time", "Flowers Die", "Here Comes The Waves", "In-betweens", "Aurora", "Give Me A Little More Loving", "Violin" and "So Divine". Within the half-realised sketches, the foundations of future gems are clearly audible, though Peter now regards the recording as a premature intrusion. Peter:

> "Basically they are the first songs I ever wrote. Half of them aren't real, proper songs, just bits of beginnings. At least with the England's Glory album, they are finished songs and although I find them a bit immature, they were a statement of where my music was at, at that time. Whereas the bedroom tape is a bit too primitive. I suppose they are of interest to people who are fanatics. Similar things have been released. I remember listening to a song of Dylan's that was taped when he was 16 years old called "Acne". It had lines like, 'You said you'd ask me, you said you'd ask me to the senior prom, but you won't ask me 'cos I've got Acne'. He was probably really embarrassed when that found its way onto vinyl."

The band practically became resident at Underhill, going in most evenings to work up their material. For a short while they toyed with the name Peter & The Pets as the US vibe permeated the walls of the rehearsal studio. Iggy had his Stooges, Lou Reed was playing with The Tots, but Peter wasn't so keen on keeping his Pets and they reverted to their original moniker.

The only break in the England's Glory practice schedule came during Lou Reed's tour, when the deadpan crooner took an interest in Mrs Perrett. At the backstage bar, some of Reed's backing band had asked the Perretts if they would like to accompany them to an after show party at a King's Road apartment. Reed seemed fascinated by the way Zena looked and the clothes she wore. He said to Zena, 'I'd really like to eat you', and she rather innocently offered him her hand. Zena:

> "Lou spotted me and took a fancy to me. He asked us back to the hotel and spent all night trying to pull me. We spent a few days in his company."

Peter Perrett may cut a slight, elfin figure but his ideals have a steely edge, like an Excalibur of arrogance that slices through the mundanity of social norms and everyday routine. England's Glory were not going to be put through the mill of paying their dues on the rock 'n' roll chain gang, working the circuit and waiting for a break. Jon Newey:

> "In those days there were two ways of going about getting a deal. Going out on the road and doing lots of gigs, or taking a demo tape around. Pub rock was coming up, there was a load of groups; Ducks Deluxe, Bees Make Honey, Kilburn and the High Roads. That was a bit shabby. We had a much sharper take on what we wanted to do. We'd heard about the Dolls and Roxy Music. David Bowie and the Spiders From Mars had rehearsed at Underhill six months before us. There was a certain feeling to it and we felt we were in that same framework. We were quite arrogant and we believed that we had a chance of becoming one of the greatest groups to have ever come out of England. When people would ask what we were like, what the songs sounded like, we'd say, 'Obviously brilliant'. The idea of doing the tracks was to take them around to record companies."

In the days before the rise of the independent label and punk's DIY ethic, demo tapes were disposable Lego bricks for the A&R demolition men. While most other bands posted their demos like calling cards bound for cassette cemetery, the England's Glory LP would give Peter and company an air of cool insolence as they casually placed a finished vinyl product onto a smoked glass record company table. In the closing weeks of January '73, Peter paid £100 to enable the band to go into Venus, a four track studio off the Whitechapel Road. They arranged a tight programme of four days' recording with the fifth set aside for mixing. The Glory boys were assisted by two more of Newey's buddies, a folk guitarist called Graham Lapwood who checked their sound balance, while Jon's flatmate Michael Kemp embroidered on some piano and organ. Backing vocals were added by a four-strong wifely chorus consisting of Zena, Penny Kemp, Menna Clarke and Harry's new bride Mary; introducing a feminine presence that would resound throughout Peter's studio work, echoing the sirens of his private life.

Aware that Peter avoided daylight and lived within a vampire-like cycle, Jon stayed with the Perretts to ensure that EG's frontman made it to Venus on time. Jon Newey:

Above: England's Glory (l-r) Harry Kakoulli, Julie, Jon Newey, Peter Perrett.

"It was always a bit of a number to make sure Peter got to the studio. He'd want to do things at his own pace. Maybe drugs exacerbated that later on, but he was always slow to get moving. We couldn't be like that with Venus booked, so I stayed over and made sure we got up early and went to the studio so we wouldn't waste the money Peter had put up. But he worked really hard, we all did that week."

Even if England's Glory's methods were a touch untutored, David Clarke observed Peter's potential and the band's progress from a more experienced vantage point. David Clarke:

"I was older than the rest of them and I think that made a difference to my attitude. I thought Zena was kind of organising Peter. He seemed unaware of minor details — like life — yet there was a determination about him that made me think he might make it one day. Although he was nice and easy going, if he wanted something in a song he would insist on it. If what we did wasn't right for him, then he would say so, he was quite firm about his music, but in other ways he seemed to be drifting.

It was difficult recording the album because we weren't all on separate tracks. We all had to play together and if one of us made a mistake we'd all have to play the thing over and over again. In the end we left mistakes in because we were running out of time and money, but it was a great experience recording like that."

The album was a candid offering with a distinctly Velvet Underground feel, both musically and in Peter's languid vocals which were delivered in a mid-Atlantic monotone. Peter:

"When people are just starting, it takes them a while to find the confidence to sing with their own voice, they sing how they've always heard music. The person I liked most was Bob Dylan, he was my hero, and also I liked the Velvet Underground. Probably three quarters of the music I listened to was American."

Amid the band's chugging enthusiasm, Peter's lyrics hint at romantic perversity with a doomy undertow, and cradle versions of "City Of Fun" and "Peter & The Pets" enjoy a spirited infancy. England's Glory received eight acetates before Peter ordered a further 25 vinyl copies pressed up with pink labels. Many of these went to his customers, some to fellow dealers, while the remainder were earmarked for the record companies. They were then approached by an eccentric young cockney entrepreneur who had connected with Perrett's scoring circle. While Zena had done most of the band's preliminary organising, the short-haired stranger won them over with his tip-top management credentials — having attempted to sail the channel in a wardrobe for a stunt, he was sure he could launch England's Glory.

Hoisting the flag, the band hired Anerly Town Hall in South East London for £50. The solid stone building with an air of Toytown majesty is situated beyond the falls and dips of Forest Hill and is just within walking distance of the spacious grounds of The Bethlem Psychiatric Hospital.

After notching up a guest list of some 300 friends, the band polished up their set and made ready for the self-promoted Anerly gig which was booked for Friday, March 23rd, less than a month before Peter's 21st birthday. When the aged wooden doors of the Town Hall finally creaked open on the eve of the band's live debut, their manager was on hand to give out shop-bought England's Glory aprons with the matchbox logo emblazoned on the front to well-wishers and helpers. Backstage, the boys got dolled up. David Clarke:

> "The thing that sticks out in my mind was Harry painting his nail. He had this one long thumb nail that he painted red when we were in the dressing room getting made up for the gig. We put on some dark eye shadow for a bit of mystery. Even though Peter is fairly wordy and poetic and we did kind of folk songs, at the gig itself we were very loud. If we would have stuck at it longer we'd have got harder and rockier."

The rise of England's Glory wasn't so much meteoric as a quick flicker before the lights failed. Within days of the Anerly gig, the band lost their manager after he voluntarily signed himself into the Maudsley Psychiatric Hospital. To this day no one can recall his name. England's Glory reconvened for one or two meetings around the managerial bedside, until they decided to hand back the business reins to the dedicated Mrs Perrett.

Zena blocked all incoming calls from the roach and roll-up regulars while she set up a series of meetings with record company A&R departments. The finished album may initially have opened the record company doors for Zena and Jon Newey, who acted as the band's hopeful emissaries, but they were consistently rebutted in their efforts to further the cause. Jon Newey:

> "RCA were interested at first, but in their final analysis, the A&R guy Alan Sizer said, 'Look I've signed Lou Reed, I've signed David Bowie,

Left: David Clarke, the temporary guitarist in England's Glory.

I don't know whether I can really take another group on of that ilk'. CBS were very keen — we'd gone up there in shirts from Alkasura and Biba boots, and they saw little glam traces in us but they'd just got Mott The Hoople.

Rocket Records, boy that was crazy, we went there and saw the head of A&R, Steve Brown. He had this amazing deck with big silver balls and an acrylic turntable, but when he put the record on, it played slow and I told him so. He glowered at me and said, 'This deck has cost more money than you'll ever see'. They passed. Island came back to us with a classic line. I think it was Muff Winwood who made the comment, 'I don't know, you could be bigger than The Beatles but it's not for us'."

After much chewing on the bait, but no actual biting by the companies, David Clarke, in a supreme act of bad timing headed for the exit and back to busking with Menna. David Clarke:

"When the album was made and the interest didn't come immediately, I left. I don't regret that. They should have got someone more committed."

Ironically, genuine interest did come following Clarke's departure. England's Glory at last broke the deadlock of indifference due to EMI's A&R man, David Sandison. An auspicious series of events began when

Newey contacted Richard Williams, a *Melody Maker* journalist. David Sandison and Williams had both been involved with Island Records' press department. After hearing of the band's career impasse and Island's dismissive platitudes, Richard Williams gave them Sandison's name and suggested that they might be better suited to EMI's odd pop taste rather than Island's fairly specific roster of English rock and Jamaican roots.

England's Glory found their champion in the genteel David Sandison, who had mastered the snakes and ladders of the rock and pop game at his own diligent pace. Having moved from journalism to A&R, Sandison was snapped up by the legendary Stones PR man, Les Perrin. David Sandison:

"I went to work for Les for about two and a half years, during which, most of my time was spent on The Stones. I also worked with Janis Joplin, Hendrix and Jim Morrison. I thought a curse was following me at one point after I met Brian Jones, they all died! I then got approached by Chris Blackwell in 1971, and went to Island to organise their press office for two years, before Joop Visser at EMI asked if I'd like to join their A&R department. It was during this period that the phone rang one day, and I was asked if I'd see someone that Richard Williams had suggested."

Sandison was intrigued that Island had passed on England's Glory, yet Williams didn't want to see the band slip through the net entirely so a meeting was arranged. Peter and Zena arrived at EMI's offices in Manchester Square and David Sandison recalls their entrance with genial fondness:

"I was immediately impressed just looking at them. They were classic wasted elegant. It's not a logical thing, but first impressions are vital and they just looked right. I didn't know that Zena wasn't in the band, she was an archetypal rock 'n' roll chick with peroxide hair, fishnet stockings and a short skirt, with this incredible, quiet devotion for Peter who she was so clearly in love with. Peter looked wonderful, and certainly after two years working with Keith Richards I thought, 'Right, we've got a genuine rock 'n' roller here', somebody who is already living it. He and Zena were rock 'n' roll animals and if you start with that and you are half way good, you can do something.

Peter was such a nice, nervous person. He was nervous because he was trying to do something with his life and going to somewhere like EMI is daunting. Every meeting is like, 'Is this going to be the one?" But I was knocked out, I thought he was wonderful, obviously very derivative of Lou Reed at that time. We chatted, I said, 'Okay, leave a copy of the record with me. I'll talk to Joop. I think it's great'."

Although Joop Visser wasn't quite as captivated as Sandison, after some persuasion he agreed to allow the band to make a demo at EMI's studio on the ground floor of the Manchester Square building. Sandison rang in the good news to the Perretts and began to make a few moves of his own on their behalf, including a droll prank that has since become a classic rock 'n' roll ruse. Drafting in *Sounds* writer Jonh Ingham to add plausibility, David enticed the star scribe at the *New Musical Express*, Nick Kent, down to his office with the promise of a preview of some stray Velvet Underground outtakes. The eloquently wasted Kent, a gaunt self-crucifixion of a man, had copped his somnambulist reputation in Keith Richards' shadow and dined on only the finest rock 'n' roll ambrosia. He leapt at the chance to sample some rare Lou Reed. David Sandison:

"Jonh and I got him in as straight-faced as we could be and said, 'Look, you've got to keep this thing to yourself, this is top secret because the contracts aren't all worked out'. There was a light in his eyes. We put on the England's Glory album. He started off thinking it was great and getting excited, then he started to spot stuff. It wasn't Lou Reed, let's be honest. Then we got to the second track on the second side, "Peter & The Pets", with that line in it, which is the worst joke ever — *'Two men from Poland keeping us apart, we're poles apart'* — Kent's eyes flickered, 'You bastards, it's great but it's not the Velvet Underground!' So we confessed."

In the England's Glory corner, however, anticipation had turned to anxiety as the band trawled through would-be guitarists, only to come up empty handed. With the EMI session looming, they placed an advert in one of the music papers. The most likely applicant to take over from David Clarke seemed to be a young woman remembered only as Julie. With her own equipment and compatible influences, she was welcomed into the fold perhaps a little too hastily. While Jon Newey was prepared to take a softer line, 'She did have reasonable chops', Peter burned on a shorter fuse, 'She was fucking useless'. Whichever way, Julie's days with the band were more clearly marked than an advent calendar.

On June 8th, England's Glory showed up at EMI, prepared to make history in the same studio where The Beatles had launched "Love Me Do" at a press conference. The old four track desk that awaited the band had been brought down from Abbey Road, and flickered into life like a rock 'n' roll time machine. A dismayed David Sandison arched his brow Roger Moore style, when he checked out the band's newest recruit. David Sandison:

> "She was all wrong for them. An ugly proto-punk in black with all these beautiful, skinny young men. Musically she didn't have it. She functioned but she wasn't as sincerely good as the others were. We did four tracks; "Predictably Blonde", "Bells That Chime", "Weekend" and "Shattered Illusion". It went like a dream. It was a four track and the problem with that is you have to pretty much record everything down into mono and maybe a stereo spread, then you have two tracks left for vocals and overdubs. There weren't any solos going on, so I just mixed it down to mono. I then took it back to Joop and he still didn't hear it. I called the Perretts and said, 'I'm sorry, we ain't getting anywhere'."

In spite of the odds, the four tracks set a raunchier pace than the England's Glory album. Julie's short-hand method of playing gave an abrupt r&b edge, while Peter's accent had begun to make its way home, having started off in New York with Lou Reed it had wound up in Sarf London.

England's Glory matured in time to meet their expiry date. Julie was given her marching orders and the band sifted through some late comers, including guitarist John Chichester (who decided to hang on to a rather comfortable post as Greg Lake's personal assistant), and an intensely Hendrix-influenced player called Alan Best. The band's impetus had floundered badly after EMI's rejection. With both Jon Newey and Harry Kakoulli struggling through divorces and Peter putting dealing back at the top of his priority list, England's Glory burned out.

The loose ends were tied up some months later, when Peter returned to Venus, with Harry, keyboard player Mick Kemp and Gordon Edwards from The Pretty Things on guitar. The studio manager was roped in to keep the beat. The casual round-up reworked two of the EMI tracks — "Predictably Blonde" and "Weekend" — along with a number called "Trouble In The World" which would crop up as the title of a quite different Only Ones' song.

For all that Peter knew England's Glory might have been his only shot at creative immortality, but with his coat pockets lined with cash from hash, he displayed a dilettante attitude to his music. Peter:

"It was just too difficult to sustain a group. It was costing too much money rehearsing all the time. So I concentrated more on the drug selling. I decided I wanted to make lots of money. I still didn't have any great ambition to be successful, just to do it for my own pleasure really. I thought if I made enough money I could just go in once a year and demo songs. It didn't really bother me at that time whether anybody else liked me. It was fun, like a hobby. Zena used to have more ambition about my music."

Before 1973 was out, the grey curtains rose on Peter's inaugural drug bust. Apprenticeship over. The name Peter Perrett was now a fully fledged entry in police files. Peter:

"The guy downstairs had been complaining about the noise and told the police, so the local CID came round and found an ounce of hash. That was my first court case. I went to court with nail varnish on and I didn't bother to have a solicitor. I got a suspended prison sentence plus a £50 fine, which was pretty heavy for a first offence. Normally you'd just get the fine. I got a solicitor, appealed against it, bothered to wear a suit, and the suspended sentence got thrown out. I just had a £50 fine."

Chapter 4 – The Turner Prize

All too often "decadence" is inappropriately used to describe rock 'n' roll antics. The epithet's true meaning has been debased by constant misconception. Decadence derives from the Latin word "cadere" (to fall) and hits a more sombre tone than the giggles of groupie geishas attending to a stoned pop emperor. What decadence best implies is a troubled spiritual condition and a corrupt eccentricity. Peter Perrett fell from grace while leaping towards his dreams.

In the 1980's, after he withdrew from public life behind permanently drawn velvet drapes, fanciful comparisons were made between Peter and the fictitious character of Turner in Nic Roeg and Donald Cammell's disturbingly groovy movie *Performance*. The Turner analogy, complete with the gorgeous nightmare setting of *Performance* — dimly lit rooms, deadly delights, the overripe scent of Patchouli and decay — is well founded even if it did arise out of speculation.

Warner Brothers originally planned to scrap the film which starred Mick Jagger, after finding it "unintelligible", but they relented and released it in 1970 with a swinging advertising campaign: *'Turner lives in a big old house furnished with antique oddities and alive with sound. He sees the world through rose-coloured smoke, and with him are two beautiful chicks'*. In a claustrophobic dope and incense fog, personalities blur as the jaded, reclusive rock star, Turner, begins to merge with Chas, a displaced gangster portrayed by the actor James Fox.

However, there was no contrivance in Peter's performance and no script to follow, except his own. The only flaw in the *Performance*/Perrett parallel was the timing. Peter was freaky, long before fame brushed him.

With the dissolution of England's Glory, Peter entered a transitional period of idleness and supine aspirations lasting throughout most of 1974. Although there was minimal creative endeavour, his and Zena's dual destiny unfolded as they became more involved in pop society. The Perretts moved out of their Forest Hill flat into a large house on Canaby Road, which balanced precariously atop the tallest hill in South East London. The young couple shared their lofty abode with Gordon Edwards and his song writing partner, Jack Green, who was playing rhythm guitar for Marc Bolan during his *Zinc Alloy* phase. Zena had left college and was concentrating on dressmaking when she was introduced to Bolan. The petite, sartorial dandy with a magpie's eye for exotic threads, swooped on the blonde seamstress. Zena:

"Marc saw what I was wearing and was quite fascinated. First of all he had some repairs that he wanted me to do, then he asked me whether I'd be interested in making some clothes for him. The band started to show up at the house to socialise. I found Mickey Finn more interesting than Marc, who was very quiet. I ended up making Marc a loose, sheer brown lurex shirt. He really loved it. At the time, he was talking about me making the wardrobe for the group but it would have been very time consuming doing it that way. Because it was individually tailored, it took me a week to make the one shirt. He gave me some of his old clothes, a sequined top and black crêpe outfit from Alkasura. They were really lovely. I was very sad when he died, because he was so enthusiastic about getting back to playing."

Not long after, Zena broke into the fetish market, designing for the mail-order catalogue, She & Me. Taking her inspiration from the snarling dominatrix that whipped their way through the pages of S&M magazines, Mrs Perrett personally adopted a hard, Madame De Sade style, which would bring her to the attention of the budding doyen of punk rock tailoring, Vivienne Westwood. Zena:

"I was wearing and designing vinyl clothes; skintight drainpipe trousers, T-shirts, stockings, gloves, all-in-one body suits. I'd already made a leather T-shirt with zips on it which Peter had been wearing. I began to go into Vivienne and Malcolm McLaren's shop on the King's Road, Let It Rock. Vivienne noticed me and wanted to know where I got the vinyl from. She'd be into what I was wearing. One time I went in with a pair of thigh-high patent leather boots on, with stiletto heels and platform soles, which I'd got made up from one of my designs at a transvestite shop. She said that she could make them up a bit cheaper, if she could borrow some of my shoe moulds — she ended up losing one of them and returned just one!"

Above: Zena Perrett modelling one of her own creations.

While Zena concentrated on her kinky collections, Peter delved into further research on new sensations, consuming each fresh delight with a voracious appetite. He had sampled to the fullest a smoky smorgasbord of hash and grass and was ready to expand his knowledge of the narcotic spectrum. David Sandison:

> "Peter's consumption was ridiculous. I'd worked with Bob Marley and Jimmy Cliff and they didn't smoke as much bloody dope as he did. I don't know how Peter functioned half the time."

The 23 year old hachischin lived like a South London sultan, cosseted from outside intrusions by a swathe of dreamy luxury. In keeping with his lifestyle, Peter added to his harem, which up until January '75 had included number one wife Zena, and Kathy Barrett who had been a peripheral fancy for the past five years. Kathy was working as a croupier at the Playboy Club, when she invited Peter and one of her work mates, Lynne Shillingford, out for a birthday drink. Lynne's introduction was to have some far-reaching effects. Peter:

"To begin with I didn't really notice Lynne but a week after we met, she phoned up and asked if I could get her any hash. I started going around to her flat. I suppose I fancied her physically. It took me a year to get her looking really good 'cos she didn't really have much dress sense. I mean she used to wear stockings, but she'd wear them with garters instead of suspenders. There were little things that needed to be altered. I got her to dye her hair blonde. But I suppose the main attraction was that she liked drugs as much as me. We were soul mates as far as the drugs went. I tried smack for the first time with Lynne. It was the best feeling in the world. We were like naughty kids together. Zena would go to bed and we'd stay up."

In May '75, Zena, Peter and Lynne moved into a house in Broad Walk, Blackheath. Completing the happy family was one of Harry Kakoulli's musician friends, guitarist Glenn Tilbrook and Peter's unofficial valet Christian Pope*(1) who lived in a room over the garage. One could only pity the neighbours when the colourful menagerie took up residence.

Slipping between the girl's bedrooms like a midnight Don Juan dispensing kisses, Peter's love triangle resonated with the gentlest of discordant notes. Peter:

"The arrangement was that Lynne had her own bedroom and me and Zena had a room, so that Zena had some privacy with her clothes. I divided my time between them roughly equally. Zena seemed to cope all right but it must have been a blow to her ego. There'd be slightly bad scenes but nothing really heavy. I thought I loved Zena but it was a very

---

1   *This marks the first appearance of a name that has been changed to protect the identity of a character. Each pseudonym refers to a specific person and no other personal details have been altered.

selfish love. I just thought I had so much love, I could give it to lots of people. I look back on that period and there were moments when it was the happiest time of my life, when everything seemed to be going smoothly but I suppose I was just fooling myself, they were only instances when Zena was forgetting."

Beyond the domestic arrangements, Peter was also seeing an Australian girl, Clare, who he first met when she went out with Jon Newey. Peter would later pen the exquisitely disenchanted "Counterfeit Woman" about her, which would appear on the *Remains* album. Zena:

"Clare was a beautiful girl and very gentle. She absolutely adored Peter. I really got on with her. I didn't used to get on with Lynne because she was very competitive and possessive, but I really liked Clare. I used to prompt Peter, 'You've got to go and see Clare, you've got to stay with her tonight'. She could cope with him being married but she couldn't cope with Lynne. She rang Peter up from the airport one day, saying she was going to America. Peter then wrote "Counterfeit Woman", which I thought was really cruel, touching upon how fickle she was."

Zena Perrett was forced to tread water in her husband's turbulent sea of love. Zena:

"If you really love someone, you don't force them to do what you want. I didn't own him. He would turn around and say, 'It's not that I don't love you, I do love you but I love somebody else as well'. Or he'd tell me that he liked spending time with other girls. Who was I to say that I was the only one to satisfy him? I don't know if it was my upbringing, not to expect too much, but I thought that maybe there isn't anything wrong with finding out how nice somebody else is. I was in love with Peter although I'd pretend to myself that I wasn't. It was the only way I could cope."

When summer began to stir, Zena opened the windows to allow some warm, fresh air to circulate around their cloistered kingdom. Peter was ready to come out of musical hibernation and once again focused his attention on getting a band together. Using a similar tactic to the England's Glory debut, a gig was booked for June 30th, but this time Peter was prepared to venture further from his own backyard. In an act of

Left:
Kathy Barrett documented for Peter's X files.

unprecedented confidence, Perrett decided to play at one of London's premier rock 'n' roll venues, the Marquee club. In his quest for suitable musicians, Peter was presented with two options — enthusiasm or experience. The choice was between Harry Kakoulli and Glen Tilbrook's embryonic band, Squeeze, and a Bristol outfit, the Ratbites From Hell who were managed by Perrett's old Forest Hill pal, Bob Whitfield. The Ratbites had evolved from the free-floating community groups on the fringes of Glastonbury festival society into a stoned, barnstorming party band with connections to the nouveau bohemian aristocracy, from the Grateful Dead to Richard Branson and artist Peter Blake who designed The Beatles' *Sergeant Pepper* sleeve.

At the core of the Ratbites' sound, was a talented young guitarist, John Perry. It was in John that Peter would eventually find a musician who could emancipate his songs. Although they were the same age, the personal differences between them cut like a laser beam. If Peter went to the Isle of Wight festival to see Dylan, the lyrical radical; then John was to be found on the same site the following year, waiting for Hendrix, The Who and The Doors to conduct lightning.

The fallen angel had met his match in the cynical cherub. Even their surnames — Perrett and Perry — are traceable back to the same West Country origin meaning of pear orchard. With a shared tendency to acute arrogance, their initial contact was not one of instant camaraderie. John Perry:

> "I'd heard Peter's music before in '73. We'd played a festival in Devon and Whitfield had come down to it. We were messing about in this field at about three in the morning, tripping, when Whitfield put the England's Glory tape on his car stereo and opened all the doors. It sounded extraordinary. I was rolling around on the ground laughing. It was the funniest thing I've ever heard but I can't be too brutal about England's Glory. I'm sure the Ratbites don't sound any better, if the tapes still exist."

Two years later, Bob Whitfield again brought word of the Perretts to the Ratbites' camp. John Perry:

> "If you were in 'underground bands' in the early '70s and you wanted to stay independent of record companies, the only real source of income was patronage, which meant either the odd aristocrat with a taste for the arts, or the new post-sixties aristocracy — popstars and dealers who were interested in financing projects.
>
> Whitfield said he knew these dealers who had an awful lot of money; the music wasn't up to much but it was worth getting a piece of it financially. I wasn't that interested but this other guy from the band, Huw Gower, who was a notably scheming individual was up for the money. It was only after I started working with Peter in the studio that I began to think that there was more to it."

When the Ratbites played a London show at the School Of Tropical Medicine, Peter and Zena went to check them out and unwittingly became the centre of a fracas when the Ratbites' conga player fell offstage and landed on Zena. Peter retaliated with a spirited bout of fisticuffs aimed at the unbalanced percussionist. For weeks after, rumours drifted back to

Somerset of the Perretts having taken out a contract for a mafia style hit on the unfortunate bongoist.

With the impending Marquee gig, Peter began to try out the musicians at Manno's rehearsal studio, situated on Lots Road, in the heart of the antiques quarter, behind the affluent King's Road. The Rat pack set up at Manno's but John Perry cast a dispassionate eye over the impish Perrett and rather hastily dismissed him as a dilettante dealer with ambitions. John Perry:

> "At that point, The Ratbites were two guitars, bass and drums and we did this rehearsal. I took an almost immediate dislike to Peter. I thought he was posing outrageously. He wasn't really saying anything. He was being very passive/aggressive. I was rather obnoxious, making loud noises when he was going to sing. Something about the situation just felt as though it needed *confronting*."

Although the animosity wasn't precisely mutual, it didn't bode well for a harmonious association, or for the surly guitarist who Zena deemed in true Saturday night talent show vocabulary, to 'lack sparkle'. The members of Squeeze might not have been as proficient but they were certainly friendlier. Peter:

> "I knew Glen pretty well because he was living at our place in Blackheath. Chris Difford, their singer and rhythm guitarist, didn't do the gig but Jools Holland played. I did a demo with them which wasn't very good."

The maverick businessman Miles Copeland was down at the Marquee, prospecting, when he caught the makeshift band's set and showed interest in them as a complete unit, including Peter. Copeland signed Squeeze to his new BTM label the following year. For Peter, the gig was yet another event in a sequence of tentative creative steps, but without discipline his aspirations lacked consistency even though his aptitude for songwriting was gaining considerable ground.

If there is something in Peter and Zena that recalls the darker tendencies of the late sixties and early seventies, without any traces of hippy sentiments, then there was also a disaffected streak that gave them some kinship to the early rush of the punk movement. Politically, Peter claims to be extremely left wing and cites Fidel Castro, the Cuban

Socialist leader, as his political hero, though it is doubtful whether the songwriter would get up early for anyone's cause. The Perretts were suburban seditionaries.

1975 was a crucial year for cultural retuning. There was a brief retro phase among the style elite which saw a Glenn Miller revival; white soul rebels, GI Joes and Marilyn Monroes rubbing shoulders in carefully selected funk clubs. At the epicentre of King's Road cult couture, Westwood and McLaren changed stock and shop moniker with each mood swing. Let It Rock had been surmounted by the Teddy Boy look of Too Fast to Live, Too Young to Die. When Malcolm went off to America to try and salvage the New York Dolls' dissipated career, Vivienne revamped the shop with a distinctly sadistic theme featuring rubber and leather wear, with a fetching sideline in tit clamps, rubber masks and other sexually threatening accessories. Westwood rechristened the shop SEX and employed dominatrix queen Jordan to work the till and terrify unwary tourists.

With their refined taste for the taboo and a continuing interest in Zena's risqué designs, Vivienne and Malcolm became friendly with the Perretts. Zena:

"Malcolm and Vivienne started coming round to the house. Malcolm had been managing the New York Dolls and had just come back from the States. I didn't know anything about the Dolls but I remember him telling us that they could have been all right but they fucked up on drugs and now he was looking for another band to manage. He gave us the definition of what he was looking for. I'll never forget it. He wanted a 'raunchy Bay City Rollers'. That was the exact phrase he used. He wanted the Rollers but he still wanted someone debauched looking, like the New York Dolls, but not fucked up on drugs... man!

He'd come round for dinner and was discussing it when I remember his hearing one of Peter's songs, "Sister" (aka "Your Chosen Life", B-side of "Trouble In The World"), it had a line in it — *'To think my mouth touched your stinking, filthy cunt'*. Vivienne was really shocked by those lyrics. They were both like, 'Wow man, what was that line?' Obviously this was before the Pistols. It was so funny. He kept telling Peter that he was looking for a frontman. It was obvious that he was

THE ONE AND ONLY: Peter Perrett - Homme Fatale

hinting but Peter treated it like a joke 'cos it was plain that Malcolm was looking to manipulate."

It is quite wonderful to imagine Perrett reinvented as Peter Rotten, Sex Pistol, and although McLaren didn't get his way, he recalls Peter and Zena with goodwill. Malcolm McLaren:

"Zena was a perky little thing, sparrow-like, into black vinyl. She was incredibly ambitious and really tried to sell herself and her ideas and all the things Peter was doing."

Due to the highly suggestive nature of some of Westwood's designs, including the classic homo-erotic dance hall cowboys T-shirt, a problem arose in finding willing outworkers to make up the garments. Zena had avoided retail censorship by employing her mother and several of Loulla's friends to make up her lascivious She & Me creations. The elderly Greek women seemed unaware of the X-rating on the clothes they were putting together, so when Zena introduced them to Vivienne, they agreed to take on her designs as well. A tapestry of anarchistic threads were fashioned over cups of tea and home-made cakes. Vivienne's frequent visits to the Kakoulli household had a great impact on Zena's restless, youngest sister. Koulla:

"I remember seeing Vivienne and thinking that she was brilliant. I was only 14 or 15 but I idolised her. We were never allowed to have pictures of men on the wall, so I put up pictures of women instead. I got into the punk movement because of Vivienne."

With both Vivienne and Zena working to a similar premise, a little artistic intermingling occurred. Zena:

"Vivienne was a good friend. I always used to go into the shop and she'd have a look at what I was wearing. One day I was a bit annoyed when I went in because Jordan was wearing an outfit and it looked like one of my designs. I asked Jordan who said it was one of Vivienne's."

Despite this, Zena and Vivienne stayed in touch, even when Westwood found more specialised outworkers. The Perretts were assured a place on the guest list when Malcolm unveiled his nihilistic version of the Bay City Rollers. Zena:

"Malcolm got the Sex Pistols together and we were invited to some of the early gigs. He'd invite everybody that he knew to fill the venue up, then he'd run around to different spots in the audience, yelling 'More!'. I thought the Pistols were great. Johnny Rotten was good on stage. Peter thought he was funny. We talked to Rotten several times but he seemed like an acid head. Really spaced out."

While the Sex Pistols were making ready to blow the decade off its musical hinges, Peter was still meandering in his pleasure garden, although he was not without purpose. In the late summer, whilst ostensibly on a business trip to Holland, Peter, Zena and Lynne managed to catch up with a Ratbites tour. Beyond the socialising, it gave Perrett and Perry time to reassess their opinions of one another.

Back in England, Peter's languid intentions suddenly accelerated into activity, when the authorities threatened to strike the hour on his liberty. Business was brisk and profitable. The only hitch had been a driver who was busted and sentenced to four years, after being caught transporting a large amount of hash into the country. Beyond that, the Perretts operated as usual, taking periodical receipt of individual trailers containing roughly 60 kilos of hash, which they would split up and store in their garage. One such consignment arrived in the early autumn. After two weeks of deliveries, 16 lbs remained, marked for customers. In the house, Peter had a large 12 ounce block for personal use. He also maintained a connoisseur's collection over at Zena's parents' place in Catford. Peter:

"As I was really into smoking, I'd kept a stash of all the best hash and grass. It was like someone who'd keep a wine cellar. There was about two lbs of different types — four ounces of Colombian grass, four ounces of Nepalese Temple Balls, four ounces of Afghani, four ounces of Leb that I'd kept over the years. Because we were dealing in large amounts, lots of kilos, lots of lbs, just having two lbs didn't seem a big deal, but we didn't keep it at home. We kept it at Zena's parents' house, in the old bedroom. I don't know why she'd left it there. She just thought no-one would ever go to her parents' place. They weren't dealing, there was no reason for the police ever to go round there, but unknown to Zena, her two younger sisters had found it and stolen bits from it. They'd given some to one of their school friends, whose parents caught her with it. So, one morning, Zena's parents got raided and her sisters told them whose it was, so they came round to us in Blackheath."

The night before the raid, Zena, who held great store by dreams and omens, awoke from a deep sleep convinced that their home was about to be raided. Although no-one else shared her premonition, or in fact believed it, Zena cleared out the 16 lbs that was left in the garage and tried to warn Christian Pope who was holding a lb of hash to sell to a friend. When the Special Patrol Group came knocking with heavy hands, the Perrett household was in reasonable order, apart from Peter's 12 ounce block and a rather suspect set of gardening scales that could weigh up to 50 lbs at a time. The police didn't believe Peter when he told them he had an interest in market gardening. Peter:

"The SPG treated it as being quite heavy. I think they realised that we weren't selling to school kids and that Zena's sisters had stolen it, but because of the scales, and the 3 lbs, which was quite a lot. Normally you couldn't expect that just to be for personal, they did us for possession with intent to supply. It carried a heavy sentence, I was facing a possible five years. They assumed that the amount would be enough evidence that there was intent to supply. We didn't say anything 'cos we were pretty together about what to do, even though it was the first time we'd been busted for anything serious. They had no written evidence or interview evidence. We had a pretty good American solicitor who had been recommended to us. We were all charged, me, Zena, and Lynne. Christian made a statement when he was arrested, saying that he was just a middle man. He didn't say where he got it from, which was cool from our point of view, but from his own it was stupid. It does freak you out when you are arrested, and lots of people just can't handle it."

The case took a year to come to court. From the moment of the bust, everything that Peter did, fell under the shadow of the judge's hammer. Posterity isn't usually a young man's concern, but as the chill November wind scattered the last of the autumn leaves, Peter was keen to get his latest compositions down on tape.

Somewhere along the line, John Perry was deemed to have regained some sparkle quotient and was recalled back into the plot. He had left Bristol for London and was living in a quiet Roehampton suburb, in a shared house with the then unknown author of *The Hitchhiker's Guide To the Galaxy*, Douglas Adams. John Perry:

> "Late in that year I got a call from Zena, saying that Peter was going into the studio, did I want to come along, and did I know a drummer? We went to a place in Tooting and did five tracks that are now on *Remains*, with the Ratbites' drummer Alan Platt, me and Glen Tilbrook doing guitars and I also played bass. We did "Watch You Drown", "My Rejection", "I Only Wanna Be Your Friend", "Don't Hold Your Breath" and "Out There In The Night".
>
> It went well. It seemed that Peter's writing had moved on from the England's Glory days. In the studio, when we were actually working on something I got on with him much better. I'd been a musician for seven years and was used to working quickly. Peter had only been on stage a couple of times, so probably I was just very impatient with his inexperience. In the studio, because they were paying for the time themselves, there was no hurry. We were better able to do the job, so we got on well from that point, we started hanging out. I'd go over to the house, and there was this running entertainment with Peter's wife and mistress. I already knew Lynne from the Bristol scene."

Peter's past work had been derivative yet charming. Between the immature uncertainties of style and content, there were glints of his songwriting potential. At the Tooting session, he found his own voice and stance, discarding the borrowed guises in favour of the truth. The more seasoned Perry also enhanced Perrett's performance, and together they touched on several embryonic Only Ones' traits — imaginative fluid guitar playing casting a net beneath Peter's veering vocals.

"My Rejection" in particular, with its lyrical contemplation of a painful relationship — '*On reflection, my rejection comes as a blessing in disguise. It opened my eyes*' — contains a slowly building climax, a device to which The Only Ones were often partial. The number closes with a curious gospel style freak-out provided by two of Zena's girlfriends, over which the band sing, '*Sweet Peter's been and gone*'.

"Don't Hold Your Breath" is a winsome essay on longing, with Perrett's voice at its warmest and most falteringly endearing. It was an unwitting yet prophetic irony that he should deliver the line — '*Heaven is so much better once you've been to hell*'. Sweet Peter had only singed his fingers in the inferno. He was to become a great deal more familiar with purgatory before he could really talk of heaven. Perrett's creative star was on the ascendant, but he was promptly brought back down to earth within weeks of the Tooting session. Peter:

"I was going into town and was driving through New Cross when I turned around this corner and there was a road block. It wasn't for me, it was just there. It just so happened that the fucking guy who was on the road block was Sergeant Clark of the SPG who busted us. I didn't think I had anything on me at all, so I was completely relaxed when I got out of the car. I was walking towards him and I stuck my hand in my pocket and as I did that, I felt this tiny lump. It was a jacket I'd put on that day. He busted me."

The incident, like so many of Peter Perrett's dramas found its way into a song. In this case, "Don't Feel Too Good" (*Remains*):

Turned around the corner
And what d'you think I see
Sergeant Clark of the SPG
I'm thinking things like this don't happen in real life
Don't ever want it to happen again
Don't feel too good this morning
Here I am, sitting in the charge room
I read the police statement
Why can't you tell the truth?
What have I ever done to you?
Went before the magistrate
He adjourned the case
And I still don't know what evils I might face
Things like this don't happen in real life
When will it, when will it, when will it all end?

It was only just the beginning.

Chapter 5 – The Sporting Life

Peter Perrett began the new year in his usual fashion. Cloaked in a faded silk dressing gown that was holed by joint and cigarette burns, he explored spaced-out frontiers. Once Peter had a taste for something, an escalation in appetite was inevitable. Peter:

> "Up until '75, it was basically just smoke and hash. I'd had odd bits of coke but it hardly did anything, it was too weak. The first time I tried it properly was when I got involved with these importers. It was 100% clean when it came into this country. I started doing a lot more coke. When you do a lot of coke, you can drink much more, and it keeps you awake, so I used to drink a lot more alcohol as well. Smack was something I took once a month, and then maybe once a weekend."

The little prince was now a petty criminal with more than one kind of record. Given the imploring tone of "Don't Feel Too Good" it is surprising — though perhaps inevitable — that he should then move into the cocaine market. He thrived on catastrophe, transforming traumas into passionate poetry. Peter:

> "I suggested to these Italians that I was working with, that cocaine was a good financial direction to go in. I'd never thought about making money but it seemed attractive. There's a certain freedom to having lots of money, to be able to do what you want to do, when you want to. Also, it would help as far as the money that was needed to get the music off the ground. It would pay for studio and rehearsal time, and equipment.
>
> One of my Italian friends went down to Bolivia, met people there and brought a kilo back, the first time just to see how it went. I got into it and we became equal partners, which meant we could invest in it and buy some. We just had one wholesaler who we sold it to for £400 an ounce. The profit margin was approximately 700%. We were selling it for £14 a gram."

Peter took to delinquency like a cat burglar to a roof. The artistic felon is not a new theme. The persecuted and provocative Lenny Bruce was crushed by obscenity and narcotic charges. Brendan Behan, the anarchic

Irish playwright, once did a spell inside for gun running. French poet, addict, mercenary and trader, Rimbaud and his fellow countryman, Jean Genet, thief, convict and writer, were amongst Perrett's spiritual forefathers. Peter was unaware of his heritage. He read very little, except for sporting papers and gun magazines. The only literature that appealed to him at school was Greek mythology. Like his artistic relatives, Perrett was a natural existential outlaw. Peter:

> "When you are young, you like the outlaw chic, fighting against society. Also, back then, the police weren't as sophisticated. It was much easier to get away with it. Because we were only dealing to one person, we didn't have to have other people around the house all the time."

Peter also showed a predisposition towards the splendid condition of poetic decline, as exemplified by the fin-de-siecle decadents who practised sensuality, enjoyment of disorder and falling into sickly stupors. Edmund White, in his fine biography of Jean Genet (or the "Jean Genie" to Bowie acolytes) perceives dandyism as a filtered form of decadence and writes that, 'The dandy topples traditional hierarchies of value and order and replaces morality with an aesthetic rule of his own devising'.

By this point, John Perry had relocated to Chelsea with his girlfriend Suze, and had become a regular visitor to planet Perrett. John Perry:

> "The first year before we started gigging was the most I hung out with Peter. We just got phenomenally stoned. The main activity at that point was coke. There would be a couple of ounces; a small mountain on the table that we'd be snorting our way through. Peter was also inclining toward heroin. Zena was struggling hard to keep him out of its orbit, although it was early days.
>
> Occasionally we'd play, but more often we'd be playing backgammon rather than music. The house had an atmosphere of its own, a suburban version of *Performance* without the literary and magickal overtones. I enjoyed it in patches but I wouldn't have wanted to live there, it was quite claustrophobic. I would get back up to London and feel like I'd fallen down a hole for a week, and would have to pick up the pieces of ordinary life again. Also, I caught the crabs."

Neither John nor Peter could be classed as 'chummy' people. Any form of bonding, beyond an initial narcotic compatibility, was out of the

Above: (l-r) "The Birthday Present", Lynne Shillingford, Peter Perrett and John Perry at an impromptu coke and backgammon party in Blackheath.

Right: Peter's cat Candy for which he wrote "Out There In The Night".

question. An amicable tension served instead of friendship, held together by a mutual esteem for the other's talent. Peter:

"I found John quite a pleasant person to be with. He was quite intelligent, and we had certain things in common, he liked drugs. He's a great guitarist and he had a lot of enthusiasm."

John Perry:

"Peter was obviously quite unique in his way. It was the reason I started working with him. It was clear that his voice was not going to be something that everybody would like — it was a specialist taste. There was a unity to the way he looked, the sound of his voice, the songs he wrote. I'd worked with people who attempted to put on a persona, that was the furthest from the case with Peter. What you see is what he is. I thought we were pretty good. One thing that Peter and I shared was a feeling that whatever we did, we were the best at. We never really discussed this, but we shared an outlook, a way of doing things and a self-confidence."

Throughout '76, the jigsaw foundations of The Only Ones fell into place. The Tooting line-up were block-booked at Manno's, trying to pin down an elusive muse. John was less than happy on bass, while Glen Tilbrook tended toward torrential riffing. John Perry:

"I wasn't going to stay on bass for long. Tilbrook annoyed me enormously. He was one of those guitarists that would play non-stop and wouldn't make space. He irritated me so much, that at one point, I pulled his jack out of the amp, which enraged him. He packed his guitar up, walked out of the room and never came back. Culturally, that was the right move."

Alan Platt was still behind the drums, although it was evident that the red-haired Scot was not a permanent fixture. When the cold weather made way for coming spring, a tall, gentle looking man with world-weary eyes, and more rock 'n' roll in his bones than calcium, ventured out to pick up his kit which had been stored at Manno's. The proprietor was delighted to see Mike Kellie again, and invited him into the rehearsal room to look over the assembled musicians. Mike Kellie:

"I stood in the room and in that instant I knew I was going to play with Peter, because his songs were great. It was just what I had been looking for. I would not let Peter go after that. As far as drums and frontmen go, I was convinced that he was my vehicle and I was his. They were wonderful, they put up with me. I was very forceful, but nobody argued the point. I was the only drummer that could interpret his songs properly as far as I was concerned. It wasn't arrogance, it was just a statement of fact."

Kellie arrived at their door with tip-top credentials steeped in the history of classic English rock. His first outfit, the VIP's evolved into Spooky Tooth, who alongside Traffic, helped to launch Island Records.

Spooky Tooth built up a solid reputation before hitting a bumpy patch which involved several personnel shuffles. Eventually bassist Greg Ridley left to join Humble Pie with Steve Marriott. Luther Grosvenor went on to play guitar for Mott The Hoople under the name of Ariel Bender, while Mick Jones turned up as the guitarist in Foreigner. Kellie jobbed around as part of Peter Frampton's Camel and moved on to session work with among others Jerry Lee Lewis and Traffic. Well into the '70s, he was touring annually with French rocker Johnny Halliday, as well as doing a spot in Paul Kossoff's Back Street Crawler.

By the middle of the decade, Kellie was floundering. He had split up with his wife and left the marital farmhouse in Berkshire for the wilder shores of the King's Road. He filled his time with pick up bands, searching for something to set his pulse racing. Now he had found it. Both Perrett and Perry took to Mike Kellie with a strange combination of bemusement and respect. Emotionally, Kellie was wide open, with certain odd beliefs that appeared to come from another, kinder age, where bands not only played together, they stuck together like family. Peter:

"Kellie was a bit of a casualty. He'd been around in the '60s and he was down on his luck. Kellie used to say how it had to be a family. John was always cynical about Kellie's ideals. At the time, I used to make fun of them but I can see what he was getting at now."

For all his apparent vulnerability, Kellie approached Perrett with such conviction that he was invited to take up his position almost immediately. John Perry:

"Peter took to Kellie straight away, thought he was a strong drummer. I was a little bit worried because he didn't appear to be able to remember titles from one minute to the next. When we were rehearsing you would see him counting a song in but he didn't have any idea which song it was, until he got going. But to give him his due, he was a strong player with a lot of character. There was no question, he was in."

One of the commonest stories told about Kellie joining also involves him moving into Peter's garden shed because he needed somewhere to stay. It is a rumour that the drummer is keen to refute. Mike Kellie:

"I haven't slept in a garden shed in my life! Not that I would mind. I slept in a kind of shed in Jamaica once, but that was a bit different. It just made sense to me for us to be together, so I moved into their house in Blackheath. It was great. I can picture it now. You'd go in, and the room on the left had a sound system, then you'd go through into the kitchen. I had a room upstairs. Christian who became our road manager also had a room. Peter and Zena were just down the hall and the bathroom was to the right."

For all the superficial domestic bliss, Perrett had just about broken the boundaries of Eros. Lynne was attempting to play tug-of-love with Peter in the middle and Zena at the end of her tether. Zena:

"Initially I thought Lynne was okay and that maybe she was more open minded than me and I shouldn't be possessive. It started to irritate me that she should be possessive while I was meant to be understanding. I didn't think jealousy was a good emotion, I used to see it in other women and I tried really hard not to be that way myself. It got to the point where Lynne said we should all be sleeping in the same bed. I didn't mind living under the same roof as Lynne but I wanted time that was mine.

I didn't mind sharing Peter but I didn't want to share my time with him too. I could respect him spending the night with her, she'd get upset about him spending time with me. The reason that she suggested we share the bed was she couldn't cope with him spending any time with me. I said I'd rather not have any of it and if Peter wanted to come and see me, fine, I'd get a flat. I rented a place in Forest Hill."

Peter was taken aback by Lynne's 'selfish' behaviour. Peter:

The Sporting Life

Above: Peter and the wolf fur coat with Zena as vixen by his side.

"It was weird 'cos when I first met Lynne, part of the attraction was that she was very open-minded, sexually. I didn't think she'd start to get possessive that early. It was a bit weird that the girlfriend should be getting jealous, rather than the wife. It was a bit cheeky that she should start trying to dictate terms.

Although I tried to persuade Zena not to go, I never really tried that hard to do anything. It's like that line in "Baby Don't Talk" (The One's *Cultured Palate* EP) where I say, *'Fools rely on natural selection'*. It's the easy way. Whoever put up with the most and stuck it out, I'd be with. For the first two months it was alright. Lynne kept me occupied. She got this girl to come and stay for a week. It was a birthday present. We were like little kids when the parents have gone away 'cos Zena was always the sensible one."

During an interview concerning this period, Peter wrote out a preamble which goes as follows:

'He picked up a hundred dollar bill rolled into a tube, leaned over the bedside and snorted a line of white powder and a line of brown powder.

> *Lynne's lips were round his penis and Jill's tongue was exploring his anus. She was a friend of Lynne's and was Lynne's birthday present to him. This was to help him to forget the recently departed Zena...'*

Like a child who had been granted a wish to stay at the fairground forever, Peter soon tired of round-the-clock amusements and began to yearn for Zena. His wife's withdrawal tilted into role reversal as she became the desired object of midnight trysts. For all the twists and turns, the Perretts were so wrapped up in each other's life that they folded into the same fabric. Peter:

"It was a shock how much I missed Zena. I realised how much I fancied her and it would be hard to leave. All of a sudden she was the mistress and Lynne was the wife at home who would phone up every ten minutes to see if I'd left. It was interesting because as the roles were reversed, it was easier to compare the two. I realised that I didn't really like the situation I found myself in.

It was coming up to the time when the lease on the house needed renewing. I let it go and didn't do anything about finding another place. I just ended up staying at Zena's more, but I kept seeing Lynne. After Zena, she was the second person I'd got most involved with. I thought I was in love with her to a certain extent, but I'm not sure if that was because we got into smack together. When you first start taking smack, it makes sex a million times better and you think you're being very emotional."

Throughout the emotional intrigue, the Perretts remained connected by their key roles in the organisation they had helped to found. One bright morning, Zena waited for a taxi to take her to the airport. Her attire was not in the usual sex vamp mode, rather she looked like any young woman in casual summer wear, getting ready to go on holiday. A ticket to Brazil was folded inside her passport. The night before, the Perretts discussed business. This was to be their final cocaine transaction. Their upcoming court case figured heavily in their decision to withdraw from risk taking. Because Peter couldn't feasibly transform himself into a straight-looking tourist, Zena agreed to go to South America to oversee their closing deal. Peter:

"It was much better for Zena to do it because she could look normal. I think she brought back nine or ten kilos, and two kilos out of it was ours. By that time we had plenty of money, and as the band had started happening, we didn't have enough time, so it was silly to carry on taking risks."

In an unusually far-thinking strategy, plans had been made for Zena's return. The Perretts would introduce their distributors into the organisation, allowing them to bow out and concentrate solely on Peter's career. Part of the Brazil pay off would be invested in the band, and Peter was keen for his wife to act as manager. Zena:

"I said to Peter, 'Are you really serious about this music? Because I'm sick and tired of you pretending. You either do it or don't, but if you do, and live and breathe it, I'll put everything into it. I will support you'.

I felt with all the things I'd done, starting up a business, working in the Brook Street Bureau, which I did for a bit, and even the Sociology course, I felt that I could do it. I'd learnt a lot since taking the England's Glory album around the record companies."

While Zena was away, Peter carried on cavorting. It was only to be expected that as Perrett showed scant concern for the laws of society, he was hardly likely to observe the Highway Code. Peter Perrett considered himself immortal, and anyone outside his personal sphere of importance was a moving target with two seconds to dive out of the way of his flying Cortina. Peter:

"I could fill a book with my road exploits, being chased by irate people. When I was young, I used to drive like a maniac with my foot on the floor all the time, full acceleration, maximum speed. I used to really like driving. I thought a car was to get you there as quickly as possible."

When Peter invited Kellie to join him and Lynne for a night out on the town, the benign drummer was in for a symbolic preview of The Only Ones' career. Peter:

"We went to an after hours club, just off Regent Street. I'd had a lot to drink. Scotch, bourbon, Southern Comfort and vodka, several doubles of all of them. We all got in the car to drive back to Forest Hill. I thought my reflexes were that good, I could always get out of the way of whatever was about to hit me, or whatever I was about to hit. You've never seen two more terrified people. I was going through red traffic lights, driving the other side of islands. They were both screaming, pleading to be let out.

I didn't have any accidents all the way from Regent Street to Forest Hill, until I drove up to Elliot Bank. I came around the corner, full acceleration, and the car started to spin on a gravel path. It just spun round and round. It was like being in a washing machine. We ended up, upside down. The roof of the car was flattened to the bonnet. We climbed out the window without a scratch on us. I was laughing, I don't know if I was hysterical. We quickly ran away 'cos I was very drunk."

Kellie was not amused by Peter's metal sandwich antic. Mike Kellie:

"He (Peter) had on this big fur coat made from hundreds of dead rabbits or something. No it wasn't rabbit, it was wolf. I grabbed him and the seam ripped and he was so upset. We were both upset. Even though I was right to be furious, we got out of the car alright. If you're drunk or stoned, you fall like babies. I remember Lynne being quite upset, but then she would have been. My argument lost all credibility when I ripped his coat. I felt so guilty and it shut him up as well. I loved him then and I love him now but he's such a spoilt little brat. All his life he's had whatever he wanted and it spoiled him. The fact that he was such a lovely guy saved him from being even more of a spoilt brat."

For all his devil child ways, Peter was bewitching. He lined his green eyes with kohl, was dressed up in the prettiest creations by his wife, and had even grown to resemble a gorgeous hybrid of Brian Jones and Keith Richards when the bloom of beauty still glowed in their hollow cheeks.

When Kellie tumbled out of the Cortina, the drummer's rage evaporated in seconds. In his youth, Peter possessed a supernatural gift for evading acrimony and responsibility. His elusive nature and delicate appearance concealed a powerful undercurrent. John Perry:

"I'd come across strong people, people who could get things done but they were always active in style. His was the first passive yet powerful orbit I'd come into. There was a time when *The Godfather* was his favourite film; he was interested in the apparent manifestation of power.

The atmosphere at Peter and Zena's had a flavour of South London villainy. Mixing with them was a completely different world from my background which was basically liberal/cultural. There was a sort of decay from which one would be well advised to maintain a separate life. I would go to the Test Match or shoot off to Cornwall with my girlfriend. But you have to remember that in the middle of this atmosphere, every Saturday, Peter would put on his football kit and trot off to play a game."

Summer passed with Perrett, Perry and Kellie incarcerated at Manno's, auditioning bass players. So far they had come up empty-handed. Their search for a good bassist seemed like a hunt for an endangered species. The band in the next room however, the Streetwalkers, had managed to lure one in for a try-out session. During a coffee break, the bass player wandered into the corridor and was captivated by the sight of two lovely ladies, Lynne and Manno Ventura's girlfriend, who were making their way into the other rehearsal room. If it had been a deliberate honey trap, the result may not have been as sweet. Alan Mair:

"I thought, 'Who are they?', and followed them to investigate. I walked in and John was playing, I thought, 'He's obviously just bought that Gibson'. Kellie I recognised from Spooky Tooth. To be honest, I thought, 'What's a seasoned musician like that playing with these people for?' It didn't seem like it was matching or something. I just left."

Kellie was almost as smitten by the unannounced visitor, as he had been when he first set eyes on Peter. Mike Kellie:

"The door opened mid-song and this head came round. I'm a great believer that you can see talent — charisma, whatever you call it, does look different. Afterwards, I got hold hold of Manno and said, 'Who was that, is he a bass player?' It turned out Alan had been a bass player all his life. I got his home number and phoned him, but he didn't want to know. I wouldn't let him go, he just had to be in the band."

Alan Mair's reluctance sprang from two sources — a somewhat flagging enthusiasm for the music business and a cultural clash. Perrett, Perry and Kellie were very diverse characters. There was no obvious

THE ONE AND ONLY: Peter Perrett - Homme Fatale

common thread between them, except something rather ethereal, for the constant Alan Mair to connect with. But these very disparities within the unit, combined with Mair's musical capabilities, made him perfect for the job. He just needed convincing.

Mair had been raised in Glasgow and cut his teeth on Tamla Motown and Booker T and the MG's. In his late teens, he played bass in The Beatstalkers, who were considered the tartan Beatles. In Scotland they met with Shea Stadium style hysteria and tearful fainting fans, but made little headway outside of their home territory. The band were managed by David Bowie's early mentor, Ken Pitt, who rented Alan a room in his London office after The Beatstalkers broke up.

Alan downed bass and picked up a sewing needle to pursue his second option; that of mod tailor and groovy boot designer, catering for the likes of Bowie, The Tremeloes and Marmalade. His stall in Kensington Market did such a roaring trade that he virtually put fellow stall owner, Freddie Bulsara (soon to be Mercury) out of business. The exotic looking Freddie came to work for Alan and eventually asked him if he would like to play in his (then unsigned) band Queen. Mair politely declined.

It took a while for the gentle-voiced Scot to regain his appetite for music but, spurred on by the success of his old friend David Bowie, Alan returned to his premier craft. By the time he reached Manno's, Mair was several years into a campaign to find compatible beings who cared for music more than money. He wasn't too sure about the unnamed outfit's intentions but he knew they had a persistent drummer. After Kellie called for a second time, Alan half-heartedly agreed to visit chez Perrett. Zena arrived back in London just in time to make Alan's acquaintance. Alan Mair:

"I got there at 1 o'clock and Peter didn't appear. He was in the bath waiting for Zena to come and wash his hair! After two hours I said, 'Enough's enough, I'm off'. At that point Peter came in and sat down and started chatting. I was thinking, 'Well, I still don't like the band anyway', but then he asked me if I wanted to hear a tape.

He put it on and I listened to "Watch You Drown" (*Remains*) and "Out There In The Night" (*Serpents*) and I just thought, 'This is fantastic'. I could hear Peter's lyrics, I could hear Peter's voice, whereas in rehearsal it had been all about the volume and I couldn't hear the texture. I loved his lyrics, the sentiments, his voice. We rehearsed together for two weeks and I thought, 'Yeah, I'm part of this'."

At 29, Alan still possessed the conventional good looks that had made him teeny pin-up material. He was the oldest member of the band, senior to Peter and John by five years, with 12 months over Kellie. He was also the 'straight' man of the outfit. Someone had to be. Alan Mair:

"At the beginning, a lot of things seemed bizarre. I like the idea of finding myself in a situation where I don't feel comfortable for a while. To my friends, The Only Ones were a bizarre band. Mentally I found myself doubling over to get my head around certain things. I mean, Peter waiting for Zena to wash his hair was beyond me. Him having a girlfriend and a wife. Even "Out There In The Night", I asked him what it was about. It turned out that it was a love song about his cat, which hadn't come home. He adored this cat, it would go in the bath with him and lie on top of him. When he told me the song was about his cat, and the cat was the only creature that gave him unconditional love, I thought, 'This guy is definitely different'."

Peter welcomed Alan's steady nature:

"He was straight, which meant he was different from the rest of us, 'cos the rest of us liked being stoned and getting out of it. In some ways it suits bass players to be solid and dependable."

In time Mair became accustomed to the quirks of his new musical comrades, and discovered that it was a matter of dealing with the sulphur and sweetness before full membership was endowed. Alan Mair:

"Peter was without doubt the most artistic person I had ever met, he was incredibly talented. If I looked at him, I could see an aura about him — a star quality. I always got on well with Kellie. In some ways Kellie was considered to be the old head in the band in the sense that he'd been there and done it. In the beginning, when Peter was a little naive, he'd listen closely to what Kellie had to say. Later this started to reverse and in some ways he held it against Kellie, that he had taken his advice. As Peter started to blossom, he would wind Kellie up because he was more vulnerable than anyone else was. I had a love/hate relationship with

THE ONE AND ONLY: Peter Perrett - Homme Fatale

John. I got to accept his bitchiness. He's a very witty guy but it's usually with sarcasm. I got to like the bit I hated about him."

Peter's days of childhood friends and vagabond players acting as insufficient backup to his visions were over. He had found validation for his lyrics with a group of committed musicians who provided the heightened dynamics Perrett's songs cried out for.

The name came to Peter in his favourite place and state, tucked up in bed, half-drugged. Washed up on the shore of dreams, he heard a whisper like the ocean through a seashell and scribbled it down on a piece of paper before drifting off again. The next afternoon, over a late breakfast, he read back the sleep scrawled memo. It said, 'The Only Ones'.

Chapter 6 – Around & Around

In a period when musical barbarism was in vogue, The Only Ones were heretics. There had been a wonderful tear-away spirit to be found in the English punk movement, and individual style was encouraged, but as punk became increasingly fashionable, rigidity of expression set in and with it came an unwritten code of behaviour akin to artistic knee-capping. The Only Ones pushed through punk's concrete playground like a morbid and exotic bloom. This wasn't pogo, this was poetry amongst the brash anarchistic sloganeering. In time, as punk's image came to be reflected in a beer can, The Only Ones shone like mother-of-pearl.

As the long hot summer of 1976 drew to a close, the punks held their coming out ball on 21st and 22nd of September at the 100 Club on London's Oxford Street. The two day festival showcased the fledgling scene's phlegm de la phlegm — most notably the Pistols, the Damned, the Buzzcocks and an early line-up of Siouxsie and the Banshees. The event had been conceived by Malcolm McLaren to present punk as a cohesive movement with the Sex Pistols as the forefront.

Some of the new groups were strenuously denying any previous musical knowledge, others were the genuine article and barely able to strap a guitar on, while The Only Ones were trawling around music shops, browsing amps and buying instruments.

Within weeks of finalising the band's line-up, Mrs Perrett had taken up the managerial reins and was paying for new equipment with part of the proceeds from her South American trip. Nobody could have equalled her dedication to The Only Ones' cause. Zena:

> "I thought I was the person for the job because I was so enthusiastic about it. If you are enthusiastic and really believe in something, you devote your whole time to it, and that way, you do it properly. It might have been easier for somebody with experience but they wouldn't have devoted their entire being to it. It was my whole life to promote this group."

An early reticence on Zena's behalf soon evaporated as she gained confidence in her role as an all-round guardian angel, prepared to work wonders for her husband's group. John Perry:

"Zena was quite a determined young woman around town at that point. She was certainly capable of intimidating people, where necessary, to get things done. At that stage, our management consisted of little more than day-to-day arrangements, and it seemed a sensible move given that no-one else had a better idea. She was dubious about it as well, at first. Her strongest advocate was Kellie, who wanted to 'keep it all in the family'."

As The Only Ones' career started to assume direction, the Perretts' relationship once again altered course. Under the guise of management, Mrs Perrett reverted to her maiden name, concealing her identity as Peter's wife for professional reasons. Zena and Peter turned a new passage in their emotional labyrinth, and took on the personnae of intimate friends, working together, a good enough idea but one inevitably doomed to failure.

In the meantime, Lynne had moved to Notting Hill, where she rented an apartment in Chepstow Villas. Peter drove hell-for-leather between bases, speeding into the horizon towards his wife, manager or mistress as the white lines merged.

With the impending court case still haunting the Perretts, Zena booked The Only Ones into the same 16-track studio in Tooting where the '75 Tilbrook sessions had taken place. Peter:

"We went into the studio and did some demos, just in case the court case went wrong. I at least wanted to have something on tape. I'd had all this time to prepare myself for the fact that I might have to go away for a couple of years."

Prior to going into the studio, Peter and Zena had been invited to a select dinner party in Queensgate, where they were introduced to Keith Richards by one of their business connections, Stefan Stone*. By the mid-seventies, The Rolling Stones had become stadium phantoms, distant, spotlit figures with more folklore than substance. Jagger had traded his threatening posture for jet-setting celebrity status, while Keith was too stoned to roll. With his heavy lidded eyes, ruined teeth and Eucharist pallor, Richards had metamorphasised into the patron saint of white, middle class junkies.

After Stefan played Richards an Only Ones tape, the guitarist developed an interest in producing the band and came down to Tooting one evening with his eight-year-old son, Marlon, to take a look at Peter and company in action.

The Only Ones had been rehearsing at Manno's almost daily and were becoming accustomed to working a number through until the moment of alchemical unity when all disparate threads come together. They transferred this method to the studio, where they put down a desolate version of "Flowers Die". After three days of musical discord, they summoned up a consummate version of "Breaking Down".

Perrett's temper was fraying with each failed take of his epic tragedy where, *'The heavens open with the sound of screaming and the smell of blood'*. The sombre tale of mental disintegration finally reached an appropriately spacey trajectory of cool jazz guitar, skimming over some wonderfully disembodied drumming. A rather tipsy Kellie had tilted back on the drum stool and was balanced precariously against the wall at a 90 degree angle, but was encouraged to keep on playing.

Several faltering attempts were made at "In-Betweens" before it was temporarily shelved. Finally in the small, stoned hours, Keith materialised to witness "River Of No Return". From a distance, the song, with its strolling bass and drums and melodic guitar hook, could pass for a merely pleasant ditty, until Perry's playing takes on a sardonic air as Peter reveals the danger of submerged women, like predatory blue nymphs inhabiting a drowning pool. The gossamer ripple of Peter's voice and acoustic guitar was a pleasing accidental effect, achieved by cranking up the reverb on the vocal mike inside the recording booth.

The Only Ones were never a particularly social outfit but Stefan was keen to foster a low-key party atmosphere for Mr Richards and laid on several bottles of Black Label whisky and a hearty dollop of cocaine. Keith was stoned on arrival and floated through the small studio like an out of body experience, oblivious to the festive trappings. John Perry:

> "Richards and Marlon came straight through to the studio floor, where we were working, into the control room. The booth was this narrow strip, and Keith realised he was trapped and couldn't walk straight out

again. The engineer was gawping at him. It was clearly the kind of situation that Richards hates. Keith's whole strategy for dealing with it was just like what shy teenage girls do, he emptied his bag on the floor and spent an hour going through it to avoid making any kind of eye contact. It was the first time I had met him but the principal impression I got straight away was, apart from his being very stoned, that he was immensely shy. Once the handbag was rearranged to his satisfaction, he split."

Keith may have given the impression of being more involved with the contents of his lavishly embroidered shoulder bag than the music of The Only Ones, but beneath the shy, stoned, aloofness, he maintained that he still wanted to produce them, and had picked out a song called "Prisoners" from the demo tape that Mr Stone had originally played for him. Ironically, any further discussion about the production of "Prisoners" had to be put on hold because of Peter's imminent court case. It was a situation that Richards knew well, given the Stones' history of drug busts, although he himself had not quite reached the zenith of judicial horrors that awaited him just around the corner like a rabid sniffer dog.

Peter removed his chipped nail varnish and pulled out a sober suit from the back of a cluttered wardrobe. In the other room, Zena clutched the telephone receiver like a lifeline as she desperately tried to reach the former England's Glory champion, David Sandison, who was now working at CBS. With his gentle air of respectability, Sandison qualified as the perfect character witness that the Perretts' eminent QC, Jeremy Hutchinson, hoped would add extra weight to their case. Hutchinson had been recommended to them as the legal rock on which they could depend, and so they made their way to the Inner London Crown Court, where Peter faced four charges of cannabis possession.

Despite Peter's understandable nerves, Hutchinson represented him like a black caped knight on a righteous crusade. Peter:

> "The prosecution presented their case, and Jeremy Hutchinson just tore them to bits. He had the policemen quaking in their boots when he cross-examined them. He got the police to handle the exhibits because part of their evidence was that the scales had traces of hash on them. He established that they handled the hash first, before the scales. Then, he

Above: The Only Ones get all fired up.

got them to handle the evidence. One policeman, when Jeremy Hutchinson handed him the hash, dropped it and it went everywhere. The jury were laughing and Hutchinson said, 'It's pretty obvious how the hash got on the scales'.

The other evidence was me saying that it was all for personal use. I convinced them that I was a connoisseur and the fact that it was all different types meant that it was less likely for resale. Also, the bit in my pocket from when I was arrested whilst on bail, I explained by saying I just didn't know it was in there, and if I had known, I would have thrown it away. As the case was progressing, this really high up policeman had come in and sat at the back, while Jeremy Hutchinson was making the police contradict themselves in the witness box. The top brass guy just got up and walked out, he was really angry."

When the trusty David Sandison took his turn on the stand, it was with a sense of déjà-vu, that took him back almost a decade earlier to the same court room, where a pale faced, shadow-eyed Brian Jones had stood in Peter's scuffed shoes. David Sandison:

"I couldn't believe it, because on the previous occasion I'd been in that court was when Brian got done for the last time and he was found guilty. I was working for The Stones during that period. The chairman of the sessions had been Reginald Seaton and when I walked in, there was Seaton sitting on the bench. Oh my God! Déjà-vu!! Peter looked fairly together, he was wearing a suit. He just looked traditionally wasted.

I basically said that I had known Peter, and that while I'd been in his company both professionally and socially on many occasions, he'd only ever once offered me any. I said, 'I don't smoke', and after that he never offered me a toke, but his own consumption was formidable. How did I explain the scales? 'Well, we've got a set of brass scales at home as well, they're something my wife bought for the house 'cos they look pretty'.

I said that I thought Peter was an extremely gifted young musician and writer and he was on the verge of a very promising career and I felt it would be really bad if something like this was going to stand in his way because he had an incredible amount of promise and could do a lot of good with his music."

During a brief adjournment, David joined the Perretts for a coffee and watched them light up an unbroken chain of cigarettes before he went back to the CBS press office. Zena and Peter returned to the court room where Peter was placed on Judge's remand, handcuffed and packed off to Wandsworth Prison for the night. Peter:

"I was guilty, I just hadn't been sentenced yet. It's different to being on remand before you've been found guilty, you're not convicted so you're allowed to wear your own clothes but because I was convicted I had to take all my clothes off. There's a doctor who is meant to examine you to make sure you're healthy, the doctor was so drunk there was a screw either side of him holding him up. Then you have to have a bath. The uniform they gave me was terrible, so were the dirty grey Y-fronts I had to wear. It was all really horrible. I didn't sleep that night, the bed was really uncomfortable and I had to share a cell with two other people. It was so frightening. I thought I was going to get a custodial sentence."

The following morning Peter was taken back to court. Fear clogged his throat like the unpleasant texture of prison issue blankets, as Judge Gibbens began to speak. A reporter from *The Mercury*, a local paper with a prurient interest in suburban shame, took down the details for a slender piece with a scandalous edge whose headline read, "Pop man faces jail on drugs charge":

> *Pop group member Peter Perrett faces a year in jail if he cannot pay a £1,100 fine for possessing drugs. Judge Brian Gibbens, QC, told Perrett, of The Only Ones pop group: 'Smoking cannabis is regarded by a number of people, and maybe this is a delusion, as no more harmful than taking alcohol or smoking tobacco. It may well be that when Sir Walter Raleigh brought tobacco to this country, if its effects had been realised, it would have been banned, and likewise alcohol'.*
>
> *Perrett appeared in the dock with his wife, Xenoulla Perrett and Christian Pope. All pleaded guilty to being in possession of cannabis, although of different quantities. Pope pleaded guilty to possessing cannabis with intent to supply others but this charge was denied by Mr and Mrs Perrett. At the end of the case, Judge Gibbens upheld a submission by Mr Jeremy Hutchinson QC, defending the Perretts, and he directed the jury to acquit the Perretts on the charge.*
>
> *Mrs Perrett was fined £150, but Pope who had a previous conviction for having cannabis, was sent to prison for nine months. Perrett was given three months to pay or face a total of 12 months' imprisonment. Judge Gibbens said: 'Smoking cannabis is considered by many to have a deleterious effect and we are not the only country to ban its use. It is up to the courts to enforce the law'.*

Peter and Zena practically danced out of the court house into the cold October afternoon. The judge's hammer had bounced like a rubber toy across their knuckles. With the legalities settled, the future of The Only Ones seemed assured.

The year drew to a close in a tabloid blaze of Punk! Shock! headlines, after the Sex Pistols appeared on Thames Television's *Today* show. Veteran presenter Bill Grundy goaded the band into a torrent of four-letter words that would subsequently go down in broadcasting history. The petty litany of insults sent the general populace into a moral panic and put the brakes on The Pistols' nationwide Anarchy tour.

The cross-country joy ride which also featured The Clash, the Damned and special US guests The Heartbreakers, was due to start in the first week of December but was held up by folks determined to stop the spread of the punk plague. Unsurprisingly the Anarchy tour ran aground, but the movement burst forth.

The Only Ones came of age in the same season as punk. While Peter and the band shared a knavish approval of the punk acts storming the barricades of the conservative music business, they had little else in common. Mike Kellie:

> "The music business did need the kick up the backside that it got from that whole period. There was this whole ivory tower of musicians and successful artists, the Rod Stewarts and so on, who were just churning it out and there were kids out there who wanted to get up and do it, and couldn't. You got people just getting up there and making noises, having a good time. Rehearsing in public."

When The Only Ones began to gather momentum and press interest, they were often considered by those outside of their following to be an aesthetic anachronism amongst the anarchists. John Perry:

> "I would say that punk was the anachronism and that we represented the median. We were a perfect expression of late '70s English rock 'n' roll and it was punk that was the oddity. God forbid that one adopts an American point of view, but to them English punk was this tiny little hiccough. There was also this rubbish at the time about guitar solos, all these stupid Stalinist dictates by people who couldn't play. I was never terribly impressed by that. We were never part of it, but at the same time we were accepted by the people who were of it, so you'd get these apologetic pieces in papers about how, 'The Only Ones play guitar

solos, but they're okay'. What do you do with criticism from people who aren't qualified to make it in the first place?"

The Only Ones carried the torch of classic rock 'n' roll into the late '70s. It was this very quality that had drawn Keith Richards to them. He was still keen to produce "Prisoners", once he learned that Peter had escaped the fate of the song's title. The Rolling Stone asked Perrett and company over to the opulent house he was renting from the actor Donald Sutherland on Old Church Street in Chelsea. John Perry:

"It was just before the Toronto bust and he was in the depth of his addiction. There was a great deal of fog to penetrate. He sat at a Wurlitzer piano and I played guitar. For about three hours we just circled this progression as he gradually locked on to the chords. There were only about seven! At one point I spoke up, 'No, that one's augmented!' But he just scowled and carried on. It was clearly better to let him take his time. From what I could gather, Keith hardly knew the names of the chords, he just worked by ear. His modus operandi was just to go round and around until he'd beaten a sequence into submission."

Time melted away with the candles that burned down in an ornate candelabra on top of Keith's electric piano, but little was achieved, save for nasal damage. John Perry:

"At that point, if you hung out with Richards, he put out many lines of coke but he wouldn't put out lines of smack. There was lots of coke being chopped out, and Peter was in this competitive mode, whereby he wasn't going to be outdone, so every line that Keith put out, Peter would say, 'Zena, put some more out!' It was like a poker game, where Peter was going to match whatever Keith was doing, and raise him. And the same chords kept on going around and around."

The rest of the band sat it out with hammering hearts, racing minds and frosted nostrils (bar Alan Mair, who always voted to abstain from substance use). As Keith sat hunched over the piano like a bent-backed vulture circling an elusive prey, a bemused Perrett was left with nothing else to do but get wired. Peter:

"I didn't know what we were meant to do, if we were supposed to join in. I was more interested in taking drugs. I suppose it would have been good to have our first thing produced by him, but it didn't mean anything to me. There were some people who were interested in us at the beginning just because we knew Keith Richards, but it didn't seem relevant to me. I was more interested in the musical revolution that was going on. I found it quite exciting, the way the music business was being turned upside down. Not that I thought the old bands should be shoved out of the way, but I did hate all the early '70s supergroups, the progressive rock things, like Yes and ELP."

While talk of Richards producing "Prisoners" carried over into the early new year, the episode came to an abrupt conclusion when Richards was arrested in Toronto for drug trafficking. The song had pressed fate's buttons one too many times, and was left to gather dust until 1984, when the posthumous *Remains* album was released. At the close of "Prisoners", John Perry can be heard teasing out the riff from Cliff Richard's "Summer Holiday", suggesting a bread and water vacation at Her Majesty's pleasure.

The stage lights rose on The Only Ones live debut in the first month of 1977. The gig, at The Greyhound on Fulham Palace Road, coincided with Zena's twenty seventh birthday, and had been offered to them by a friend of Alan Mair's.

The band walked into the small venue with a typically haughty aplomb that belied their pokey surroundings. Zena, her youngest sister Koulla and Lynne flounced in behind them, showing off their specially made up Only Ones T-shirts. The punters scanned the trio of bleached blondes, cunningly deployed to add a touch of feminine glamour and suggest that if an unknown band already had such a tasty following, then they must be good.

A fair sized collection of friends were in attendance, and for that extra touch of weirdness, Stefan Stone brought along Doris Day's son Terry Melcher. The former Byrds' producer, with ties to The Beach Boys, had fallen foul of Charles Manson and his homicidal family, after he promised a recording deal, but failed to deliver. In '69, Melcher's recently sold house became the site of a bloody massacre, when the pregnant actress,

Sharon Tate and three of her companions were murdered by members of the Manson Family.

In the beer and brimstone charged atmosphere, The Only Ones opened with "The Guest", which had been radically made-over since its tepid beginnings as an England's Glory number, and now roared into action with a whacking great intro crossbred from the Sam and Dave's Stax classics "Hold On, I'm Comin'" and "Soul Man". At the back, Kellie's sticks sliced through the air like twin propeller blades, as he kept up the song's impetus. The Aries/Libra logo on the front of his Ludwig kit, symbolising the reckless ram and the enigmatic scales, shook slightly in the mounting rumble.

The Only Ones played their first gig as a five piece, augmented by Barbara Dixon's pianist boyfriend. John Perry:

> "It was a practical move by Peter. I don't know if he was worried about whether his own rhythm guitar playing would be strong enough. I suppose having a keyboard player was a safety measure. He was a competent professional musician who stayed in the background and did a good job but he wasn't really necessary."

Peter's insecurities dispersed within seconds of stepping on to the narrow stage. The Only Ones' early shows were tunefully raucous affairs that rocked liked caged lightning. At the centre of the storm, Perrett clutched a white Stratocaster borrowed from John, and appeared to flicker like a stubborn flame whipped by the wind as he fought to project his reedy vocals above the maelstrom.

He held fast throughout a set that included a quirky uncharacteristically submissive love song, "I'm Yours" — a psychoanalyst's joy, brimful of worrying conclusions and the repeated refrain, *'My mamma loved me, then she died'*. A rowdy version of "As My Wife Says" followed, with John Perry keeping the tale of domestic disdain in check with a tight r&b loop.

In his Somerset C.C.C. sweater, white shirt and jeans, Perry looked as though he had just wandered in from the Test Match. His cricket schedule had been shot to pieces by band commitments. All of Zena's attempts to doll him up, Perrett fashion, for the gig, had failed. John Perry stood his ground, a glowering guitar anti-hero who let his Les Paul make all the flamboyant gestures. To his right, in a black leather jacket, Alan Mair hammered home the bass runs.

All the songs that had bounced around Manno's and Tooting, were unleashed — from a brash "Oh No", with its tongue in cheek nod at punk, to spirited renditions of "In-Betweens" and "Lovers Of Today". Sparks flew in the dark, feedback howled, the rhythm section throbbed like a monstrous pulse. Peter's hair tumbled around his shoulders, his mascara ran, his white suit was soaked in sweat. When the spell was broken by the house lights, and the audience were banished into the night, he remained in transition between lucidity and dreams, in a delighted satiety.

CHAPTER 7 – The Wraith's Progress

Jim Carter-Fea had made a living out of letting the good times roll. In the late sixties, his intimate West End venue, The Speakeasy, reached mythical status along with its habitués, who included The Stones and Jimi Hendrix. The rock aristocracy turned the low-lit Margaret Street establishment into the narrow portals of paradise. Carter-Fea became the confidant of Brian Jones and many of the starry regulars who hung out in the club's ruby gloom until dawn broke and they were helped into limousines by their sleepy chauffeurs. Ten years down the line, several of the club's former customers were now famous ghosts, haunting the fading fun palace, yet The Speakeasy retained a spectral charm and jaded reputation.

It was the perfect setting for The Only Ones to pursue their craft and develop a live profile. Zena appealed to Carter-Fea for a one-off spot with the hopeful allocation of further dates, if the band met with his approval. Exactly seven days after their Greyhound debut, The Only Ones played The Speakeasy on January 21st, and immediately secured a six week residency. In becoming the club's semi-permanent house band, they scored instantaneous credibility points from the more hip divisions of the music industry. John Perry:

> "The most important run of gigs we did throughout that year was at The Speakeasy. Its glory days were over but it was still the only London club I really enjoyed. It was a great place to have a residency, and the music business people still came down there."

There was also a cliquey Speakeasy social order with a lingering snobbery that precluded the baser elements of the music scene riff raff. John Perry:

> "The Speakeasy was like a youth club for the bands who were working around London. You'd find some of the Pistols, The Clash, The Heartbreakers, but you would tend not to find the other punk bands down there. It was as though there was some unspoken policy. It was a musician's place."

Although John and Peter are generally reserved characters, they found a rare kinship with The Heartbreakers, and in particular their frontman, Johnny Thunders, with whom they both established a long term association.

Boasting two former New York Dolls in the line-up — Thunders and drummer Jerry Nolan — The Heartbreakers had been asked over to England to join the Anarchy tour by Malcolm McLaren, and had found themselves slung into the same punk bag as the rest of the bands on the bill. The essential difference between Thunders and his gang and the UK punk acts — apart from the fact that they could actually play — was that The Heartbreakers were genuine street punks who brought with them all the bad habits of New York's mean streets. The Heartbreakers walked it like they talked it and could play up a storm that left grit in your eye. John Perry:

> "I enjoyed The Heartbreakers shows more than any of the other bands. They were a good r&b band. Jerry Nolan had a great idea of how r&b shows were presented — no breaks between numbers and keep the tempos up. Punk was the anachronism, not us or The Heartbreakers, so in that sense, The Heartbreakers were the only band we felt any affinity with. They'd been musicians before it happened. All good rock 'n' roll bands, from The Stones to The Who, have a sense of the dynamics of r&b. Some of the punk groups had little idea about those things."

While Peter can be utterly charming and superficially accessible, he is a very insular man with few friends. On occasion he has been known to take a shine to this person or that, but it is more often than not a passing phase that concludes in his eventual disillusionment. With Johnny Thunders, he forged an authentic relationship. Although their alliance had a narcotic core, there was a mutual level of respect, attraction and affection, that was unusual for either of them. Both Peter and Johnny were charismatic, self-destructive rakes-on-the-make in the rock 'n' roll arena, but the parallels stop there. Peter:

> "I met Johnny at the first or second gig we did at The Speakeasy. He was wearing a red leather jacket and he came up to me, and with this drawl he said, 'Hey man, I really like your voice'. Then he said his name was Johnny Thunders and it clicked with me because Vivienne

Westwood had asked if I wanted to go and see Johnny Thunders and The Heartbreakers playing at The Roxy, but I hadn't made it.

I'm not sure if by then I realised he had been in the New York Dolls. I'd thought the cover of their first album was good because I was into wearing make-up then, but I only heard the record once and didn't like it. I didn't take their music seriously. As soon as Johnny spoke to me, I was interested. I made a joke about how, 'I'm allowed to give you coke but my manager doesn't allow me to give people smack, so I won't offer you any'. We just became friends. Pretty soon after I got to know that he was into smack. We started scoring together."

As Thunders and The Heartbreakers zoomed off around London playing punk-friendly venues, The Only Ones made The Speakeasy their main base, sometimes performing two shows a week, for the first three months of '77. The only aberrations from The Speakeasy run were a further four gigs at The Greyhound, and one night at central punk HQ, The Roxy in Covent Garden, where Peter, John, Alan and Kellie brought a halt to the pogoing and introduced the shocked crowd to the concept of musicianship. On March 28th, The Only Ones unintentionally ousted Siouxsie and the Banshees from a support slot to The Heartbreakers at The Marquee. Peter:

"Johnny had invited me to see his band, they were playing at The Roxy again. I'd seen quite a lot of the other bands, and apart from the Pistols, I thought they were the best band I'd seen. He asked me if we wanted to play with him at The Marquee. The Heartbreakers were at the height of their popularity then, and although I knew it would be a purely punk audience, which wasn't ideal for us, I was into doing any gigs, whether it was a confrontational crowd or not. Apparently Jerry Nolan had already promised Siouxsie and the Banshees they could support, and the rest of the band were on Jerry's side. I was quite pleased when Johnny shouted and put his foot down that we were going to support him.

I remember lecturing the audience about replacing one uniform for another uniform, that it wasn't intelligent of them and that everybody should be an individual. That was what the punk movement was about, being yourself rather than copying everybody else."

Although The Only Ones had begun to acquire a small following of discerning disciples, there were still plenty of vacant spaces at their shows. Hidden treasure is hard to come across by chance alone. It wasn't until the release of "Lovers Of Today" b/w "Peter And The Pets" in early June, that the press put the band on the map and a sizable cluster of punters started to congregate at the gigs.

The Only Ones cut the two tracks at Basing Street studio in Westbourne Grove. They entered the converted church over the Easter weekend, disturbing the celestial spheres with their electric rites. The single's A-side, "Lovers Of Today", is an autistic romance delivered by Perrett in a suitably deadpan fashion, although the lyrics languish in ennui:

If we ever touched it would disturb the calm
Physical effort often causes mental harm
I don't have the energy
You could say things get pretty tranquil with me

The rhythm section agitates against the sentiments of inertia and Perry's guitar playing jabs at the song's structure with polished talons. The B-side resurrects "Peter And The Pets" to searing effect. While England's Glory may have originally lit the song's fuse, it was The Only Ones' rendition that brought about the explosion.

During the course of the weekend, the band worked with the in-house tape operator, Robert Ash, who received a co-production credit on the single. From that point onwards, Ash became a regular fixture at many of the band's sessions over the next two years.

They released the single on their own label, which Peter christened Vengeance. Peter:

"We had enough money to exist by ourselves. We were in this great position where we didn't have to think about record companies at all. Back then, it was at the height of being able to do things yourself. There were all these home grown labels. I called it Vengeance 'cos that's what it felt like. When I'd been in England's Glory and Zena had taken the demo album around the record companies, no one had been interested apart from David Sandison. I thought it was a rejection. I was totally naive. I didn't realise it was to be expected, so the name Vengeance was my way of saying, 'I don't need the record companies'."

The Wraith's Progress

Above: The cover for "Lovers Of Today" with the original flirtatious artwork.

Kellie still shudders at the memory of the malevolent moniker:

"I can't believe I was on a record label called Vengeance. A lot was democratically decided but some things were not. That was one of them. Vengeance."

The Only Ones' business affairs were also taken care of by Vengeance Ltd. In time, a Vengeance Ltd signpost would pierce the soil of the Perretts' overgrown garden outside their Forest Hill mansion.

Five hundred 12-inch copies of "Lovers" were pressed up and then bagged in a plain white sleeve with a 7-inch size picture stuck on it. The first widespread pictorial representation of the band presented them as a warped quartet. Kellie looks like a mournful vampire in a long dark coat with a gothic batwing collar. Alan pouts in the middle and John appears to be covered by a fishnet body stocking. Peter stands at the forefront, wearing a leotard, tights and too much eye make-up. Alan Mair:

> "I always liked the cover of "Lovers Of Today". I thought it was quite bizarre. John didn't like it because he looked like he was wearing a big stocking. Peter and Zena were very particular about what the band wore. The first Only Ones' tour poster was a picture of Lynne and Koulla standing against a wall, wearing stockings and suspenders. For the sleeve of "Lovers", Peter cut off most of our clothes, left our heads and placed it over the print of Lynne and Koulla, so there were bits of stockings and suspenders everywhere."

After the first run sold out, a new batch of 7- and 12-inch records were pressed up. Miles Copeland caught the sweet smell of hot cakes and traced it back to Vengeance where he offered Zena a distribution deal through Bizarre records, with an option for further pressings. While Vengeance was financially rewarded, there was an alleged disparity between how many copies were accounted for and how many were actually sold.

As "Lovers" began to woo their potential audience, The Only Ones made ready for their first out-of-town dates. The day before departure, on June 2nd, the band gathered at Manno's to record on to a couple of Revoxes what would have been a typical twelve song set of the period. With Stefan Stone acting as tape operator, they revved through "I'm Yours", "This Ain't All It's Made Out To Be", "Prisoners", "As My Wife Says", "The Guest", "Watch You Drown", "Lovers Of Today", "In-Betweens", "Another Girl, Another Planet", "The Whole Of The Law", "Oh No" and "Peter And The Pets". They interweaved old and new numbers with a turbulent verve.

The Only Ones were a highly competent outfit from inception but there was a rough hewn element in their early performances which maturity would distil into honeyed venom. Sharing a similar spirited vigour, Zena propelled the band onto an almost perpetual cycle of gigging that lasted throughout the rest of the year. Zena:

"They didn't have an agent, so I concentrated on getting them work. I found out where all the clubs were in England and phoned them up. I had the gift of the gab because I used to sell advertising space. I got them a tour of Wales. They played at miner's clubs and working men's clubs, but they were gigs and they paid. Instead of me paying for rehearsals, they were being paid to play. It was very hard work for them."

A hand-picked road crew were selected to assist the band on their travels. John Perry:

"Our first roadies were Christian Pope, Peter's butler who made the tea and made the beds, and he recruited a psychopathic razor-killer called Les. Chris was a drunk, three cans of Special Brew for breakfast and Les used to shoot Tuinol, so this pair would come toppling downstairs, dropping everything. They crashed the van. Ran out of oil. Everything."

The first lap of the out-of-town gigs were arranged like crazy paving around uncharted backwater venues in South Wales. If the rest of the band were stoic in the face of hardship, Peter greeted the venture as if he were a hyperactive baby banshee sworn to reek havoc on the indifferent or hostile until they reacted. John Perry:

"Peter is fond of the idea that a band should play live just to get itself together — it doesn't matter where — so you just book anywhere. But the first dates we did outside of London were the most disparate bunch of gigs I've been involved in. We played a pub outside Bridgwater, Somerset followed by a miners' club in Abertillery called The Six Bells.

The Bridgwater gig was the only time I've ever seen Peter drunk on stage. Some kid brought him a double scotch, put it down at the front of the stage and Peter drank it. It ended up with someone putting a line of double scotches out on stage, which Peter proceeded to drink off. He played rather wildly that night.

The gig in front of the miners was extraordinary, bearing in mind we were playing a bunch of unknown, original material at a social club on a Saturday night, it went surprisingly well. There was a long period of uncertainty but in the end they seemed to be won over by the aggression or the enthusiasm."

Although John would only smash a guitar when driven to a cold fury, Peter was made of more flammable fabric and unable to contain frustration without igniting. Peter:

"We did a tour of fucking South Wales, rugby clubs and social clubs. I don't think there was anyone under the age of 45 in the audiences. The bottles coming at the stage were the least distasteful thing about the rugby club gig. The toilet was knee deep in sick and piss and the rugby players hated the fact we had the nerve to come into their club and make this horrible sound. It was an experience playing to audiences that hate you that much. There was a feeling of us against them. Our gigs became very chaotic because quite often we were surrounded by a sense of violence, that's how we started smashing our equipment up, which was a problem for the first two years. I was the chief culprit, I just used to get tense and worked up about the situation."

Lynne added to the fever pitch by assaulting Perrett and any hopeful groupies that she feared might make overtures to her already part-time paramour. Peter:

"Lynne used to get upset. There was this one Yugoslavian girl who started hanging around and Lynne pulled a knife on her. I took Lynne to a gig in Swansea once and I started kissing a girl and Lynne went crazy. She started slapping me around which really annoyed me. It was the only time she hit me and I didn't hit back."

As the pace intensified and the band spent more time together in transit, certain divisions and issues became apparent. Alan Mair:

"I think the nucleus of the band became Peter, Zena and I. We were the eternal optimists. We would be doing crummy tours of Wales and John would be going, 'Fucking hell, why are we playing all these bogging places?' Kellie was never that optimistic either, whereas we had blind faith that we would get there. I felt I had a very strong relationship with Peter."

The overwhelming adversity of the South Wales expedition made the band's summer approach on the more regular rock venue circuit seem like an easy ride even if they performed at the same furious gallop. Peter:

"We played a gig in Birmingham (Rebecca's) and I smashed Kellie's drums up with my guitar and he grabbed me around the neck and pushed me up against the wall. He was really upset about it. I'd run out of things to smash up. I'd jumped off the stage on to the tables and kicked over the audiences' drinks and there was nothing else for me to wreck, except his drums.

I was doing something that I believed in and if people hated it, I hated them. It was like forcing it down their throats. Play it as loud as you possibly can. We tended to play the raucous songs, "Peter and The Pets", "The Beast", things that would build to great climaxes and go on for ten minutes. I don't think we started getting tuneful until the album came out."

The first enthusiastic reports of The Only Ones exploded over the narrow black margins of the music papers. While one or two of the journalists appeared to be thrown off their hobby horses by the literate and musical qualities of the band, the rest of the hack pack polished their pencils and made with the praise. "Lovers Of Today" scored a hat trick by becoming Single Of The Week in the *New Musical Express*, *Sounds* and *Record Mirror*. The live reviews were equally gilded. The *NME*'s Max Bell gave the band their earliest half page write up in the July 16th edition of the paper, where he chronicled a gig at the Rochester Castle:

"Where other recent discoveries fall short, they shine. They can play the obligatory three chord trick and all the harder ones too. The combination of Perrett and lead guitarist John Perry is more than a summation of the high energy, three-minute cliché; it sparks with a force generated by the arrangement and material while oozing an on-stage tension lying dormant in the personality of the group and its peculiar approach; something that was hitherto the property of Television and Talking Heads."

One young journalist who would devote himself to writing streams of newsprint glorification to the band was Pete Makowski. After making "Lovers" Single Of The Week in *Sounds*, he caught the band live in London and was instantly seduced. Pete Makowski:

"They were just brilliant. They played so well, really good songs. It was a great night and I met them afterwards. I met Peter and I was like, I won't act excited but I was buzzing. I said to him, 'I think you're brilliant, I think you'll do really well'. But then he got upset about it because I told him he sounded like Lou Reed. He went, 'I don't like Lou Reed. I never listen to Lou Reed'. It was a classic. I was trying to backtrack and make out it was a compliment but he got really offended."

In spite of Makowski's Lou Reed faux-pas, Peter warmed to the *Sounds* scribe in the light of such apologetic adoration. The sweet-faced, unsure 19 year old made easy company when Peter needed an occasional social sidekick to collude in his adventures. Pete Makowski:

"At one time I became a cover for him with Zena. I was his alibi. Peter intrigued me. He'd tell me little stories about himself, drifting in and out of vulnerability. When he got comfortable with you, he became very animated. I got as close to him as anyone could get.

We used to go driving about in his Jag. He sort of flew from place to place. We'd end up in Forest Hill and there'd be a house and council flat. He seemed to have property everywhere. There was this girl (Lynne Shillingford) and we'd go over to her place in Notting Hill as well. I knew Peter must have spent a lot of time there because there were lots of Lou Reed albums, loads of Dylan and piles of England's Glory albums holding up the speakers. One evening I remember this big scene going on at the Notting Hill flat. Customs & Excise were apparently watching the place and Peter's Jag. He had to ditch the car.

I got into heroin at that time and Peter was the best tutor. He didn't get me into it but I did it round him. He used to teach me little tricks, like you don't drink orange juice, you drink passion fruit juice, then you don't puke up. We used to score then go out. One night we went down The Nashville, we were having a line of something in the toilet and these people got really upset. They thought we were having a scene.

I remember there were more blokes interested in him than girls. I was sitting down with him at The Speakeasy, and he was wearing his leopard skin coat and eye make-up. There were two creepy geezers looking over at us, I thought they were policemen until one of them pulled me up and wanted to know if he was my boyfriend. It was weird. A lot of women like that fragility. He reminded me of Marc Bolan."

In the August 20th edition of *Sounds*, Makowski also compared The Only Ones' elfish front man to Syd Barrett and early Kevin Ayers — 'Both parties write almost narrative lyrics that don't follow the conventionally accepted styles'.

That summer the band left the sun-baked capital for Escape Studios in Kent. The former oast house had been converted into a 16-track studio with comfortable live-in quarters. Over a five day period, The Only Ones captured "The Whole Of The Law", "Another Girl, Another Planet" and "Special View (aka Telescopic Love)".

The bewitching influence of Aleister Crowley permeated Peter's writing at this stage, and is evident in some of the songs on the band's first album. John Perry had lent Peter a copy of Crowley's *Diary Of A Drug Fiend*. First published in 1922, the book was received by a shocked public. It is a candid exploration of cocaine and heroin addiction based on the author's own experiences.

The main characters — Peter Pendragon and his exotic wife Lou — whirl around the high spots of Europe sampling the finest of substances until the spell is broken by dependency and despair. They eventually recover through the strength of willpower and the application of practical magick. John Perry:

> "Peter didn't seem to be a particularly great reader from what I could see, but large parts of *Drug Fiend* deal with heroin so I lent him the book. My memory of the time, is of taking it away from Peter before he finished it because it seemed to be exerting such a baleful influence on him. It's one of the few times I've seen Peter completely hooked by a book. He seemed to be taking to it so literally and living out the content of the pages that it seemed the safest thing to do was take it away. It certainly showed up in some of the lyrics."

Crowley's preface to *Drug Fiend* closes with the line 'Do what thou wilt shall be the whole of the Law.' The Magician's most oft quoted phrase has a brimstone background dating back to the French 15th century writer Francois Rabelais, who was also of the opinion that one should, 'Do what thou wilt', as were the unholy brethren of the 18th century Hell-Fire Club, who dedicated themselves to black magic orgies and political conspiracy. The eminent transgressors regularly gathered at a ruined abbey located on the bank of the Thames near Marlow. Inscribed over the abbey's entrance was, "Fay Ce Que Voudras" (Do What Thou Wilt).

In spite of the Crowley influence on its title, "The Whole Of The Law" is not an occult discourse but an ardent love song. Perrett audibly pines, as he proclaims that he will swim the length of the ocean, plumb the depths of every sea and escape from chains to reach his beloved. The band delicately colour his sentiments in gentle tones, perfectly accompanying the lyrical longing.

The following afternoon at Escape, Peter strolled up to the microphone and started to sing the opening lines to one of his latest compositions:

I always flirt with death
I look ill but I don't care about it
I can face your threats, and stand up tall and shout about it
I think I'm on another world with you, with you
I'm on another planet with you

Alan Mair:

"We got "Another Girl, Another Planet" straight off. We just started playing and we'd never done the intro like that before. I came in on the off beat and I looked at Kellie to come in. It was a magical moment."

John Burns, the studio engineer suggested the atmospheric backwards cymbal intro giving the tune a spacey surge that was embellished by Perry's warning guitar flashes. The rising adrenalin of Alan's bass and Kellie's drums hastens "Planet" into orbit and the sudden unfurling of all-out passion. Peter's strangled dove vocals fly dizzily above the ravishing melody. John Perry's performance is a staggering display of stratospheric mastery coming from the same galactic plane as Hendrix's "Axis Bold As Love".

The final track from the Escape session was a dreamy, voyeuristic yarn, "Special View". The lackadaisical lilt which Perrett applies to the lyrics masks conflicting emotions of excitement and betrayal as he spies upon an unfaithful lover:

On some occasions I lose my patience
And I slip out of alignment
If I say I'm sorry

Don't take this pleasure from me
This is something really thrills me
But same time it kills me

Like mocking minstrels serenading the unfair lady, the band's commentary on the lyric is given its fancy edging by John Perry's Spanish style mandolin strumming. The recording was briefly interrupted when Perrett was called away to the phone by a member of the Escape crew. Peter:

> "It was Jeremy Ensor saying that he was from CBS and he didn't know if we were close to signing but they'd like to state they were very interested in us and they'd like a chance to speak to us before we signed to anyone. We were quite flattered that they'd gone to the trouble of finding out where we were."

That August, exactly one year after their line-up was finalised, the bidding season on The Only Ones was gloriously opened. The band were in no hurry to get hitched until they had played the field and checked out all of the record company suitors that came to court them. As Peter told the *NME*'s Max Bell:

> "We ain't signing anything yet. I've always done things my own way because I must work with people I can trust as friends. Also we're looking for the right producer. He exists somewhere on the planet."

Record company representatives started to stalk the band as they continued a hectic itinerary of gigging that veered from the North to the South. The music press were also in attendance, adding their voices to the rising buzz that surrounded The Only Ones. One curious manifestation of the press gang's attention was the unnecessary categorising of the band under the New Wave flag. New Wave was the definition bestowed upon any non-specific genre act of the period that fell outside of the perimeters of punk. A whole section of creatively diverse bands fell into the vast New Wave canyon due to lack of media imagination and the need for easy classification. The Only Ones made their *Melody Maker* debut as part of a series on up-and-coming New Wave bands, where Alan threw the issue even further left field when he told Ian Birch, 'To the hippies we were punk and to the punks we were hippies'.

THE ONE AND ONLY: Peter Perrett - Homme Fatale

also came running. Stein had established his company after a sweep of the burgeoning New York scene, where he had cornered The Ramones, Talking Heads and The Dead Boys. One of the bands most often compared to The Only Ones was Television, who Stein had initially pursued but ultimately lost to the more affluent Elektra. When Seymour made contact, Peter decided to give him a taste of home grown hospitality. Peter:

> "Stein took us out to dinner with one of his groups, The Dead Boys, and they were being really childish, acting like slobs in this restaurant. Afterwards he took us back to the flat he was staying at. He smoked hash so I gave him these hot knives which is a very strong way of taking hash. You cut the bottom off a plastic bottle; that's the implement the hash is to be smoked through. Then you get two knives and heat them until they're red hot. You then get a lump of hash and put it on one of the knives. You need another person to do that for you. The person waiting to inhale stands there with the bottle and you put the other knife onto the hash, and the extreme heat makes it explode in a puff of smoke Stein breathed it in and it completely wiped him out. He was unconscious on the floor. I should have taken that as a hint that he was someone I could talk to."

Then came Kellie's former label from his Spooky Tooth days, Island. The company's proprietor Chris Blackwell was keen to make a deal, even though there were one or two people in the A&R department, including Muff Winwood and Howard Thompson, who weren't quite as enamoured of the band as their boss. In spite of a little backroom scepticism, Island would probably have been the most compatible company for the band in the long term. It was a belief that all the members of The Only Ones would concur with even before the benefit of hindsight set in. Peter:

> "We went to see Chris Blackwell in his office. The thing I really liked about him was his attitude. I should have sensed then that I had at least got something in common with the guy who owned the company. He said he wanted to get involved in our careers the same way he did with Bob Marley and Steve Winwood. He'd had this guy, John Martyn, on the label for years without any commercial success, yet he didn't put

any pressure on him. He let him make the albums he wanted to. I think Island would have been the best."

Island's main rival in the race for The Only Ones was the vast CBS corporation. Peter:

"Bob Dylan had been on CBS and I suppose psychologically it seemed like a real record label to me. Great records had that orange label. I thought I could get free Bob Dylan records!"

In a last ditch attempt to prise The Only Ones away from CBS, Blackwell flew to a gig at Leicester University on December 3rd, where he offered to match the CBS deal but with a different scale of payments. Alan Mair:

"Some of the Island artists hinted that they weren't receiving their payments on time so we thought we might as well go with the Bank Of England. CBS. Terrible mistake."

Just before Christmas curtailed all trading until the new year, Zena darted into the plush CBS building in Soho Square with a briskness that defied her lethal stiletto heels. She checked her reflection in the mirrored lift, and applied a second coat of murder red lipstick before going in to parlay with a top team of CBS players. The A&R division of Dan Loggins and Jeremy Ensor awaited her, along with a gruff corporate solicitor. Zena:

"I went into negotiate the deal and they offered us a ridiculous amount of money. I then came out with my figures and the solicitor said they were telephone numbers. I said that I'd worked it all out and went through the figures to show how I'd reached that sum. Everything was worked out to the exact penny, from how much the album would cost to the band's wages. I told them I couldn't knock one penny off it, otherwise we'd have to forget it. He said I would have to forget it, and if I walked out of the room, the deal would be off. I said fine and walked out. When Maurice Oberstein, the managing director came back from Midem, he personally phoned up and asked me if I would come back in. They offered us £10,000 more than I had asked for, just to make sure they got the band."

Zena secured The Only Ones a mighty £70,000 contract with a further quarter of a million pounds to be paid out over the ten album deal. Stories of the band's good fortune and their manager's cool business acumen were soon splashed across the music industry's trade papers.

After a lively gig at The Roundhouse on Christmas Eve with Eddie and The Hot Rods supporting, the band went their separate ways for the holiday season. Outside the venue, Peter pulled a raggedy fur coat around his wraith-like physique and surveyed the sleeping neighbourhood where Zena had once been taken in by the National Council for Civil Liberties while he had been left to roam the streets. In spite of the icy wind that stroked his pale face, he felt unusually secure. Peter:

> "The naiveté of it. You think that's it. Now you're signed to a record company, all the hard work has been done. You imagine that they are going to sell millions of records for you, and all you've got to do for that money is make great records."

Chapter 8 – The Late Show

The world seemed to tilt on its axis in order to bow at Peter Perrett's dainty feet. News flashes announcing the signing of The Only Ones to CBS and of work in progress on their debut album, appeared in all of the January editions of the music papers. The band were hot property and their ethereal frontman the object of media rapture. Like blood on fangs, the dark ink sank into the white paper of the CBS contract. Instead of a surge of power, a growing sense of unease crept up on the group members as they became more familiar with the corporation who were supposed to ensure their musical immortality. John Perry:

> "The day we signed, there was a party. It was clear, straight-away, from the attitude of the people I talked to in the CBS building, that they didn't know who we were. They were a fairly lame lot, they weren't very imaginative or bright. People don't have to be into the same things as you, to get on with you or not be intimidated by you. We had no sympathy for them and vice versa. It was a total mismatch from the beginning."

Working under the mistaken premise that true talent would triumph over (corporate) adversity, the band were at their most optimistic during the first quarter of the new year. John Perry:

> "The atmosphere within the band was good. I think there was a general assumption that things were going to happen. We were getting great press. We were on an upward curve. We had a batch of good songs to choose from to put on the album. I wasn't particularly ambitious, my vision was, if the band was working and getting a good reaction, that was good enough for me. All of that was happening, at that time."

The band went through the finishing stages of their patchwork studio policy as they moved towards the album's completion. The only piece of the fabric that they failed to pin down was an appropriate producer. Bob Ezrin, Matthew 'King' Kaufman and Chris Blackwell were all short listed then dropped in the final skittish decision. Peter:

"We produced it ourselves. It would have been good to work with someone who could have contributed because there were great producers around. But while someone might do good work with another group, it's scary to commit yourself to someone who is actually going to influence what the record will sound like. It wouldn't be so bad if you could turn around to the record company and say, 'Well, it just didn't work. We're going to have to start again', but you can't always do that. You get stuck with it. I suppose we avoided having producers because we were scared."

They checked into the CBS studio on Whitfield Street, where they cut three tracks including the beautiful "Someone Who Cares". Peter pulls the broken heart strings and the band respond in a luscious cascade. "It's The Truth" hits a similarly poignant note of Perrett romanticism, skillfully enhanced by Perry's guitar work which evolves from a delicate flutter to a full-blown embrace at the song's close. The session concluded with the open self-analysis of "No Peace For The Wicked" which conjures a solitary vision of Peter behind closed doors and curtains as he poses the questions:

Why do I go through these deep emotional traumas?
Why can't I be like I always wanted to be, carefree?
Why can't I be happy like everybody else?
There's no peace for the wicked

The gloomy self-absorption is lifted by the band who break through their frontman's shadows like a ray of golden light. The wonder of the rhythm section was down to Kellie and Mair's aptitude for coming up with unobtrusive yet sympathetic structures that balanced the whole.

The rest of the material and the final embellishments were done at Basing Street over several weeks. Peter:

"The first album was just like finishing it off, because we'd done it in bits. We booked the time, went in and did it from start to finish. We worked quite efficiently. John would go in and lay down loads and loads of guitar tracks, then me and Alan would spend time on the production."

Raphael Ravenscroft, the man responsible for the memorable sax intro on Gerry Rafferty's top ten hit single of that year "Baker Street", came down and blew up a warm breeze for "The Whole Of The Law". Former consort Gordon Edwards added the swirling Hammer House of Horror synthesizer on "Creature Of Doom". A live version of the same track, taken from a December '77 gig, had already been previewed on The Hope & Anchor *Front Row Festival* album. The double 'New Wave' sampler incorrectly listed The Only Ones' number as "Creatures of Doom" much to the annoyance of Mr Perrett.

The backing vocal belladonna was sixteen year old Koulla, who had recently absconded from home and joined Peter and Zena at their Forest Hill abode. Koulla Kakoulli:

> "I used to go into the studio with Zena. I loved hanging around with them. On "City of Fun" Peter would say, 'It's up to you', and they wanted a female voice to reply, 'No, it's up to you'. They asked Zena to do it, then they asked me. I did it in one take and from then on I never looked back. I think it's because I did everything so quickly, and also our phrasing is quite similar. The way he spoke, I'd speak — and the way he'd sing, I'd sing. It wasn't intentional, we just complimented each other."

Amidst the overall fine tuning, the frantic "Language Problem" knocked the dial into distort mode. Peter lathered up the lyrics with a series of unintelligible garbles to purvey his frustration in a relationship where, *'Taking drugs is one thing we've got in common'*. As the band feel their frontman's mounting rage at a communication impasse, Perrett pulls off a noisy guitar tantrum which snarls at Perry's melodic undercurrent. The closing track on The Only Ones' eponymously titled LP was "The Immortal Story". The glory and terror of meeting ones' dreams in reality are interpreted by a whinnying rumpus of bucking guitars, galloping drums and a wild electric stampede that destroys everything in its path.

If the album was a chronicle of Peter's vivid emotions and imagination, then the saga of "The Beast" was his most unwittingly prophetic moment. Penned whilst in the studio, the lyrics take their cue from Crowley's *Drug Fiend* and plays on the Magi's self-designated epithet of 'The Great Beast'. Smack had long since upstaged cocaine as Peter's drug of choice. He wrote the song while still in the lingering honeymoon stages of the habit. Even though there was an awareness of the potential for personal

THE ONE AND ONLY: Peter Perrett - Homme Fatale

Above: 'You may know the next one — it's called "Lovers Of Today". If you feel like singing along, don't.' John Perry.
The Only Ones playing in Brighton at the CBS yearly convention.

addiction, Perrett like so many who'd embarked on the same course, somehow considered that he alone would master the drug that was beginning to take its toll on those weaker than himself. Peter:

> "As a song "The Beast" is the only one that is totally about drugs. There are other songs that allude to drugs but only if they affect the relationship that the song is about. As soon as I took smack I knew how dangerous it was, just the fact that I could like something that much. But I genuinely believed that I wasn't going to succumb to it. The song is written from a point of view of strength or imagined strength. I'm warning other people about it, but in the song I'm saying, '*I know it's not going to happen to me*', because I could see it happening to Lynne and other people around me. I wouldn't have carried on with it, if I'd really believed it was going to happen to me. I've known a couple of people who wanted to be junkies, who thought it was glamorous, but I never wanted to be a junkie at all."

The Late Show

Once the album was in the can, Peter began to dream up wildly impractical visions for the cover art. During the brief period when the band were thinking of calling the record "Special View", Peter and Pete Makowski devised a delirious design incorporating 3D badges with eyes on them that would dilate when held up to the sun. One can only imagine the delight of CBS when hearing of such a suggestion. In the end, 'straight' group shots graced the front and back sleeves. Even then there is something amiss about the cover portrait, other than the double exposure, as The Only Ones line up inside Basing Street studios like unusual suspects.

Although the media were heralding The Only Ones as the 'next big thing' and CBS had coughed up a decent advance, very little altered in the respective lifestyles of the band members, financially or otherwise. John Perry:

"The CBS contract was supposedly worth a quarter of a million, I think, for 10 albums. It was a fairly demanding contract, we got the money in lumps. Zena had already spent quite a lot of money so she had to be repaid for what she'd spent. It wasn't one of those situations where you got the advance and started buying cars. We played better venues, but we'd have done that even if we hadn't signed a record deal."

It was Kellie with his lack of emotional insulation and tatterdemalion past who was bruised with the realisation that the band was never going to be a family concern. Mike Kellie:

"I think we might have got £500 each. Some of the money from CBS went on equipment. We got a great PA even though we spent more on it than we needed to. There was never enough to set ourselves up. Alan's always been comfortable in his own right. John and his girlfriend Suze had their flat in Fulham and were very good at surviving, anyway.

The only independence any of us had was the independence we brought with us. I had no inheritance from Spooky Tooth, never had two pennies to rub together. I stayed in one of Peter's old flats in Forest Hill. I lived there with Christian. Peter and Zena lived up the road. It was their territory, it was their show. I'd given up my independence because I believed in the band. I'm not feeling sorry for myself but I remember the frustration of it. It wasn't terribly fair but life isn't fair. You want fairness, go to hell. If you want justice, become a Christian."

Far removed from Kellie's philosophy, Peter continued his dalliance with decadence. The first martyr to his excesses was Lynne Shillingford. Like a slighted Pre-Raphaelite mistress who resorts to laudanum (opium in alcohol) and madness when neglected by her lover, Lynne alternated between rising hysteria and retiring under the swans-down coverlet of heroin relief. Her unbalanced state was further compounded by an abortion at Peter's behest and his return to Zena on a more-or-less permanent basis, although the affair continued with a heightened sense of clawing desperation on Lynne's behalf. Peter:

"Lynne was getting crazier and crazier. She always used to attack me in cars. One time she wanted me to stay with her but I was going off with Zena somewhere, and as I drove off she jumped on the bonnet of the car and started taking her clothes off. Another time I was driving a friend's Mercedes while he was out of the country. Zena was in the front, she would always be in the front and Lynne would be in the back like number 2 wife. I suppose it was horrible putting her in the back, she must have felt left out. Anyway she had stilettos on and she started kicking me in the back of my head. I drove the Mercedes into a lorry and completely smashed up the side of the car."

Zena had carefully refurbished the basement flat that she had originally taken up when seeking sanctuary from Lynne's increasingly possessive demands upon her husband's time, during the fraught period when they had all been living together. The dark warren of rooms at the bottom of an impenetrable Victorian house was within yards of Albert and Amelia Perrett's place, yet it might have been continents away for all the contact Peter made with them. Zena decorated the subterranean lair in rich rust colours with hints of Art Deco. She prepared a tiny room fit for Thumbelina, inside a cupboard with a ladder leading up to a bed, for her youngest sister. Before Koulla moved in, Peter had read her the house rules. Koulla Kakoulli:

"He said, 'One thing you've got to learn before you move in here, is how to skin up'. He taught me how to skin up. I was really made to feel welcome. Peter took me under his wing. I told him that I wanted to be the best female guitarist there had ever been and he told me it wasn't impossible. He'd wake me up at 3 a.m. after he'd been out and teach me how to play guitar. He took what I wanted to do seriously and we worked together closely for about a year."

As Koulla became used to the Perrett's idiosyncratic way of life, she shared in the everyday chores. For all the unconventional aspects of Peter's behaviour, he takes comfort in particular preferences and rituals. Koulla Kakoulli:

"Peter is a very strange person to live with. These were my duties — apart from skinning up. I had to know exactly how his breakfast was made. It was like a ritual. He'd have his coffee in a small bone china cup. He'd have eight spoonfuls of sugar and the cream for the coffee had to be poured over a spoon so that it floats on the top. His toast had to be buttered into all the four corners and if he has marmalade or honey, that also had to be spread right into the corners, and then taken into his room. If it was wrong, he'd go, 'Zena, Zena!, she hasn't stirred the coffee'. It was unbelievable. I got used to it. He still does it. He's never changed. Zena is still making his special coffee and toast. She carried on being his mother. She's always looked after him, too much sometimes."

Another more unfortunate habit that Koulla became familiar with was one that seemed to be sweeping a whole clique of people in and around the vicinity of The Only Ones and Johnny Thunders. Koulla Kakoulli:

"Back then my heroes were Peter and Johnny and the bands who were out there looking thin and wasted. There was even a band called Wasted Youth. Everyone was using drugs. It was trendy to look thin and white. I started using heroin when I was living at Zena's. There was some on the table and I took a bit and I was gone. I thought, this is brilliant, you just need a taste and it gets you mashed. I didn't realise that you'd be using grammes and grammes a day and it would be hundreds out of your pocket. I just thought a fiver's worth and you'd be mashed all day. Peter tried to warn me but I wouldn't listen."

A network of rock 'n' roll opium eaters emerged. Some, like Johnny Thunders and the *NME*'s Nick Kent had more established habits. Others like Koulla and the members of Wasted Youth were apprentices, enamoured of the mystique they thought they could share with their heroes. Even though Peter had not yet fallen prey to the full brunt of total dependence, he was mesmerized. Separately from Perrett, John Perry was also imbibing on a regular basis.

Heroin addiction is not a static condition. Rather, it is a gradual submergence with invisible depths. Some people are just able to tread water for longer. Years after Sandison's attempt to pull off the England's Glory/Velvet Underground scam, Nick Kent caught up with Peter Perrett in person. Nick Kent:

> "As a drug addict Peter was a really nice guy and that's very rare. I also found that he was weak. I wanted to slap him sometimes. He had Zena who was devoted to him and so was her sister. I remember when the guy took a bath, they'd be in there, rubbing his back. I wasn't in the same room, mind you!
>
> He was a good looking guy and he had everything too easy, and in the process, it had made him weak. Don't get me wrong, neither of us were at our best. He was smoking a hell of a lot of dope and snorting heroin. He was just out of it. At that time we were all out of it. But because Zena had made herself indispensable, he was in this cosseted situation were he didn't have to go down on the street in order to score. It was very cushy for him but I'm sure it got worse. It always does get worse, the longer you stay addicted."

After their first encounter, Perrett reckons that Kent left behind an empty methadone bottle and all of his notes for an article which he then had to ad-lib in print, while Kent recalls Perrett being over an hour late for the meeting. Of course, none of these factors deterred them from further contact. As fellow travellers on the road to the land of nod tend to intermingle, several avenues led to creative, if somewhat dilettante collaborations. While the most significant of these was with Johnny Thunders' Living Dead and the *So Alone* project, on which Perrett and Kellie guested, Kent also invited The Only Ones (without Alan Mair) into the studio. Because of the mutual connections, Kent was made privy to Peter and Thunders' relationship. Nick Kent:

> "Peter and Johnny were very close. Johnny loved Peter and saw him as a superior songwriter. At one point he even wanted to become the

guitarist for The Only Ones. Can you imagine? For him to abnegate his ego to that point, which shows you how much he respected Peter. They were a good pair, but Johnny let the lifestyle corrupt him, whereas Peter didn't. I never saw him trying to rip anyone off, but it started to slow him down.

I did some music with him when I was with The Subterraneans. I went into the studio with Peter, Mike Kellie, John Perry and Tony James, the bass player from Generation X. We recorded a couple of things which have since come out on bootleg (*Punks From The Underground* — SkyDog). I'm kind of embarrassed about them. One of them, "Chinese Shadow", is a dub kind of thing with me talking.

Peter was great in studio situations, a very good rhythm guitarist and organiser. But another time, when I was arranging stuff and he had the facility to record several tracks on a basic recording console at home, I'd turn up at his house and he'd just be getting up. Zena would then have to go out and score for him. Eventually he'd be ready to focus on music at 1 o'clock in the morning. He was getting slower and slower and of course this was leaking into every aspect of his life. He was always late to everything."

Most of Peter's extra-curricular musical activity with Thunders took place in the lull between the completion of *The Only Ones* album and its release date in the early spring. After the dissolution of The Heartbreakers, Johnny strung together a casual revue called The Living Dead in an attempt to keep his fingers in the fire until something more permanent came along. Once again Peter returned to the small stage of The Speakeasy which had become the duchy of The Living Dead. Peter:

"After The Heartbreakers split up, Johnny wanted to form a band with me. I was happy with the way The Only Ones was going, but I liked playing with Johnny. I liked playing his music, it was a diversion and it was fun not being the frontman. I used to get really out of it at those gigs, because at that time I wasn't getting stoned for Only Ones' gigs. It was the first time I was getting out of it on stage. It was a laugh, the freedom to just not be professional."

As The Living Dead was a fairly loose concern, the line-up was liable to alter from one gig to the next, however the main participants tended to be Peter and Kellie, the raven-tressed New York chanteuse Patti Palladin, Eddie and the Hot Rods' bassist Paul Grey, and French teenager Henri-Paul, who deputised on bass or guitar depending on the evening's truants.

The Speakeasy reverberated with a set that consisted of covers such as Gene Vincent's "Be Bop A Lula", The Chantay's echoing instrumental "Pipeline", The Shangri-La's "Great Big Kiss" which was often corrupted to "Great Big Fix", as well as a selection of Thunders' own songs. Clamouring to get on board The Dead train was the hapless Sid Vicious, upon whom Perrett took pity. Peter:

> "Sid was like a little kid, he seemed to have the mind of a twelve year old. There'd been all this publicity about how vicious he was and how he'd attacked Nick Kent, which was pretty nasty, but I think he was easily manipulated. Because Johnny was his hero, he really wanted to play with him. I think Sid used to get stoned with Johnny and he promised Sid that he could play this one gig.
>
> We did a sound check and he was meant to be learning the songs — one of which was "Stepping Stone" which the Pistols sometimes used to do — but he was totally hopeless. Maybe they played it in a different key. I said to Sid, 'Just play E'. He didn't know where E was on the bass guitar. To try and teach him, I put his finger on the fret and moved it about, but it didn't seem to sink in. After the sound check Johnny said, 'He's too useless, I'm not going to let him play'."

Knowing how dejected Vicious would have been, Peter pleaded for clemency on his behalf, but when it came to the actual gig, Sid's amp and speaker were quietly unplugged by a roadie. Peter might have softened to Sidney, but not to ever-loving girlfriend, Nancy Spungen. Peter:

> "I thought she was loud-mouthed American scum, she didn't have any class about her at all. For a laugh, Johnny told her it would be really good if she went out topless and introduced the group. Johnny probably didn't even notice but Sid was really hurt by it, which was ironic because half the world had probably already seen her like that. She went out topless, introduced it, then said all our names.
>
> For the first three or four songs, Sid really got into it, he was jumping up and down, posing. Then I think he must have listened out for what

Above: Leopard-skin and leather. The Living Dead — Peter, Johnny and Patti Palladin at The Speakeasy.

sort of noise he was making, 'cos all of a sudden he realised that nothing was coming out of his amp. He thought that somehow it was broken, I don't know if he realised it was sabotage. He started calling out for a roadie to fix it, but Johnny walked up to the mike and said, 'Thanks very much Sid, now we've got Henri-Paul coming up to play'. Sid slinked off the stage, it was like he'd been substituted and thrown off. He was a very sad character."

More often than not, The Living Dead were supported by The Snivelling Shits. The band had been formed by two young men with their fingers on the slowing pulse of the mile high club, Pete Makowski and fellow *Sounds* scribe, Giovanni Dadomo:

"The Living Dead was an inevitable marriage. They were all on the same circuit and they all took smack! But I think we all took it for the purest of reasons — to explore feelings. It was a romantic thing. It wasn't to get out of it, it was to get into it. There's a sublime difference between trying to nullify your life, as Lou Reed said, and trying to expand the borders of your knowledge. The irony is that smack originally gives you the illusion that you are expanding your consciousness but what it really does is close it up. I've always felt that it is like an oriental fan, and when you take that particular drug, it seems like your emotional spectrum opens up. In fact it gets narrower and narrower until all you think about and live for is what Burroughs calls "the algebra of need". Ultimately it's tragic and it's boring."

In that year, the plumage of the fan was spread wide like the feathers of a peacock. In each opulent fold there was another line of creativity that would eventually be smothered when the fan snapped shut.

As John and Kellie had taken to hanging out at Island's St Peter's Square canteen, they came into contact with Robert Palmer, and ended up writing and recording a track called "Tall Stories" which also featured Palmer on bass. But most of The Only Ones' extra mural pursuits tailed off as CBS began to pull the big levers on the publicity machine for the imminent release of their single and album. The Living Dead were terminated at roughly the same time, when the former proprietor of Anchor records, Dave Hill, signed Johnny Thunders to his new Real label. The contractual details of the one-off album deal were carefully negotiated by Zena on Thunders' behalf. Unfortunately, all the hours of discussion to ensure the guitarist a sizable advance were blown in a moment's desperate need, when Johnny traded waiting for the full amount due to come to him, for a small cash-in-hand payment so he could score. Peter:

"Zena was furious and I was really pissed off with him. He'd gone out and bought either a quarter ounce or a half ounce of coke or smack but he hadn't even got a good deal. Whenever he gave you drugs, he was really pleased because normally he was broke and on the scrounge, so when he was the person to give it to you, it made him feel good. He asked me and Kellie to record the album with him but we were only available for a week."

The Only Ones embarked on a hectic promotional schedule which started at the beginning of April. The first flag on the agenda was another

The Late Show

Peel session, for which they planned to play "The Beast", "No Peace For The Wicked", "Another Girl, Another Planet" and "Language Problem". As their career continued, their frontman went from being fashionably late to practically posthumous. While Peter had always been tardy at best, he reached a point where he consistently failed to differentiate minutes from hours. Perrett now subscribed to the dislocation of heroin time, which runs outside of the 24 hour routine of 'straight' life. While the rest of the band adapted to the inevitable delays, and to some degree synched in with it, their dilatory conduct often caused consternation from those unused to it — which was how the band's second Peel session became the stuff of legend at the BBC's Maida Vale studio. Alan Mair:

> "If there was nothing going on, Peter would just stay in bed all day. Then he would anticipate that it would only take him half an hour to get ready. Being late doesn't matter, that's not important to him. It's funny because everyone else adapted to this.
>
> One of the nicest stories that came out of the chaos that surrounded The Only Ones, was at one of the Peel sessions. We had to be in the studio by 10 o'clock, so I thought, 'I'll get there at 12 o'clock because that will be when everyone else arrives'. I was the first there, then Kellie. John turned up at 1 o'clock, but by 2 o'clock Peter still wasn't there. The producer (Malcolm Brown) was going nuts, suggesting that we cancel the session, but the engineer who was a fan of the band was going, 'No, we can make up the time'. People were starting to get mega pissed off. Eventually, Peter arrived at 2.30 p.m. Within 40 minutes we'd put down the four tracks. We played fantastically. Everything was forgiven. It was finished and mixed by 8 o'clock. The engineer tells me they still talk about that famous session. If anyone's late, they say, 'Yeah, but no-one's ever as late as The Only Ones!'"

In the countdown to the launch of the band's first single on CBS, "Another Girl, Another Planet" b/w "Special View", The Only Ones encountered one of the few genuinely friendly faces that the record company had to offer. With a vastly differing roster of acts allocated to her that included the Blue Oyster Cult, The Vibrators and the bard of Manchester, John Cooper Clarke, press officer Judy Totton took to The Only Ones despite foibles which worked against them in the less tolerant sectors of CBS. Judy Totton:

"My main memory of The Only Ones during their CBS days was how late they always were for meetings. Zena who was brilliant at business and Peter were the worst culprits. Perhaps it's unfair to say they were *always* late but they were certainly late enough, often enough, to cause a certain amount of upset. Eventually I think people got a bit fed up with them. That's not to say that the label didn't believe in the band, they did. They just weren't the easiest of acts on the roster to deal with. I looked after the band from their first single through a couple of albums.

I loved the music. I always got on well with Zena, she cared about people. I remember her coming round to my house late one night to tell me about a vivid dream she'd had about a car crash and warning me not to drive for a couple of days. I remember Mike being really nice. Alan was very funny and John was quiet. Peter was the mysterious, charismatic frontman. He summed up a whole attitude, a model that many bands have since looked to. It was a kind of decadence, a sort of jaded stance; late nights, dark rooms, black eyeliner, a faded velvet grandeur, enhanced by drugs."

Peter's wan beauty and lyrical dispatches of high altitude romance and despair stirred the imagination, but behind the 'faded grandeur' there was a lack of moral energy. In 1888, the novelist and cultural observer, George Moore, whose *Confessions Of A Young Man* reflected upon themes of spiritual malaise and fatal enchantment, described the work of the French poet Baudelaire as being 'Beautiful flowers in sublime decay'.

Peter had made his bed of blood red roses.

CHAPTER 9 – Out Of Eden

Peter Perrett's stellar poetry and the atmospheric arabesques of "Another Girl, Another Planet" have strong parallels to the opium reveries of the eighteenth century Romantic circle that included De Quincey and Coleridge. In a later study on the output of literature under the influence of opium, *The Milk Of Paradise* (Abrahams, 1934) the author states that the drug 'affected the patterns of imagery, resulting in abnormal light perception and extraordinary mutations of space'. He might have been reviewing the single.

While the critics, cultists and elitists swooned over "Planet", the record flew over the heads of an indifferent public like an unnoticed UFO and barely made its presence felt on the Top 50. The people's choice throughout April '78 was Brian and Michael's hideous tribute to the painter Lowry, "Matchstick Men and Matchstick Cats and Dogs", which festered for weeks at the number one spot. "Planet" could never have competed with such vulgar mundanity but the wallpaper flowers that decorated the record sleeve were just as stilted as any of Lowry's paintings. John Perry:

> "The "Another Girl, Another Planet" cover was going to consist of a photograph of Peter in the middle, with a planet in each of the corners, and a girl's face on each planet all looking at Peter. When I suggested that maybe this wasn't such a good idea, it was replaced by the wallpaper cover. Peter was being hounded by the police and had to disappear. No mean feat — to disappear whilst attempting to maintain a profile in the papers and do gigs. He'd been holed up in a borrowed council flat and staring at the wallpaper. He said, 'If I can't have the cover I want, I'll have the wallpaper I've been staring at'. Peter came up with the idea as a default sulk."

"Planet" is now viewed as one of the finest moments in pop history, yet at the time Peter's strange, plaintive voice that so endeared him to his admirers, alienated a broader audience as did the morally subversive content of the lyrics. The band were justifiably taken aback when "Planet" broke-up on impact with that immovable object — mass acceptance. Alan Mair:

> "We were, and still are in some ways, shocked that "Another Girl, Another Planet" wasn't number one. I think that took the edge off the band. It affected Peter deeper than he ever said. Radio One wouldn't play it. They thought the lyrics were too heavy. '*Space travels in my blood*' wasn't quite to their taste in 1978. Also, Peter's voice was an acquired taste. He was very self-conscious about it. He always wanted a lot of reverb on it. You either love or hate his voice. Personally, I love it, always have done."

To promote the single, The Only Ones took a support slot for the duration of a short UK tour with Television. Fronted by the gaunt Tom Verlaine who adopted his surname from the decadent poet Paul Verlaine, Television were the one band with whom The Only Ones shared an aesthetic sensibility. John Perry:

> "That was a reasonable match. I got on well with their guitarist Richard Lloyd. Tom Verlaine struck me as being a little wound up. We toured on a coach, and Verlaine who was tall, was walking along the aisle of the coach when we went over a bump. He got a great chunk of his hair caught in a sky light but he was too self-conscious to say, 'Help, get my hair out of this'. So in the end he wrenched it away and walked off, obviously in great pain, with this great chunk of his scalp left hanging from the skylight. Poor man."

The Television/Only Ones jaunt which stopped at Newcastle Town Hall, Manchester Apollo and Birmingham Town Hall, should also have included Bristol Colston Hall on the list of destinations, however the gig was cancelled after the truck carrying the equipment crashed, killing the unfortunate driver. John Perry, who had contemplated taking a ride with the equipment so he could get to Bristol overnight, had a narrow escape when he changed his mind at the last minute and stayed in Birmingham. The tour concluded in London at the Hammersmith Odeon, where an appreciative if spartan audience dotted the medium-sized venue. As John Perry told *Zigzag*, 'We played to half empty halls, I think it was mostly a fifty/fifty audience to see us just as much as Television'.

While it may have been an inspired pairing, neither The Only Ones nor Television had wide appeal, but the dates caused quite a stir amongst the Rock intelligentsia who greatly favoured both bands. As Max Bell wrote in the *NME:*

> "There had been a certain interest generated in the double billing of former coterie darlings Tom Verlaine and Richard Lloyd versus, in the blue corner, the Brit wunderkids Perry and Perrett, especially as both Verlaine and Perry are credited with a love of jazz structure, while everywhere you looked people were telling you how Television sounded like the Grateful Dead and how Perry had played with Dead lyricist Robert Hunter some four years back. What did John learn about his trade then from our American visitor? 'Absolutely nothing. I spent a week in the guy's proximity and only learnt from the papers that he had similar tastes to mine. Guitarists who listen to Coltrane to influence their licks are few and far between'."

In mid-May an obscure campaign for The Only Ones' first album appeared in the music papers, featuring a full-page picture of a sphinx. While the reasoning behind this baffling campaign remained as inscrutable as the icon itself, The Only Ones, like the sphinx, were placed on a pedestal by the press who lavished the record with the highest of praise.

> "*The Only Ones* is a superb album. Can you say 'very superb'?" Giovanni Dadomo, *Sounds.*

> "There is a compelling self-confidence behind The Only Ones' vision which attracted me from the outset, this starting with Pete Perrett's haunting songs and brazenly unorthodox singing, and stretching through to the resolve and unity of the players themselves". Nick Kent. *NME.*

> "I rate The Only Ones as one of the most stimulating and original bands around. That word 'original' has been sorely taxed of late, but if ever its application was justifiable, it is here and now." Ian Birch. *Melody Maker.*

Left and right the critics waved their wands and bestowed five star ratings on the album. A gallery's worth of photographs of the band stared out from every paper; Alan, John and Kellie in relatively sober threads to

THE ONE AND ONLY: Peter Perrett - Homme Fatale

Left: Koulla Kakoulli playing with Lonesome Nomore.

their frontman's leopard-skin pillbox chic. In a business where managers seldom receive much public recognition, Mrs Perrett cut a sympathetic yet tough figure, able to make it in the predominantly male-orientated world of the record industry. Zena:

> "I didn't really like being interviewed. I didn't like the focus. I wanted them to focus more on the band. The trade magazines were quite impressed that I'd got such a big deal, and when I first went into CBS, I think they just thought I was for show, rather than knowing what I was talking about."

Zena took on the press with great aplomb and a somewhat re-edited history which she shared with Bart Mills from *Music Business* magazine:

> "She became the group's manager when she saw that an old South London school mate, Peter Perrett, had failed to interest the music industry in his songs. 'I asked myself why his talent wasn't being recognised', she recalls. 'Maybe this was an opportunity for me. I went

round to see Peter. He was a lazy good-for-nothing, living very decadently in a house with two girlfriends. He played poker for a living and would get involved in games with rich Arabs that would last up to a week. He already had what a lot of guys go in to pop to get — girls, thrills and money. Yet I knew he was very frustrated and I told him so'."

From a feature in *Cosmopolitan* to an article in *The Sunday Observer*, Zena was hailed as one of the forerunners of a pioneering breed of women staking a claim in the music business. Mention was also made of a new band, Lonesome Nomore, that Zena had just taken under her wing. Named after a Kurt Vonnegut book, Lonesome Nomore was to be Koulla Kakoulli's vehicle for the big time. She put the band together with her future husband, bass player Malcolm Hart, before recruiting 15 year old drummer Nick Holmes and guitarist Billy Duffy who eventually went on to join The Cult. Koulla Kakoulli:

"It was a really good band. We were all young and fresh. Zena managed us at first, but obviously The Only Ones were just getting bigger and bigger."

Despite the critical and intellectual acclaim laid at their feet, and an ever growing phalanx of devotees, The Only Ones consistently failed to catch a commercial wave. They were not a band made for whistling along to, nor for turning the lyrics into simple stadium refrains. Mike Kellie:

"We were loved by the music press from day one. I don't think we ever had a bad review. Unless it was later on when Peter was too stoned and mumbled his words. We were loved by the press but it didn't mean a thing."

The band's sales might not have met expectations but their live shows always did. The rough hewn elements of the early gigs had been burnished to a rare sheen. While Peter's artistic genius sometimes manifested as a strange form of neurosis during day light hours, by night, on stage, he was a prowling poet, pitched into the ravishing musical affray. John Perry:

"The key thing for me throughout the band, the touchstone if you like, was playing live. What worked best about The Only Ones live, is that it was like a four way scrap amongst equals. Kellie was the most powerful drummer I'd ever worked with. In retrospect my respect for him grows and grows. Alan was completely solid. At good gigs it always felt to me that Peter was having to fight to make himself heard above it, and having to fight to get up front. I think that is probably where some of the strength of it came from as a live band."

Throughout their career, The Only Ones kept up a tumultuous cycle of gigs, spinning like a big wheel through town and city. Alan Mair:

"We were always doing gigs. We had our own PA system so we never stopped playing. After the first album — I think it only went to number 22 in the charts — everyone got a little despondent that we hadn't achieved the chart success we should have done. In some ways it got harder from that point onwards. After that there were more drugs around, there was more chaos."

In honour of The Only Ones first CBS-backed English tour, the company's art department devised a poster campaign showing individual silhouettes of the band, sitting on a very rocky bay where they appear to be fishing. Perhaps it was meant to be a visual pun on catching the big fish of the New Wave, more than likely it was just a dumb idea. The 11-date excursion, straddling the end of May and the beginning of June, went reasonably well, apart from an incident at the under-attended opening gig, Barbarella's in Birmingham. Kellie's chums, Robert Plant and John Bonham, decided to drop by and toast the occasion. Predictably, the excitable Led Zeppelin drummer became drunk and disorderly.

Record Mirror's roving reporter Bev Briggs, a staunch Only Ones advocate, missed Bonham's barbarity but learned of 'Peter's Premonition':

"Barbarella's had the aura of a pick-me-up night club, everything drowned in a deadening red light. The band's last gig in Birmingham had been a virtual sell-out, so Barbarella's should have posed no problems except for 'Peter's premonition' as they call it. He anticipated the lack of audience. A couple of hours later, he was proved right. The Only Ones took to the stage at about 11.30 and play to no more than a handful of kids.

Perrett's premonition was justified, maybe it was the total lack of advance publicity. The set they played was unusual and certainly not typical of The Only Ones live. The brashness of a perfect set would have probably cost them the little audience they had, so the whole affair was low key. "Any requests?" Tuning up/constant intimacies with the kids who were there. It won them a strong following."

In and around the tour, Peter and Kellie contributed to Johnny Thunders' *So Alone* album sessions, which were split between the familiar territories of Island Hammersmith and Basing Street studios and utilised the Living Dead ensemble plus a further gathering of guests, including several Sex Pistols, Phil Lynott from Thin Lizzy and the former Small Faces ace, Steve Marriott. Koulla also joined the scattered company, teaming up with Patti Palladin and Chrissie Hynde to recapture the chipped innocence of the vintage girl groups which were so favoured by Thunders.

Peter and Kellie participated in five numbers — "Ask Me No Questions", "(She's So) Untouchable", "Subway Train" and the sensitive "You Can't Put Your Arms Around A Memory" which is considered by many to be Thunders' finest moment. The title track, which was shelved by Real Records as incomplete, surfaced over a decade later when the album was released on CD. Peter:

"Me and Kellie ended up doing the first half of the album. I played guitar and sang backing vocals. The session was as together as anything Johnny was involved in, like during the "So Alone" track itself, in the middle of the lead break, he fell over. He just fell backwards into Kellie's drums. The lead guitar stops and there's a great big crash. I thought they should have put it on the record because it summed up how things could get with Johnny.

When the sessions moved to Basing Street and we'd finished the tour, he asked me to play piano on one of the tracks. I thought I'd teach him a lesson, because previously he'd been so out of it that it had been up to me to teach the songs to the musicians. I got really out of it and fell asleep on top of the piano. He couldn't move me. Normally, when I was working, I was very conscientious."

So Alone met with a good critical response and added romantic dimensions to Thunders' bad boy image, but the album's alternative significance at the time was missed. *So Alone* represented the late '70s hip clique of heroin users (very few of the artists involved were not partaking of the drug). The record's inner sleeve photo montage of the contributors by Michael Beal is like a high school yearbook of a time before most of the class were dismissed into arduous addiction, and in certain cases, drug-related deaths.

On June 13th, The Only Ones' stature was further enhanced by their first television appearance on the *Old Grey Whistle Test*. The late night music programme's circular logo hung behind them as Peter stared deep into the camera, kohl-rimmed eyes peering out through a long curling fringe. As he intoned the lyrics to "No Peace For The Wicked" and "The Beast", the band played with seasoned grace, John Perry teasing out perfect notes with total detachment. John Perry:

> "What I hated most were people who were visibly nervous about being on television, and grinning inanely. I thought it was better to stand still and concentrate. From the point of view of the three musicians, as opposed to the frontman, we'd been doing this for a long time. We were good at it. We didn't have to wear fancy dress or behave like Devo or The Clash to make an impact."

In the first week of July, the band recorded a short set featuring splendid renditions of "The Immortal Story", "Lovers Of Today", "Someone Who Cares", "The Beast" and a new number "She Says" (later renamed "No Solution") at the Paris Theatre on Lower Regent Street for a spot on Radio One's *In Concert* series.

With an ever-increasing workload and a major US tour being planned for the autumn, the band had to keep abreast of the momentum. Musically and lyrically they were a supreme team, with an aristocratic assurance in their craft, but they still had certain shadows to keep at bay. Appreciation of The Only Ones took a certain aesthetic. In August, John Perry told the *NME*'s Max Bell that, 'We are in danger of becoming a musician's band or a critic's band'.

Like the group's career, Peter was also in peril of becoming stymied by prevailing forces. The boy who had sped through life with wings on his feet was fettered by heroin addiction. He took the chance to clean up after winning a lengthy game of poker. In Peter's house of games, poker was one of his favourite pursuits. Peter:

"I first started playing in 1975. It's a real buzz. I only enjoyed long games because if you play for a couple of hours, luck can come into it but if you play for a long time luck evens itself out and then it's just down to the skill of the player. I used to play with friends who were serious about it. I used to make quite a lot of money sometimes. I won two grand once, that's how I paid to go to Brazil. I played with two associates of mine who were going to Brazil on business. They wanted me to go for a holiday, part of the reason was because I'd won this money off them. They said they'd rather pay for a flight on Concorde which was £1,500 at the time, but it was also to get me well. By the summer of '78, I'd started using everyday."

The image of the cigar-chewing card shark with rolled up sleeves and steely eyes doesn't sit well on Peter's slender shoulders. The lost prince with his naked vulnerability, closing in on his opponents like a wolf in leopard print clothing, presents a paradox. John Perry:

"It's hard to pin down. It's a mixture of shyness and unbelievable candour which is disarming. At the same time, there is another tension between great naivety and a very effective calculation. There is another axis there between adult calculation and an almost childlike persona. You have to look in terms of paradoxes."

After recovering from a week spent in a tiny fishing village, coping with the aches, shakes and the copious snuffles of heroin withdrawal, Peter visited Rio and Sao Paolo. He returned to London with a less pallid complexion and "From Here To Eternity" — a solemn song of cautious deliverance.

I see a woman with death in her eyes
But I don't have the time to pray
For her salvation or for her soul
She walks her chosen way
But in the darkness and in the light
I have found some hope of me getting out from this underground
I can't wait to get back home

Any shadows of doubt receded with the band's aspirations for their second album. Once again an assortment of producers and engineers received call-ups to audition. For a time, John Peel's in-house engineer, Mike Robinson, was tipped to participate in the project. Peter predicted a change in the creative course to Max Bell:

> "This time Perrett would like to come up with, 'Some dumb hummable tunes. A hit single will sell the album. But we are an album band and I couldn't write anything I didn't feel'.
>
> Alan took up the subject with firm resolution, 'I know that the next one has to be rougher, with more energy, the sound of the band now. The last album was good but it was a compilation of old songs — a backlog. It had got to be fiercer to improve and we've got to find the songs which succeed in creating mood. What's old to Peter is new to the rest of us'."

The boardroom machinations of their record company ensured that The Only Ones would receive even less support than usual as they prepared for the album. "Planet" was re-released, backed with "As My Wife Says", on a 12-inch format. Once again it orbited around the charts without making any great impression. John Perry:

> "They released "Another Girl, Another Planet" a second time and it didn't happen again. That record is never going to be a top ten hit no matter how may times it is re-released."

Major record companies sometimes exude a vaguely patriarchal air and CBS was no exception. Those acts who play the game without too much dissent are amply rewarded, especially if sales meet expectations, while those who go against the grain will be in for a rougher ride. The Only Ones were misunderstood sons, the Cains of the corporation. Of course Peter was a profoundly willful character but he was unstintingly dedicated when it came to making music. John Perry:

> "For all of Peter's singularities and demands, he always turned up on time for the shows. He wasn't sloppy drunk or sloppy stoned on stage or out of tune. As far as working goes, he was always completely responsible. He cared passionately about how his music was presented.

The original pro-Only Ones fraternity within CBS that had lobbied for their signing had now broken up. Zena:

Above: The Only Ones share a joke.

"After six months, the guy who signed us, Dan Loggins, left to go to America. Although Maurice Oberstein was interested, he was too far away to really get behind the band. You need an A&R guy behind you. Even our production manager died of cancer."

The band's status within the organisation was already on shaky ground, but was impaired further when Muff Winwood and Howard Thompson (both of whom declined to be interviewed for this book) moved from Island to CBS. As John Perry puts it, "We were now being looked after by the people we'd turned down". Peter:

"I felt that Howard Thompson didn't like us. He signed The Psychedelic Furs. He was just trying to promote the bands he signed. He wasn't interested in the bands that were there before."

Mike Kellie however, considers that Muff Winwood did his best for the band. Mike Kellie:

"Muff was our A&R man at C&A. I mean CBS. It might as well have been C&A. Muff, brother of my dear friend Steve Winwood, was the head of A&R, which was an irony for me, because having come from Birmingham and with Muff having played bass in the Spencer Davis Group, we were all mates. Muff was so gentle and patient with us. I'd have kicked us out of the door months before he did."

As the summer reached its golden apex, the season of open air rock bacchanalias were declared open. A festival in Hyde Park which was to have featured The Only Ones, the Buzzcocks and Steel Pulse was killed off by the Department of the Environment but the two day West Coast Ashton Court Free Festival ran smoothly. With a lively crowd who danced even when one of the generators broke down, Bristol's vast hippy tribe gathered to see 38 acts play on 3 stages. While the ex-Gong guitarist Steve Hillage was the main attraction, The Only Ones turned in a sparkling set which was witnessed by the faithful Max Bell:

"Perrett's rhythm guitar understanding is now so improved that you can love this band on a dozen different levels; witness the punky duetting of Perrett and Koulla Kakoulli during "The Immortal Story", itself followed by a "Horse Latitudes" revisited guitar barrage ending. The Only Ones are far and away the most creative source to tap off the new freedom. The Clash, Buzzcocks, the Banshees are still learning things musicians of this calibre left behind years ago. As one kid said to Perry after the show, 'You make it look so easy'. They do too."

In preparation for the "Planet" tour, which would keep the band on the move up until the end of the year, organisation within their own camp was tightened up. Converting the long, narrow hallway that runs through the Perrett's basement flat into an office space, Zena took on a much needed staff member. Zena:

"Linda Quinn was a friend from school. She was quite efficient and she acted as my personal assistant. She kept the whole office together and Peter's father used to do the accounts."

To keep the on-the-road madness down, Les with the taste for Tuinol was jettisoned. A permanent crew was acquired consisting of Chris Reynolds, a quiet young Welshman called Barrie Evans, and the ebullient Digby Cleever, an archetypal rowdy roadie. In spite of a new order in the ranks, all manner of incautious behaviour still dogged The Only Ones' best laid plans. John Perry:

"We used to devise songs on tour about the amount of equipment left behind. On the first day of touring the road crew lost Peter's Strat. They used to lose this horrible CBS display board which was a bitch to carry. They'd leave it behind in clubs and just when they thought they'd got away with it club owners would come running out behind them, 'You've left something inside!'"

Following warm up dates at Harlow Technical College (September 22nd), Birmingham Barbarella's (23rd) and City Of London Polytechnic (30th), the band launched the "Planet" tour at London's Lyceum on the Strand on Sunday October 1st, supported by Bram Tchaikovsky's Battleaxe and The Business. The evening clouded over early. The Only Ones seemed unusually fatigued and their grand finale "No Peace For The Wicked" was jarringly discordant due to the misguided efforts of Television's former guitarist, Richard Lloyd, who came out to join the band for the last number. Peter:

"Richard was totally out of tune, completely different key. It was the worst guitar playing I've ever heard. That's how the evening started with him. I should have realised that he wasn't alright in the head then."

The sound of ice cubes crashing around empty glasses drowned out the conversation at the after show party, where assembled guests found themselves left thirsty in an unexpected alcohol drought. Judy Totton:

"There always seemed to be misunderstandings. The band thought CBS was supplying the drink for the party and I thought we were just bringing whatever happened to be left over from the 'invited guests' box at the show. So I arrived at the party with just a few bottles of wine. I promptly had to rush to the nearest off-licence for more, which is not that easy at that time of night on a Sunday."

When the party eased off in the early hours, Peter took Richard Lloyd back to his Forest Hill hospitality suite. Lloyd turned out to be a most unfortunate guest given the circumstances. Peter:

"Zena was in bed with a threatened miscarriage. She used to have lots of trouble with pregnancy. Me and Richard were sitting at the end of the bed. I gave him a line about an inch long of smack. I know he'd been drinking, I think he'd taken some downers as well but even so, it was still a minute amount. He snorted it and after about five minutes he just fell backwards. Within 30 seconds his mouth had turned blue. He was totally fucking completely gone. There was no walking him around the room or anything like that. He was fucking heavy, Zena was trying to stop him falling off the bed. It was the last thing she needed, at 6 o'clock in the morning, with a threatened miscarriage. He was too heavy for me to do anything about it by myself.

Luckily Kellie lived in an old flat of ours just down the road. I phoned him up and he came straight over. We carried Richard out into my Daimler Sovereign. I drove at a hundred miles an hour to Lewisham hospital. Kellie jumped out, got the trolley people and told them what had happened. As Richard was being wheeled into the hospital they had to start heart massage. He definitely owes his life to me because if we'd have waited for an ambulance it would have been too late."

With the worry that Peter's Daimler was about to become a hearse, Zena began to hemorrhage and was whisked off by ambulance. Zena:

"I lost that baby, I was very upset. It was the first pregnancy I'd had since I'd been managing the group. I remember the doctor saying that I could have another one but I thought, 'I'm definitely not going through with this again'. The weird thing is that I used to see this Egyptian guy who read my Tarot cards. He told me that the group was going to be successful and that I was going to get pregnant and lose the baby, but not to worry because I was going to get pregnant again and it would be a son who would be very gifted."

Whatever the personal predicaments, the "Planet" tour kept rolling. From nightclubs to student venues, The Only Ones played the circuit in a flourish of lights and shadows, illuminating the crowds that stood before them.

On October 12th, Johnny Thunders staged his one-off "All-stars" gig at the London Lyceum. Featuring most of the *So Alone* collaborators, including Perrett and Kellie, the show was intended as a grand gesture before Thunders returned to the States. Leading the on-stage parade, Peter and Johnny cut the air to ribbons with their tandem guitarwork. The following day, news broke that Sid Vicious had been arrested in New York for the murder of his beloved Nancy Spungen. Thunders flew home to review new prospects and offer his condolences to the woebegone Vicious.

Week after week, more dates were added to the "Planet" schedule. Hundred of miles, autumn into winter nights. Nottingham, Dudley, Bristol, Harrow, the band picked up hard-core fans at almost every port of call, pinning Only Ones promo badges, bearing a red rose with a barbed wire stem, close to their hearts. As the Christmas lights were switched on all over the country, the tour finally wound down.

Still reeling from the effects of post-Planet centrifuge, Peter crashed his car on the way to Central Recorder studios in Denmark Street. Perrett was unhurt but the car suffered a grand's worth of damage. He was delayed for the session where the band were laying down the new single "You've Got To Pay", which was more or less what the garage mechanic told Perrett on receipt of the dented vehicle.

The luscious "Someone Who Cares" had been a strong contender as the follow up to "Another Girl, Another Planet" but the catchy roll of "You've Got To Pay" was a more obvious choice. Perrett was in brilliant lyrical form as he charts a failing relationship.

> *Our flight path's a gradual descent from the firmament*
> *I can tell by the tone of the letters you sent*
> *What was once sacred is now filled with hatred*
> *How come such love can be dissipated?*

While the song holds up a two way mirror to Peter's stormy affair with Lynne, the sheer quality of his words have always been able to reflect further than the immediate autobiographical source. Kellie's drums rattled the windows of Perrett's domestic intrigue, while Mair banged at the shutters. John, who was less than enamoured with its choice as a single, only plays on the song's coda.

Somewhere between a valentine and an arson attack, "Flaming Torch" was was also ignited at Central. The band laid the sizzling hearth from which their frontman's sentiments glow like burning flowers and acrid embers:

True love is your guiding light
It's like a flaming torch
You can see the magic in the night
As the flames start to distort

The groundwork for "From Here To Eternity", Peter's favourite song from the upcoming album, began its passage through a haunted darkness which is then lifted by Perry's guitar playing as Peter's lyrics reach almost biblical proportions:

Such a tender age to sell her soul
To dreams that don't come true
She's like a woman whose whole life has dissolved
She's the living proof that all that glitters is not gold
And even serpents shine

The Only Ones took the creature out of Eden and into the title of the second album — *Even Serpents Shine*.

CHAPTER 10 – Serpent's Kiss

Inside the basement flat, it was warm and dark. Peter's kittens, Angel and Isis — a Christmas present from Kellie — dozed in a corner of the bedroom. The phone rang shrill in the hall. While the kittens dreamed on, Peter rather warily went out to take the call. It was Michael Beal for the third time in as many hours. In his official capacity, the photographer was attempting to illustrate the wilder shores of Peter's imagination for the cover of *Even Serpents Shine*. But for that night only, Beal's unofficial role was as an on-line go-between for Lynne Shillingford, who had been told not to call her paramour at the flat. Exiled at her mother's house in Bristol, Lynne was repeatedly threatening to end it all if Peter didn't contact her. As the evening wore on, so did the effects of the downers she was gulping like sweeties. Each further call was a secondhand SOS relayed by Beal. Before Lynne could slip over the edge of no return, the photographer warned her mother to confiscate the rest of the pills. Peter's advice, which didn't come from The Samaritans' handbook, was for Lynne to go ahead. Throughout the recording of *Serpents* their relationship had been declining. Peter:

> "After we stopped living together, the relationship was stormy because it was based around her wanting me to be with her all the time. Anytime I wasn't with her, there'd be lots of problems. She'd come down to the studio and make a scene by dressing up in the clothes that I liked, stockings and suspenders, and she'd take her clothes off and try to seduce me in the studio. She was on the point of a nervous breakdown. It wasn't sane behaviour — it wasn't the real her because she became so unattractive then. Her crying became more and more childlike. The less I saw of her, the more smack she'd take, and the more smack she took, the less respect I'd have for her. I felt guilty because I was the first person that gave her smack. She started interfering with the band.
>
> When there are scenes like that going on, it's hard to concentrate. To Zena, my music always came first, no matter what problems we had, whereas Lynne seemed to me to be selfish. She wasn't thinking about

my music. In March '79, I finally decided that was it. I saw her intermittently after that, on rare occasions, but it wasn't a regular thing."

Like the first album, the mosaic of *Serpents* was made up of a mixture of older and more recent numbers — old gems like Peter's stray cat lament "Out There In The Night"; plus "Someone Who Cares", "In-Betweens" and the curse of "Curtains For You" which lyrically plunges down a shaft as black as a mine while propelled by a venomous musical shove.

Once again the sessions were recorded in different studios. The backing tracks were split between Central Recorder and Tony Visconti's Good Earth studio in the West End. "Programme" drips with icy perspiration, guitars and words thrash about in an indefinable yet clearly nightmarish sequence, the rhythm section tearing like the hounds of hell after the wide-eyed victim.

"No Solution" opens on to the romantic ruins of Peter's life, where *'Love is just destruction disguised under another name'*. If "From Here To Eternity" is *Serpents'* crown then "Miles From Nowhere" must surely be its bejewelled sceptre. Peter's angst grows electric:

I wanna die in the same place I was born
Miles from nowhere
I used to reach for the stars
But now I've reformed

It's carried along on a whirling current of music, down into the rapids of Perrett's psyche. He later told Max Bell that:

"Miles From Nowhere", that's the feeling that I want to be untouched by everything. It's hard to retain the things you thought were important. I try not to let life affect me."

The final number on the album is a transcendental piece called "Instrumental". With a strong flavour of the mystic East and a percussion part recalling Pharaoh Saunders' "Japan", Peter whispers across a night desert of wind chimes, bells and writhing snake charming guitars, reminiscent of The Doors' introduction to "The End", willing the serpent to dance.

On January 3rd, the band took a break from recording and braved Siberian style storms to keep an appointment in Newcastle. Contingency travel plans had to be activated when Heathrow Airport closed down in the inclement conditions and The Only Ones had to take the train. At Tyne Tees television studio, the producer of new rock programme *Alright Now* waited anxiously for their arrival. Hosted by Den Hegerty, the former front man of doo wop outfit The Darts, *Alright Now* was the forerunner of *The Tube* and its theme tune was "Another Girl, Another Planet". The band eventually arrived with snow on their boots which had thawed out for the filming of the programme's opening sequence.

Once the band were back in London, Zena continued discussions with Miles Copeland's brother Ian, who was scouting for the US rock agency Paragon. After securing American tours for Ultravox and The Police, Copeland was hoping to do the same for The Only Ones. He flew home with Zena's pledge that the band would be ready to make their US debut at the end of January.

With commitments for the New Year starting to fill their diary, The Only Ones rapidly entered into the mixing stages of the album at CBS and Basing Street studios. As before, Koulla contributed the backing vocals. The rippling Hammond organ came from a chance encounter with John 'Rabbit' Bundrick, formerly of Back Street Crawler and the Eric Burdon Band, who had wandered into the studio, admired the material and was invited by Alan Mair to join the session.

While Robert Ash was in attendance as chief engineer, The Only Ones still hadn't elected an outside producer. Eventually the album evolved into a Mair/Perrett production. John Perry:

> "If you listen to *Serpents* today, it's the densest sounding of our albums. Every track was filled up, sometimes it seemed just because they were there... The sound got further and further from the strength of the live four piece and I lost interest in the sessions. I'd do my parts, stay and listen out for anything else that might need doing, then head off to a girlfriend's place and leave them to it. It was turning into process for process sake. I'd put up *The Peel Sessions* album as the antithesis of *Serpents* — single sessions of four songs *completed* in 8 hours!!"

THE ONE AND ONLY: Peter Perrett - Homme Fatale

For Alan Mair, the chance to produce was not just a matter of keeping control of the music within the band, but was also a valuable experience for life outside of The Only Ones' camp. Alan Mair:

> "I was very heavily involved in it, that's why I pushed to get production credits on it. I'd done the same thing on the first album but that didn't seem important at the time. I was very interested in producing — I wanted to go on from The Only Ones. *Even Serpents Shine* was my production. I mean Peter would always say, 'I like that, I don't like that', but I felt that if I pushed for it just to be an Alan Mair production everyone would probably oppose it, but I thought if I put Peter's name on it, it would be accepted."

The middle portion of the month was taken up with buffing *Serpents* to a dark finish. The album has a certain baroque feel in common with The Doors at their most mesmerising. The single "You've Got To Pay" was teamed up with a number dating back to the pre-Only Ones Tilbrook period — "This Ain't All It's Made Out To Be". With the album virtually complete, The Only Ones set off for two Irish gigs — Dublin Trinity College and Cork University — plus an appearance on PTF Television. As the band were boarding the plane, two members of the Special Branch nabbed Kellie and issued him with a warrant pertaining to a two year old driving offence. Kellie was later taken off the "Most Wanted" list and released in time to make the dates.

A couple of days later, the band were ensconced on a plane with a more distant destination. New York in winter is mean and merciless, the icy whip of the wind comes down like a dominatrix lash in a Times Square sex show. The Only Ones landed at JFK in the midst of a howling blizzard. Making up the rest of the party were Zena, Max Bell and the road crew. It would have taken a vast stretch of the imagination to describe conditions on the tour as anything approaching luxurious.

The Iroquois Hotel on Sixth Avenue had seen better days when the staff outnumbered the cockroaches, which might explain why no food or drink was served on the premises and the band's first meal out in Gotham City was at a Burger King.

The following evening, a frost-bitten crowd queued up outside Hurrah's, a converted discotheque, waiting for the doors to open and The

Above: The rhythm section walk the New York beat.

Only Ones to play. Backstage, the band were huddled around a one-bar electric fire and trying to inhale the warmth from numerous joints which circulated the small room. Apart from a handful of Only Ones cognoscenti who had sought out their records on import, the audience was predominantly made up of New Wave fans eager to sample anything from the second coming of the British Invasion. While fresh converts to the band spilled out into the night after witnessing a fine set, the stragglers in the crowd were thrown by The Only Ones' esoteric character. The Clash and Dire Straits had been easy to catagorise and their US sales figures had risen accordingly, but The Only Ones were perpetual outsiders in a marketplace where "unique" was not a saleable commodity.

When the band were flaked out in the cold comfort of their Sixth Avenue flophouse, sleeping off jet-lag and post-gig exhaustion, another Englishman in New York, well known to Perrett and company, was succumbing to 'The Beast'. Sid Vicious, while out on bail, fixed up $160 worth of pure smack and bought a one way ticket to the other side where

Nancy awaited him. Reviews of the band at Hurrah's hit the stands on the same day as a plethora of Vicious obituaries.

Even though CBS had minimal input in the tour, which was financed by Vengeance, The Only Ones greeted the press at Columbia's NY office and came away with a fervent full-page spread in *The New York Rocker*. The interview coincided with the release in England of "You've Got To Pay" b/w "This Ain't All It's Made Out To Be". A palpable disillusionment already tailed the single, as Mike Kellie told *The Rocker*:

> "We're split on being happy with the new single. It was like our attempt to make a good single. It's very much an image thing. People don't buy the record to listen to how good it's played. It's played okay but, after "Planet" and "Lovers Of Today", it's not up to standard. I wouldn't be surprised if anyone thought we'd sold out."

Although it wasn't considered to be 'selling out', many found the single to be a slight offering after "Planet". The group's stab at commercial compromise had missed the mark.

Taking advantage of the trip, Peter spent a little time in New York getting further acquainted with his step-sister, Edith. The mystery of the photograph of a familiar-featured, yet unknown child, in his parents' bedroom was finally solved for Peter:

> "I first met Edith in the mid-seventies. She looks like my mother. She's ten years older than me. There was always a picture of her in my parents' room, so I knew that somewhere in their past was this little four year old blonde girl. It wasn't until I got into my teens that my mother thought it was safe to tell me that she'd been married before and had a child."

Even if it was years too late for any real sibling bonding, Peter and Edith maintained a long distance relationship.

After a second show at Hurrah's, the band moved on to Boston but got blocked en-route by an unwieldy parade of snow-ploughs. They broke through the line of diggers within minutes of a nervous promoter at the packed Paradise Theater having to cancel the gig. In an unusual act of faith, Columbia in Canada released The Only Ones' debut album to coincide with their appearance at The Edge in Toronto on February 7th. Despite an enthusiastic crowd milling around the club, Peter's long orphan's face looked more pinched than usual. New York and the last of his junk was three days behind him. John Perry:

> "Peter's starting to feel quite ropey. He's cross and in a mood to take anything if he can't have what he wants. Some kid shows up in the dressing room and says, 'Have some THC man'. Now THC is the active ingredient in cannabis but it's quite a rare drug. In fact the stuff was almost certainly PCP, which is elephant tranquilliser and a common drug in North America. The kid puts out two big lines of elephant tranquilliser which Peter duly snorts and we take to the stage. Peter's stage demeanour was usually pretty taciturn but at the show, after the first song, he suddenly starts chatting to the audience, going on and on. We finish the second song in the set and he starts going "great-audience-and-we-love-you-so-much-it's-fantastic". I'm yelling '1! 2! 3!' counting in the next song — and then after the gap it would happen again. Peter was transformed into this very vocal peace and love exponent. It was hysterical and I wish someone had a tape of that night."

By the time the band returned home, Peter had come down from the clouds and was ready to promote the new album. To the UK press, The Only Ones presented themselves as a united front with shared dreams and ambitions as they began the big push on *Even Serpents Shine,* which included a mighty three month cross-country tour. This time the band were determined to transcend their cult status and bloom into public consciousness. Mike Kellie told the *NME,* 'We don't want to be a cult. We haven't got this far for purely artistic reasons. We want success, to be rich'.

The odds seemed stacked against them. "You've Got To Pay" like "Planet" didn't get on to the all-important BBC playlist and an edgy CBS were considering calling in a producer of their own choice to give The Only Ones a more marketable flavour. Alan Mair aired the band's concerns to Max Bell:

> "Most people think we're an oddity. We need a hit to get them attuned. It wasn't until Pink Floyd broke through with "Money" and *Dark Side Of The Moon* that they won their elementary mass appeal. I sometimes wonder if we're too indulgent, but we try and keep the balance on any obsessions. We feel the songs are outstanding so we've got to graft and

THE ONE AND ONLY: Peter Perrett - Homme Fatale

Above: Crooked men outside a crooked house.

wait. Sometimes it seems that we don't have the organisation to hard sell, or we aren't capable of a commercial hit."

Although they were artistically unsurpassable, the band were being overtaken commercially by their contemporaries, such as Elvis Costello, The Police and Ian Dury and The Blockheads, who were all enjoying chart success and growing public acclaim. The Only Ones sparkled like a jewel box full of hidden secrets, but somehow they had yet to catch the eye of the multitude.

For all of his bluff cynicism and tart quips, John Perry told the *NME* that he had grand visions for the band:

"We've got to stand on our own ground, however small, because the band's been together long enough to exist in its own right. We should present ourselves in a way appropriate to the number of people. We want thousands screaming because the band works better in concert, we present ourselves as a unit. I want riots, fans rushing the stage, falling equipment, crushed bodies. We never wanted to get stuck in little clubs, that punk ideal was never shared by us."

While it seems unlikely that Mike Kellie would advocate apocalyptic riot scenes, the drummer concluded the three page *NME* article with a rallying flourish:

"There can't be any more splits in ideals. We've got to share the ambitions, go through the shit together, and we'll do it."

Unfortunately, the golden serpent that they had adopted as an emblem for the album was slowly poisoning the communal cup. John Perry:

"We started out as a band and more and more it became Peter and the musicians. During the second album things were much more dispersed. You could have drawn the line between Kellie and Alan who were straight and Peter and I who were getting high, but the division in the band never came down that way. Even though Peter and I nominally appeared to possess the same interests, we were pursuing them separately by the time of the second album."

Michael Beal's interpretation of Peter's ideas for the cover of *Serpents* culminated in a feverish concept of volcanic eruption and lava splashes in violent reds and oranges, banked by an ash coloured valley. The bizarre nature of the sleeve with its flight into the unknown was a declaration of high cult. With the best will in the world, it seemed as if the band were unable to escape their destiny. For Kellie, who was portrayed on the cover as the guardian of a cave full of snakes, the serpent wasn't shining quite as brightly as it might have done, in spite of his carrying the torch for band unity. Mike Kellie:

"It wasn't as good as it could have been, I knew that all along. Often with first albums, it just all pours out. It's the second album that's the crunch. I remember that we never captured the spirit of "Out There In The Night" that we caught on an earlier demo. *Even Serpents Shine* is a combination of satisfaction and dissatisfaction! The cover was a marketing man's nightmare. We were a record company's nightmare."

The album, which is Peter's favourite from The Only Ones' collective output, was released on March 9th with the CBS marketing department on red alert. Extensive advertising appeared in the music press for a four-week period. A national window display campaign ensured that high street record retailers were crawling with *Serpents*, as well as badges, T-shirts and stickers. The album slithered to number 42 in the charts and sold roughly 30,000 copies in the first six months of release, almost exactly the same as their debut platter. No matter which way the band threw the dice, a snake was always writhing above them on the next ladder of progress — despite the warm encouragement still coming from the critics.

> "*Even Serpents Shine* is an alluring mixture of focussed emotions and assured performance: and they really are the only ones doing it." *NME*'s Phil McNeill.

> "It just occurred to me that the Perrett songs I enjoy most are, on the one hand, when he is so happy about being guilty, and on the other, where he is so guilty about being happy". *Record Mirror*'s Peter Coyne.

> "*Even Serpents Shine* is The Only Ones captured in their prime. Confident, strong, arrogant. A tale of survival, growth and the goods." *Sounds*' Dave McCullough.

On March 1st, the grand *Serpents* tour was preceded by a magnificent Peel session featuring "Miles From Nowhere", "Flaming Torch", "From Here To Eternity" and "Prisoners". The rest of the month was almost entirely devoted to gigging. Taking Lonesome Nomore with them as their support band, The Only Ones' electric odyssey opened at York University, before moving on to Glasgow, Newport and Hull University, where the *NME*'s Emma Ruth caught the band casting pearls before students:

> "The Only Ones always mean business but here they weren't given full opportunity to do anything more than break even. Between lecturing ageing punks ('Stop spitting — it's very childish') and putting the encore to a vote ('You sure you want to hear more? You weren't shouting very loud') they nevertheless played with a meticulously urbane blend of guts and finesse. And certainly, if looks are anything to go by, The Only Ones are as polished a set of professionals as you're likely to see this side of the Royal Marines: leatherclad Perrett is even beginning to look like Lou Reed, while stately John Perry

(ermine-bedecked, like a Tudor king) and Alan Mair (red-laméd, in the style of a Showaddywaddy refugee) provide the technicolour.

On a strictly musical level everyone should already know that The Only Ones are among the more inventive emergent bands, and would have been superstars by now had they not had to compete with all the no-talent junk outfits vying for positions all down the line. From a career opportunity point of view, The Only Ones will not be denied for much longer — but gigs like this can't do them any good. Communication is only possible between equals, and playing the kind of 'entertainment night' venues they're still apparently doomed to, they get less than they deserve."

As if the Devil himself was pulling the strings that made them play, the tour wound its way through Scotland then back to the North of England. On March 19th, they stopped off in Manchester to record three tracks for the *OGWT* — "No Solution", "In-Betweens" and "Programme" — before returning to their rudderless voyage. They were borne along to Sheffield, Middlesborough and Newcastle, then shared an unlikely Rock Against Racism bill with the Leyton Buzzards and Barry Forde, at Lancaster University on the 25th. The band played out the month at Barbarella's where the stage was reduced to a sodden hulk by a torrent of spittle from a tubercular crowd. Koulla Kakoulli:

"We did the whole tour with them, and Peter used to always ask what the audience was like. We went to Birmingham and I got spat at, someone got me in the eye. Then they spat at Peter, I remember he kicked some bloke in the head for it and then he said, 'Look if you really want to do something, I'd rather you pissed on me because I'm into water sports'. After that no-one spat and the band carried on playing."

April was brimming with the same madness — Bristol, Liverpool, Manchester, Loughborough, Lincoln, Oxford. Temperaments flaring like distress signals in the night. Koulla Kakoulli:

"Peter wouldn't go out on stage unless the food was laid out properly in the dressing room. I think he really did start to lose what he was there for. He was there to make music and it started getting silly. There was one gig at a university where they hadn't provided chocolate cake and Peter started saying he wasn't going to play."

As an unpalatable side order to the chocolate cake, CBS dished out some sour grapes when they released the new single, "Out There In The Night" b/w "Lovers of Today" and "Peter & The Pets", with little consideration for the band's wishes. Peter shared the bitter aftertaste with *Record Mirror*'s Chris Westwood:

"...."Out There In The Night" is their (CBS) choice. I wanted to bring out two unreleased tracks on the B-side, they didn't let us have anything to do with the cover, or the fact that it's on blue plastic. There are a lot of people, obviously, who don't have "Lovers Of Today" but I would still have preferred to put out two unrecorded tracks."

After all the intensive road work, the band were at a physically low ebb as they approached the climax of the tour at The Rainbow in Finsbury Park on Saturday, April 2nd. Once the support acts, Lonesome Nomore, The Leyton Buzzards and John Cooper Clarke had done their turns, The Only Ones stepped out on to the stage of the cavernous, baroque theatre. While the ornate setting suited the band, the venue was only two thirds full. Row upon row of scuffed velvet seats remained vacant as The Only Ones' faithful followers congregated together. Nick Tester from *Sounds* found a pot of gold at The Rainbow in spite of the absent crowds:

"The critical flag has been raised above The Only Ones for some time now but a proportionate (and deserved) following still cruelly drags behind. Saturday's showcase sadly reflected the public's continued hesitancy — rather than hostility — to herald this outstanding band. Praise is worth repeating. Live they are an increasingly overpowering proposition, and with two superb albums already flying high among the best, their low commercial appeal is as absurd as it is also obvious. The Only Ones execute, with minimum flash or fuss, music where shock is substituted for subtlety. Even better they avoid the all too often crude demand to be packaged and sold from a particular marketable angle. So the missing fans stay away and really that's their misfortune and not The Only Ones."

As if the band hadn't done enough gigs on the *Serpents* trail, in May they set off on the "Missing Links" tour, filling in the gaps of all the venues they hadn't played when promoting the album.

The rock 'n' roll summer season opened with the release on Arista of *That Summer* — 16 New Wave nuggets including The Only Ones' "Planet", Richard Hell and The Voidoids, the Patti Smith Group, The Ramones, Elvis Costello and Ian Dury and The Blockheads — which was pressed up on sunshine yellow vinyl. The soundtrack from the Columbia film of the same name made for the ultimate post-punk celebration, but Peter had become increasingly deadened to the more jubilant qualities of the outside world. A heroin pall cloyed the atmosphere around The Only Ones. Alan Mair:

> "After *Even Serpents Shine* there were just too many drugs around. It seemed that everywhere I went, everyone was pinned. To all intents and purposes, The Only Ones were trendy and successful and it really set a precedent to a lot of people to think it was cool. Most of the people who supported us or came into contact with us ended up doing the same thing. I never ever touched it. I thought it too dangerous a drug for me to take. Peter used to say to me, 'If ever anyone puts some out, if you went to take it, I would physically pull you away from it because you'd like it'. Even though Peter took the drug, he still disliked what it was. John had a different attitude, he could bounce in and out of it without being very deeply affected but Peter had a different constitution. It was a sorry state for the band to be in."

When the band played six dates in Holland, they took their troubles with them. Alan Mair:

> "It was reaching the stage where instead of arriving in Amsterdam and rehearsing for the gig, Peter and John would end up trying to score some dope and end up in the heaviest places with the heaviest people, who Peter would bring to the gig. His romance with the drug had been and gone. That's when you get into a real rut. I remember saying to him, 'If you're going to be really stoned all the time on stage, I'll leave'. Zena was trying to stop him. It was just a no-win situation. You can't win with that drug. I thought I could blackmail him by saying I'd leave, I would have done anything to stop him. I even remember taking stuff off

him and throwing it away, knowing that we were losing him. He had been a really magical bloke but that aura had gone."

Following Nick Kent's comment that the band were "indolent", a reporter from *Zig Zag* unwittingly tested the validity of Kent's description when he visited the Perrett's Forest Hill flat to do an interview with Peter, only to find him tucked up in bed and unwilling to come out from under the covers. Instead, the interview proceeded with John and Zena touching upon the possible direction of the band's third album. Zena explained:

"Peter's still writing but his songs are a bit stranger. I think they are going to be quite a shock, they're very weird. There's one, "Why Don't You Kill Yourself?", which is amazing. It's not morbid. It's just the way it sometimes appears to people. His mind works in a fragmented way and his songwriting is like that."

Somewhere along the way, John Perry must have become psychic:

"I don't think there's anyone at CBS who knows what we are or how to represent us. I think they'd spend a lot more time, money and effort on us if they knew how to present us. I suppose the worse thing that could happen is that we'll be remembered as a band that should have done better, should've been bigger and people will write great retrospective reviews."

Zena ran the managerial sideshow like a hyperactive humming bird, constantly darting here and there on the band's behalf, whilst acting as a buffer between Peter and the mundanities of everyday life. With a history of miscarriages, Zena left it in the hands of fate when she once again fell pregnant. Perhaps the Egyptian Tarot reader she visited, who had predicted a son, really opened the veils of prophecy. When her slender figure began to take on the ripe qualities of pregnancy she broached the subject with Peter in her usual taut manner. Zena:

"I'd had nine miscarriages and I didn't realize, even when I lost my daughter, how it affected me because I didn't show any signs of emotion. If anything bad happened to me, I guarded it. I didn't show any sign of emotion. I just carried on, and having Peter's career made it easy for me to deal with that, because all I did was focus on it. And then suddenly I was pregnant. Peter wasn't very keen on it, so I said to him,

'It doesn't have anything to do with you, I don't expect anything from you. I'm going to go through with it'."

Peter in his mentally disassociated fashion was removed from the situation, but potential fatherhood gradually took on a novelty aspect with some unexpected bonuses. Peter:

> "I thought it would be a fringe thing, Zena's problem. Zena asked me if she could have it. I knew I was going to be friends with Zena for the rest of my life and she'd make the perfect mother. She said it wouldn't infringe on my liberties in anyway. I thought that was great, she can look after it. I enjoyed the first two or three months of her being pregnant because her body looked good then, but as soon as her body started getting out of shape, I just wasn't turned on — also there was the worry because she gets ill in pregnancy."

When Mrs Perrett informed CBS that she would have to go into hospital for six weeks to sort out some minor 'female trouble', they merely thought she'd put on a bit of weight. Duly excused she gratefully sank into the starched sheets of a hospital bed, confined to a strict regime of rest and more rest because of her tendency towards toxemia. Peter Junior was born two and half months early and delivered by Cesarean section on June 20th 1979, weighing just 2 lbs. He was rushed to the premature birth unit and put in an incubator for the next ten weeks. The short life of their firstborn Nicola came back to haunt the Perretts, as they looked upon the helpless being in the tiny glass box which was keeping him alive. While Zena was in hospital, she signed the contracts for ownership of the Big House where Peter's parents still lived. Peter:

> "We knew that the person who lived on the bottom two floors was going to move to Ireland. Because my parents were sitting tenants, we got it cheap, £33,000. We moved my parents up to the top floor and we were going to move into the other three floors."

Once little Peter was out of danger, his father succumbed to a pure rush of parental response. Peter:

> "It was an awe-inspiring thing. Playing with his little feet, everything was new. It was such a novel thing in my life. The moment you are

THE ONE AND ONLY: Peter Perrett - Homme Fatale

hooked is the first moment there is a communication of feeling between the two of you, the first time that you see that it recognizes you."

Zena kept her affections in check. She barricaded her heart so that no stray emotions might shatter the enforced calm that was her coping mechanism. She couldn't afford to open the floodgates for fear of being swept away by long repressed torrents of pain. Instead, after two more weeks in hospital, she left for New York to finalise details of The Only Ones' second US tour. On her return, a nanny was installed to tend to the baby. Zena:

"I didn't really bond with him. When he cried for something, there would always be someone else to pick him up. It was only years later when the group broke up that I was left in the role of a mother."

In spite of acquiring the Big House where Peter had been raised as a child, and the birth of a son, the three d's that Peter Perrett had so tenderly courted — decadence, despair and decay — were treacherous muses which would soon engulf him. The echoes of the last notes of The Only Ones were discernible in the background.

Chapter 11 – Castle Built On Sand

Although it would be several years before the Perretts moved from the basement flat into their new home, they took pleasure in gradually refurbishing Number 3. The large Victorian house, with a narrow driveway and enough parking space for all the Daimlers Peter could wish for, had neatly tended front and back gardens which Albert Perrett had looked after for many years. The property itself possessed a secluded period charm, the occasional turret and many light and airy rooms, but Peter Perrett's domain was rapidly to metamorphose into a kingdom of disorganisation. Between Only Ones' engagements, Peter and Zena would frequent King's Road antique auctions, bidding for an eclectic array of exotic fancies and furnishings which they stockpiled in the vacant rooms. Peter:

> "I never really thought about furniture until I started to consider the house. I started going to auctions, finding out what I liked. I like oriental art, oriental paintings, oriental ceramics, oriental furniture and oriental carpets. I also liked French furniture, Louis XVIth style chairs. I had lots of gothic oak and tapestries. It was a variety of things that worked together well. I didn't like modernish things at all, Zena liked Art Deco, but it was too modern for me. I liked a bit of floweriness. We had loads of nice things. We bought all this Art Nouveau stained glass for a conservatory. We had grandiose plans for the house."

To protect their stately home from the forces of the law, the Perretts devised a security system strong enough to withhold a battering ram and the entire drug squad. Peter:

> "Whenever the police came round, it would take them an hour to get in. There were loads of doors to get through. There's the big wooden front door, that's the first door you come to, it had a really solid frame. I mean it's not as solid now because the police have had millions of goes at it, but you couldn't get through that. Then you'd go up the stairs and there'd be another door, you'd open that and there were two more doors — one for that floor and the other one went up to the top floor. The top

floor door had locks on it, and on the other side of it we had these enormous planks of wood jammed up against it. The police never got in by breaking the doors down. We'd always eventually let them in, after taking our time to do whatever."

Unfortunately, the doors were the only things in Perrett's life of any lasting durability. Peter:

"We employed loads of cowboy builders. My father kept telling us that the builders were doing it wrong and we didn't listen to him. He liked to poke his nose in everything and because of that, we tended to ignore him. He was like that over my career, wanting to know everything, making suggestions when he didn't know the first thing about it. But as far as the house goes, it was the one thing he did know about 'cos he was a building contractor all his life. Everything that was done in the house either fell down or wasn't done properly. We weren't protected legally, none of them were registered builders."

The temporary stage at the Glastonbury Festival where The Only Ones performed on June 22nd, was more secure than most of the fixtures and fittings that were being erected in the Big House. Before the month was out, the band returned to Holland to play four dates — Utrecht, the Pink Pop Festival, a Rock Against Racism gig and an open air festival in Nondel Park (Amsterdam) supported by the Gang Of Four. July was an unusually quiet period for the band as they straggled towards their third album, rehearsing through humid evenings at Summa studios. Where once there had been sublime magic, discord reigned. Alan Mair:

"After *Serpents,* I thought Peter's stuff was becoming too druggy. Every time we came to rehearsals, the songs were all really slow, just too drug orientated. Not so much in the lyrical content but in the attitude."

Another album deadline loomed, but The Only Ones were no longer a cohesive unit pulling in the same direction. All their efforts hadn't paid off. Sure, they'd made exquisite music, toured almost continuously and touched on heaven in live performance, but it wasn't enough. The band were almost as burned out as Icarus. Peter:

"If we'd have taken six months off, just to be apart from each other for a while, maybe we could have got it together. It was silly going ahead and

Above: The Chairmen of the Bored. The band wait for a press conference.

making the album. If we'd had a better relationship with the record company, I'd have been able to go in and say, 'Listen, we're not getting on very well at the moment. It's best if we just have a break to sort out our internal problems and then get the album together'. But I didn't feel there was anyone I could talk to. I felt that we scared the people at CBS, that they thought we were really untogether and if there was a hint of anything more untogether, it would freak them out."

In August the band sought a shady retreat in Romansleigh, North Devon, where the former Yes guitarist Steve Howe owned an 8-track studio in a pretty farmhouse. The well of songs that the band could draw from had not yet dried up, but the creativity flowed less freely when recording began at Langley Farm. Peter:

"We went to Devon to get the songs together. We recorded "Me And My Shadow", "Trouble In The World" and a song that ended up being called "Devon Song" (*Remains*). In the end we used the Langley Farm version of "Me And My Shadow" on the album, because when we tried to do it in a studio we couldn't get the same feel, so we dubbed that recording. "Trouble In The World" was re-recorded later on and "Devon

Song" got left off because I never finished writing it, which is why it's got the same lyrics on each verse. Quite a lot of the other songs were in a similar state."

The week spent in Devon was a warm-up to the main bulk of recording which began in earnest back in London. Following a gig at the Lyceum on September 2nd with Toyah and The Psychedelic Furs supporting, the band plugged in at Utopia studios with producer Colin Thurston. CBS were keen for Thurston, who had previous form with Duran Duran and The Buzzcocks, to work with The Only Ones. Thurston was foisted on the band rather than voted in. Peter's favourite candidate for the job had been the Manchester-based Martin Hannett, who had imbued both Joy Division and Magazine with an atmospheric ambience. Although Hannett would have been the better choice, insofar as understanding the musical aesthetics of The Only Ones, it was the "straight" man who ended up getting production credits. Peter:

"We spent a day in Advision Studios with Martin Hannett and we only got two backing tracks down — "The Big Sleep" and "Oh Lucinda (Love Becomes A Habit)" — which is not much work. There was no urgency involved in it at all. It was more like getting stoned, mucking about and occasionally playing a bit of music. He just let things happen, he didn't try and organise anything. Certain members of the band thought we were chaotic enough as it was. I think it was mainly Alan who thought Colin would be better. He was the exact opposite of Martin. He was very straight — a slave driver — which made it uncomfortable for me. He tried to take off all the rough edges. I think it would have been a better album if Martin Hannett had done it, but I think the first day we spent with him frightened everyone."

With his sandpaper technique and strict regime, Thurston began putting the band through their paces. Work started at Utopia on their fifth single "Trouble In The World". Despite the song's pessimistic title "Trouble" gallops along at a cracking pace. There was unforeseen trouble on September 13th, when Alan Mair's Dan Armstrong bass guitar was stolen from Olympic studios while the band were recording the single's B-side, "Your Chosen Life". The track, which was deemed "obscene", appears to have evolved from a much earlier number "Sister" which had shocked the fluorescent socks off Vivienne Westwood and Malcolm McLaren some years before.

A sloping jazz background gives no hint of what is to come, neither does Peter's voice until the song winds towards its conclusion and his revulsion is made plain. Any further recording had to be put on hold for over two months, when the band left for their second tour of the States.

The 26-date trek coincided with the US release of *Special View*, a compilation of the first two albums which met with enthusiastic reviews from coast to coast. But a hitch in the distribution process meant that *Special View* wasn't always in stock at local record stores when the band hit various towns on their itinerary.

The tour kicked off with two nights at Hurrah's. New York welcomed The Only Ones back with some highly suspicious flyers featuring snapshots of the band with a collage of narcotics and associated paraphernalia framing them. Placed between the cocaine, capsules and a syringe, a Fender guitar pick was the only indication that this was in fact an advertisement for a rock band rather than a flamboyant syndicate of dealers. Gigs in Boston and Philadelphia followed before The Only Ones did a detour back to New York to play CBGB's. The downbeat joint came as a shock to Perrett and company who were more familiar with the club's legendary status as the throne room of the New York underground scene, rather than its sleazy reality. Peter:

> "We said we'd play CBGB's, but we were really shocked when we got there. It was unbelievable, a terrible place. It was the worst place we played in the whole of New York."

Peter got a closer look at the city's grimy underbelly when he reconnected with Johnny Thunders who took him on a trip, deep downtown, for some deals on wheels. Peter:

> "I spent quite a bit of time with Johnny. He used to score on the lower East side. It was real scuzzy basic street scoring. The reason why all Americans fix is 'cos it's like about 2% of the strength we'd get in England. It just doesn't work if you don't fix it. Going to score was really scarey. One time we went down to the lower East side. Only certain cab drivers would go there. They knew exactly what you were going for. What happened was that the cab slowed down, the thing was

THE ONE AND ONLY: Peter Perrett - Homme Fatale

Above: Kellie explains theosophy to Perrett and Perry in Washington DC.

not to stop, because stopping was too dangerous, but you'd slow down and you'd have these people running next to the car, they'd show it to you and whichever one of them had a good deal, you'd reach out and give them the money, then speed off as soon as it was done. I'd never encountered anything like that in England. What was weird, was that the cab driver treated it as normal. I tried to make up some pathetic remark about, 'The trouble you have to go to get some grass these days'. I was trying to pretend it was just soft drugs 'cos I felt embarrassed."

After New York, the touring party which included Zena and Peter's former fancy Kathy Barrett, who had been taken on as baby Peter's nanny, headed for the scene of Perrett's previous angel dust encounter, The Edge in Toronto. This time The Only Ones' frontman was a little less delighted to be there, as Alan Niester reported for *The Toronto Globe*:

"Personally I thought it was quite clever when the drunk in the corner yelled out, 'Are you the only one?' to the lone figure testing the mikes on the stage. After all, it was a group called The Only Ones we were all waiting for, and the 9:45pm unofficial starting time had long come and gone by that point. The British new wave outfit were making their second pass through Toronto. Their first appearance here was met with generally favourable response but unfortunately their stand started out with a few rough edges. First, there was an unspecified hold-up at Customs, which somehow manifested itself in a 10:53 set start. Then there was the radio interference, which resulted in John Coltrane coming loud and clear through the amp, and ultimately the speakers, which in turn resulted in Peter Perrett leaving the stage. With order restored at 11:10, we finally got a chance to determine if it was all worth the wait. It was."

The next date, at The Phantasy in Cleveland on September 26th, had to be re-scheduled for the following evening, after Peter, Zena and Alan missed their flight. Alan Mair:

"We were leaving Toronto to go and play in Cleveland and Kellie was late, he'd stayed at a friend's ranch. We were all to meet at the airport. We were all there except for Kellie, and I had his passport. Suddenly Kellie rushed in, I gave him his passport and he went through the gate. All the luggage and guitars went through the check in. As I turned to go through, the airport attendant shut the gate and said, 'I'm sorry, the plane's gone'. We were supposed to be playing Cleveland in five hours. It was a one hour flight. So Zena, the baby, Peter and myself were stranded in the airport surrounded by a mountain of equipment. In the end Kellie's friend hired a big estate car. We drove to Cleveland and arrived as they were cancelling the gig."

The rest of the month and Detroit, Chicago and Milwaukee passed without any significant incidents. October was a different proposition altogether. The fun started in Minneapolis, which John Perry confused with Indianapolis and thought that he'd try out for the 500. He was awarded a ticket for speeding and a night in the slammer. Later on down the trail, when the band were en-route to a gig at Brothers in Birmingham, Alabama, they witnessed a small plane crashing into a pylon, but there were still plenty more sparks left to fly when they arrived at the venue that night. Early in the set, the club's tetchy owner issued an ultimatum to the band, to either keep the noise down or get out. With cavalier derring-do, The Only Ones ignored his request. Sometime later, the neighbourhood good ole boys, complete with baseball bats, turned up to "escort" Peter and company off the premises. The police were called in and order was barely maintained.

The tour reached its emotional nadir in Atlanta, Georgia, where Peter found the inspiration for "Baby's Got A Gun":

> *I found love in Atlanta, Georgia*
> *I said 'Baby I don't think I can afford ya'*
> *She said, just for me — she'd do it free*
> *Can't you see your infatuation's*
> *Gonna mean unusual complications*
> *You're in danger — baby's got a gun*
> *Baby's got a gun*
> *She's gonna shoot you down*
> *She's gonna shoot you in the ground.*
> *You know she's gonna be the ruin of your life*
> *You don't get worried 'cos it happens all the time*
> *But you can never see through evil when it smiles*

Peter temporarily lost his heart and the plot midway through the tour when he met a local girl. The events recalled in the song are as clear as forensic evidence. Alan Mair:

"We had to leave Peter behind in Atlanta. He just got so out of it, he didn't know where he was or what he was doing. We waited half a day for him to show up, but then we had to go on. He'd met this girl and gone back to her place and when he got ready to leave, she got a gun and tried to rob him."

There is a double-barrel metaphor to be found in the song's lyrics. Although Peter had a habit, he chased the dragon rather than fixed. Smoking junk is a less cost-effective method than shooting up, where a small amount lasts longer and the rush is more intense. Miss Georgia Peach introduced Perrett to the needle. Peter:

"The first time I had a fix was in Atlanta. This stripper that I met fixed me. It's a slightly sexual thing, being injected by a female. Drug taking is very ritualised, and I think the ritual of fixing is a lot more dangerous. Although smoking drugs on foil is a ritual, it's not as obsessive as fixing. I'd seen Johnny Thunders fix water just 'cos he wanted a fix and there wasn't anything else. I've had people give me injections but that was only through desperation because either their stuff wasn't strong enough or I couldn't get enough to make it work. Mainly that happened in America."

On his home ground, where the smack was of good quality and rarely in short supply, Peter was able to chase the dragon right into its lair. Peter:

"Most of the people that I knew that got into fixing on a permanent basis seemed to step over a line where they just don't give a shit about anything anymore. I always did things to an extreme, the way I approached drugs was by taking as much as I possibly could. With smoking, if you put a quarter gram on a piece of tin foil, it takes 10 or 15 minutes to get to you. It's a much slower way of taking it into the system. Whereas with an injection it is much easier to OD. Luckily I've always had enough. That made it easier to resist fixing. I'm not saying that I'm stronger than other people just because I didn't fix, I was just luckier that I didn't have to resort to it."

He eventually found his way out of Atlanta and picked up the tour which wound through the West Coast before concluding back in New York with a gig at the Irving Plaza. The next day, John Perry was interviewed on WPIX FM. After selecting some favourite tracks including the Stones' "Tumbling Dice", Dion and The Belmonts' "Baby, You've Been On My Mind" and "My Friend Jack Eats Sugar Lumps" by The Smoke, the DJ asked John, 'Who are the other members of The Only Ones?' To which he replied, 'I don't know but I wish them a lot of luck, whoever they are!'

The disintegration of The Only Ones took place by degrees. The scenario was as fatalistic as one of Perrett's songs. A less intense group with more outside guidance might have been able to work through their problems and eventually even found chart success some five or ten years down the line, by holding to a steady course. The Only Ones were made of finer fabric and they were coming apart at the seams. Yet, from a distance the damage was barely noticeable and in performance they were undiminished. John Perry:

"Through the second American tour, we were doing good shows and the ensemble playing was getting better. The only thing that wasn't

THE ONE AND ONLY: Peter Perrett - Homme Fatale

happening was any kind of structured consolidation of the career. There should have been management capable of looking ahead rather than just reacting to things as they happened. It seemed to me that by that time, the only thing that was going right was the live shows. In personal terms I was happy. I was making a living playing in a good live band. My response to chaos has always been to laugh at it. I rather enjoyed each new disaster as it came along, I thought it was funny and very right for the band, which isn't a good attitude if you are ambitious. We did better gigs while stuff was falling apart all around us."

John stayed on in New York for a further week, to see the sights with his girlfriend Suze, while the rest of the band returned home. On October 27th, they re-grouped in Paris for a gig at Le Palais and a television appearance. Holland was next in their autumn almanac. The Dutch had always given The Only Ones a warm reception and the five shows at Amstelveen, The Exit in Rotterdam, Arnheim, Appeldoorn and The Paradiso in Amsterdam exceeded their enthusiastic audience's expectations. If, according to John, the band thrived off a certain amount of chaos, then they were triumphant in their turmoil, as The Paradiso gig which was later released as a live album testifies (*The Big Sleep* — Jungle Records '93).

Peter's angelic corruption of "Silent Night" was recorded for Dutch radio during their stay. After sticking to the traditional first verse, he breaks into his own version of the carol:

Silent night, holy night
Oh dear Jesus, help me fight
Give me salvation
Show me the truth
All I ever wanted to do
Is sleep in heavenly peace
Sleep in heavenly peace

The sincerity and delicacy of the performance is breathtaking, and if Jesus had heard it, he surely would have taken Peter for a moonbeam. The Only Ones' frontman got left behind in Amsterdam by the rest of the band when he refused to be disturbed from his heavenly peace. Alan Mair:

Castle Built On Sand

Above: The whole crew in Lawrence, Kansas — (l-r) Digby Cleever (roadie), Chris Reynolds (roadie), Peter, Barrie Evans (guitar tech.), Alan Mair, John Perry, Mike Kellie.

"We'd done the last gig and the plan was to drive, then catch the ferry back, but Peter wouldn't get out of bed. I said to him, 'If you don't get up, I'm going and I'm taking the car'. I went back to his room five or six times, then finally I said, 'Peter, this is the last time, we're ready to go'. Zena wasn't with us. John, Kellie and myself left him in bed in the hotel. Later on, Peter got up, realised we'd gone and phoned the police to say his car had been stolen and that John or I was driving it. We got the ferry and got back to England. Apparently Peter had no money on him, but I just didn't care, I wanted to get back to England. When Peter got home, he threatened Kellie, he was going to shoot him or something like that, then he phoned me. He thought we were going to have a fist fight. I said, 'Any time Peter, where do you want to meet up, Hyde Park?'."

Once order was restored, the band went back to Summa rehearsal studios to work on the material for the third album which was to be called *Baby's Got A Gun.* The original release date of "Trouble In The World" b/w "Your Chosen Life" was put back after CBS withdrew the single on the grounds that the sleeve photograph was unsuitable. The shot featured the band sitting around a table with a large antique crucifix on it, and drew criticism on the grounds that John Perry looked too out of it. "Trouble" was finally released on November 16th with a new picture that parodied The Doors' first album cover. The single garnered mixed reviews but one thing was certain, Colin Thurston and The Only Ones were not compatible. Nick Kent, writing for the *NME* duly noted the off pitch partnership:

> "The basic problem is one of arrangement and production. The band's instrumental strengths have always come from their stoutly individual utilisation of the two guitars, bass and drums set-up, but "Trouble" comes galloping forth in a blur of tinny synthesizers. Perhaps Thurston is attempting to recreate the textural momentum of Bowie's "Heroes" which he engineered but here it simply falls flat."

It was too late in the day to alter the course of the album. The proceedings surrounding the recording, which lasted through most of December, swerved this way and that until the producer/navigator lost the map and the battle-weary squadron went down fighting amongst themselves. Although Thurston managed to moderate most of the musical thrusts and parries, the manifest power of two songs — "Why Don't You Kill Yourself?" and "The Big Sleep" — overcame his soft rock and synthesizer tendencies. Naturally "Why Don't You Kill Yourself?" is brimful of paradox, the up-tempo tune clearly recognises Booker T. Jones and William Bell's Stax classic "Private Number" — without the lyrics. Once Perrett interjects his message, however, emphasised by a female chorus, the entire tone of the piece changes to a sneer campaign as he proclaims:

> *This ain't no missionary speech*
> *Just some friendly advice*
> *Why don't you kill yourself?*
> *You ain't no use to no one else*
> *Why don't you kill yourself?*
> *You ain't no use to no one else*
> *I heard you had your stomach pumped four times already this week*

"The Big Sleep" is a chilling descent into oblivion. The rhythm section holds the pace as if they were solemn pall bearers while John Perry wreathes a forlorn masterpiece with some filigree fretwork. Perrett, like a lazy Lazarus, seems content with the seductive internment the lyrics imply:

> *I don't have the strength to break an empty shell*
> *And I surely don't have the strength to mend it*
> *I don't ever want to sleep again now that I've found love*

Out of the twelve songs on the third album, only "Why Don't You Kill Yourself?" and "The Big Sleep" share a sense of total completion. Peter:

> "Apart from the three songs we did in Devon, we hadn't worked out any of the others, we just learned them in the studio. It's a lot of half ideas. It could've been a much better album than it was. There are some good songs on it but it doesn't seem complete. The first and second albums seemed rounded and finished, whereas that album, maybe because I knew how it was made, seems a bit up in the air. There is nothing to take it to its conclusion. It just reflected the disintegration."

As usual Koulla was on hand to add a feminine touch but this time she was paired with Pauline Murray. The former Penetration front-woman possessed an ethereally pure voice that counter-balanced Koulla's stronger, more earthy tones. The down-home flavour of the Grand Ole Opry was introduced at CBS studios, when Peter and Pauline duetted on the Johnny Duncan country & western number "Fools". Like a last chance vision of Donny and Marie Osmond sucking lemons and swigging Jose Cuervo, the lonesome twosome mourned love's slings and arrows, while refusing to dodge the blows. Midway through the month and the album, the sessions moved to Red Bus studios in North London. The lovely "Oh Lucinda (Love Becomes A Habit)", Peter's farewell note to Lynne, was all but signed and delivered:

> *Take the crutch away from you*
> *And watch you fall down*
> *It's a shame about a girl like you*
> *Always falling down*
> *I see the way you're looking*

It's a silent rhapsody
I know there's something cooking
I know I've seen that film before
The end is so predictable
You've got to learn to live again

Colin Thurston's light-weight production gives a superficial sheen to the number which, when performed live, reached a far greater depth of emotion both vocally and musically. The Peel session version created much more of an effective Perrett melodrama, complete with pushy bass runs, knock-about drums and cracking guitars. "Me And My Shadow" also came into focus at Red Bus — an Edgar Allan Poe story set to a Bo Diddley beat with Kellie's drums pumping like a tell-tale heart while Peter flees his own shadow. It wasn't just Peter's shadow that was playing up. The rest of the band had thrown down their gauntlets in a neat row. There was mutiny on board at Red Bus. Mike Kellie:

> "There was never any room for any of us to write. I've always written songs. Alan and John wanted to write. I'm not talking about who was better than Peter, because there was never any competition. There was an autocratic side of the band that I was never comfortable with."

As Kellie, John and Alan were pushing for more creative control of the album, Peter was withdrawing. Peter:

> "There was very little input by me. Okay, I did the vocals but I spent very little time at the studio. There were days when they'd wait four or five hours for me to turn up."

Alan Mair had written a couple of songs including "My Way Out Of Here" which he hoped would find a place on *Baby's Got A Gun*:

> "I said I wanted to put some songs on, and we started rehearsing, but Peter wouldn't play. I thought that was very childish. "My Way Out Of Here" was my song, although on the first print of the album it was credited to Peter. Peter wasn't turning up for rehearsals or for studio time. Colin Thurston was quite into what I was doing, so we ended up recording them but Peter never played on them. Then, overnight, he came in with four or five songs; "Happy Pilgrim", "Re-Union", "Strange Mouth", "Deadly Nightshade" and "Castle Built On Sand".

Castle Built On Sand

Above: A black cat crosses paths with The Only Ones.

"My Way Out Of Here" appears to summarise Mair's feeling towards the situation he was in. The bass player had for some time been considering leaving the band but was unable to make the final separation. The song itself is a breezy little rocker, but the really curious aspect is that Mair delivers it almost exactly like Perrett, minus the unique plaintive lilt. Peter:

> "What annoyed me is the song had vocals very like mine, he sang as much like me as possible. CBS made a mistake on the label and put all songs by Peter Perrett, so if you didn't know otherwise you'd just assume it was me."

The inclusion of "My Way Out Of Here" meant that there was no room left for the title track, "Baby's Got A Gun", even though the lyrics were printed on the inner sleeve. The brewing insurrection prompted Peter into coming up with some new material. Prior to the recording period, he claimed to be making a conscious decision to pen more uplifting lyrics, but there is little evidence to bear out a sudden influx of sweetness and light. "Happy Pilgrim" vaguely touches on optimism but the love that

Perrett desires is one that will shield him from evil. Given Peter's proclivity for melancholy and melodrama both in public and private, there was little chance of him ever finding his way out of the dark woods where eternal shade eclipsed the warmth of the sun and strange flowers grew amongst the thorns. The fatal bloom of "Deadly Nightshade" was plucked for the album:

> *Stars are your companions*
> *And the darkness is your friend*
> *It protects you from the gaze of any would-be hired assassins*
> *Oh deadly nightshade*
> *After dark you blossom*
> *You flower in the night*
> *You smell of roses*
> *But sometimes you taste bitter*
> *Almost like deadly nightshade*
> *My belladonna*

The three remaining songs, "Castle Built On Sand", "Strange Mouth" and "Re-Union" are perfunctory efforts. Everything was in place — the decadent doctrines, esoteric, doomed lyricism and virtuoso playing, but the passion had been stifled by prevailing forces. The sessions and the band's internal problems came to a head within days of Christmas. John Perry:

> "The divisions were apparent. Peter was the sole songwriter; our modus operandi meant that the band worked up the songs organically. Nobody disputed Peter's role as composer but there needed to be *some* recognition of the arrangements, perhaps 10 or 15% of the publishing set aside and divided up four ways between the band — something to the effect of 'Songs arranged by The Only Ones'. Either that, or there had to be consideration of songs from other sources, especially as Peter's output was lessening by this point.
>
> I pushed for one of Alan's songs to go on the record and that wasn't very well received. Peter wouldn't talk to anyone, went off and then turned up unannounced at Red Bus one evening with a bunch of teenage musicians with whom he'd had a rehearsal. It was news to us and the producer. They weren't very competent but evidently to Peter they

represented Raw Enthusiasm as opposed our Urbane Cynicism. The session collapsed after about 90 minutes when the noble savages, unused to the rigours of studio life, abandoned the unequal struggle to tune their instruments."

As well as the band's external grievances, there seemed to be several strands of personal discord. The musicians were unhappy with the way the credits and spoils were divided. Peter, however, believes that the band went into decline chiefly because of drugs. Perhaps all the reasons were merely hostages taken in the last stages of a failing cause. Peter:

"There were all these arguments. Alan wanted to do "My Way Out Of Here" because they wanted to start getting publishing royalties. I started playing with a couple of other guitarists because I was worried about my relationship with John. We just weren't getting on well, mainly 'cos whenever I stopped using, he'd bring stuff on tour or whatever. I started playing with people that were friends of friends, but there wasn't anyone I seriously thought of playing with. I just wasn't happy playing with who I was playing with."

John contests Peter's drug theory when it comes to the decline, but he agrees that drugs affected his sound — literally. His guitar was hollowed out specifically for the transportation of his own gear but it's an aspect that Perry considers to have little influence on the band, other than possibly adding to its heroin aura. John Perry:

"Peter is always very keen on citing drugs as the problem which led to The Only Ones' break up, which is nonsense. The major cause of the break up was maladministration. Plenty of people keep an efficient organisation going through far more involved drug usage than we had. Drugs are a convenient catch-all excuse to blame for a whole variety of stuff. In my view, the whole time the band was going, it made Peter a bit late for setting off to gigs sometimes, but we rarely missed any gigs and I don't remember scenes where Peter and myself were incapable. I turned up on time and stayed in tune, and beyond that, my view was that my personal life was my own."

The band went their separate ways for the festive season with little cheer. For Peter and Zena, the Christmas break should have been a

THE ONE AND ONLY: Peter Perrett - Homme Fatale

peaceful family occasion. Instead, the basement flat became the chaotic site of a police stampede, as truncheons tangled with tinsel. The raid came as the result of three kilos of cocaine being brought into the country by the drug syndicate Peter and Zena had been affiliated to. Events escalated after a translator for the organisation, Billy*, cut a side deal with Zandro*, a Bolivian friend of the Perretts. On Boxing Day, Billy contacted Zena, who went to visit Zandro. All three were netted by Customs. Zena was released after 3 days, while Billy was detained. The basement flat was also turned over and Peter was unceremoniously carted off to prison for the night. Peter:

"It's horrible spending that time of year in the cells 'cos the cell and the blankets are all covered in sick from people getting drunk at Christmas."

Koulla was preparing dinner and expecting Loulla and Dimitris to call round when the front door came crashing down. Koulla Kakoulli:

"Customs and Excise smashed the door in. It was terrible. We were expecting my parents. I rang Zena up and a Scottish man answered. When I asked if he'd get her, he said she was doing something. Peter told me I should have woken him up and told him what the guy on the phone had said. I heard this crack and then this guy with long hair and an axe came running down the passage. I didn't think they were police. There was five guys and one helmet. When I saw that helmet, I thought, 'Thank God'. They ripped everything to bits, including the settees. It was a nightmare. Poor Peter. It was about six in the evening, he was still in bed. They woke him with an axe over his head. He was so cool, there was a bottle of linctus (methadone) by the bed, and he went, 'There's 400 mills of linctus in here'. Opened it and went glug, glug, glug. While they were searching the premises, he watched the Benny Hill Show. He used to love Benny Hill. He was sitting there with his little round glasses on, watching Benny Hill."

Chapter 12 – Mourning Glory

The basement flat had started to take on the appearance of a besieged bunker. Several windows were boarded up and the steel plated front door bore the random damage and hatchet dents of the Perretts' Christmas callers. Mercifully the season of ill-will to all men was over, but The Only Ones as a group were slow to respond to the demands of the new year. Alan Mair was busy consolidating his production credentials working with a young Scottish band, Another Pretty Face, which included future Waterboy, Mike Scott, in the line-up.

Peter meanwhile, was assisting Wasted Youth who were about to make their second single. The sickly runts of the decadent litter had sent Perrett a demo tape. After catching one of their gigs at the 101 Club in Clapham he agreed to produce them. The Youths scurried off to their rehearsal cellar in Canning Town to work on the three songs in which Peter had shown most interest — "I'll Remember You", "All My Friends Are Dead" and "Do The Caveman" (Bridgehouse Records) — before transferring to Basing Street studios where Perrett awaited them.

Wasted Youth's former guitarist, Mick Atkins, recalls Peter's sweet-toothed tutorials:

> "The recording went reasonably smoothly. Not only did Peter produce, he had a fair bit of input as well. He wrote the lead guitar intro for the single's A-side "I'll Remember You", which our vocalist Ken Scott played. Peter had taught him some music theory that he'd worked out himself, based on a mathematical formula. He also played the bass intro on it. For the B-side, "All My Friends Are Dead", Peter did backing vocals on the chorus using backwards echoes, it was quite an ethereal, ghostly sound and he played rhythm guitar at the end of the track. For "Caveman" he didn't play anything, he just produced. It's the kind of song where there is a verse and a pause, which is really difficult to do, but out of the five verses he found the tightest one, then looped it. Musically he was very professional, even though I'm sure he was stoned. We all were. The other thing I remember is that I kept coming

across half-eaten Kit-Kats and Lion bars that he'd left on the desk or lying on a chair. I was always sitting on bars of chocolate by accident."

The first Only Ones' dispatch of 1980 came in the form of a full-page *Sounds* interview, during which Perrett unburdened his gloom with a view onto journalist Dave McCullough who described his visit to the Perretts:

"Last week I got a 176 bus to Forest Hill, where Peter Perrett lives in an unspectacular basement flat and where I entered, past a suspicious girl, into a room filled with heavy clouds of dope and the stinging, attacking sound of new product from The Only Ones. This is where I found a half-dead, half-alive, half-naked Peter Perrett. This is where I saw him in his cage, dissatisfied, disillusioned, like some exiled, fairy-story prince or an upstart, unproclaimed poet sifting through some ashes, looking blankly at a book of cut-price furniture, and longingly glaring at the bars of his cage."

The band's future was evaporating as fast as breath on a mirror. Judging by the tone of the article, it would have taken an extraordinary act of faith to even suggest that The Only Ones were going to last much longer into the new decade. Perrett clawed at the chance of getting a hit single like a man reaching for a lifeboat, but at the same time his reckless nature compelled him in the other direction — to go swimming with sharks. Peter summarised the prevailing market forces to McCullough with slighted brevity:

".... 'Now, I think there's only a very small percentage of the population that needs music to survive. I think most people just hear something on the radio, and if they hear it again they'll just go out and buy it. The market you've got to get across to is pretty stupid'. His mood alters slightly when Zena walks in holding the baby and he talks of immortality through children and cutting back on extra-marital liaisons but the palpable discontent never lifts."

The narcotic reputation which developed around Perrett and the band that had previously only been alluded to by the press, was now an absolute fact, open to discussion. Peter told McCullough:

".... 'I don't like it when people contact us with drugs. It upsets my mother for one thing. She keeps inspecting my arms. It's bad for someone like Alan who doesn't even drink. It would be terrible to get the sort of reputation that Keith Richards has got, a celebrated junkie'."

The band made their first public appearance of the year a week later at The Lyceum with Simple Minds and Martha and the Muffins in support. Pauline Murray and Koulla joined the band for a lively encore of "City Of Fun" and "Me And My Shadow", but already Koulla was preparing to beat an exit.

Lonesome Nomore had picked up a small but steady following and signed to Dick James Music for a one-off single, "Tuned Insane" b/w "Do You Think I Care". Photos of Koulla looking like a punk version of Jean Harlow, with bleached curls and painted lips, often graced the live review sections of the music press. Despite the exposure and Koulla's role as Only Ones' ingénue, Lonesome Nomore were still starlets struggling to be stars and their front-woman was growing impatient. Koulla:

"There was quite a lot of arguing between me and Zena. Peter was butting in, saying I was ungrateful and that most bands would have appreciated having a manager like her. But Zena really wasn't putting the time into us and it was hurting me because I knew we could have got somewhere if someone would have pushed us."

Baby's Got A Gun was released on April 11th and eventually peaked at number 37 in the national charts. Both the front and back sleeve photographs by John Whitfield summarise The Only Ones' collective despondency. The cover captures them in the Big House, while the excellent back sleeve shot, which was co-ordinated by Michael Beal, was taken in the Charlie Chaplin suite at The Savoy Hotel. The band are gathered like a contingent of dodgy conventioneers. The girl with the gun in her mitt, who was strategically placed in a wardrobe, was the partner of Steve Nicoll, the drummer from Eddie and The Hot Rods. Another babe with a gun in his hand, and the barrel in his rose-bud mouth like a lethal dummy, was two year old little Peter Junior. The poster, which advertised The Only Ones' up-coming tour and album release, triggered a moral outcry and several record shops protested. A further bout of controversy was caused by the second track on the album, "Why Don't You Kill Yourself?". When some wanna-dies began writing to Perrett, CBS started pressing the panic buttons.

THE ONE AND ONLY: Peter Perrett - Homme Fatale

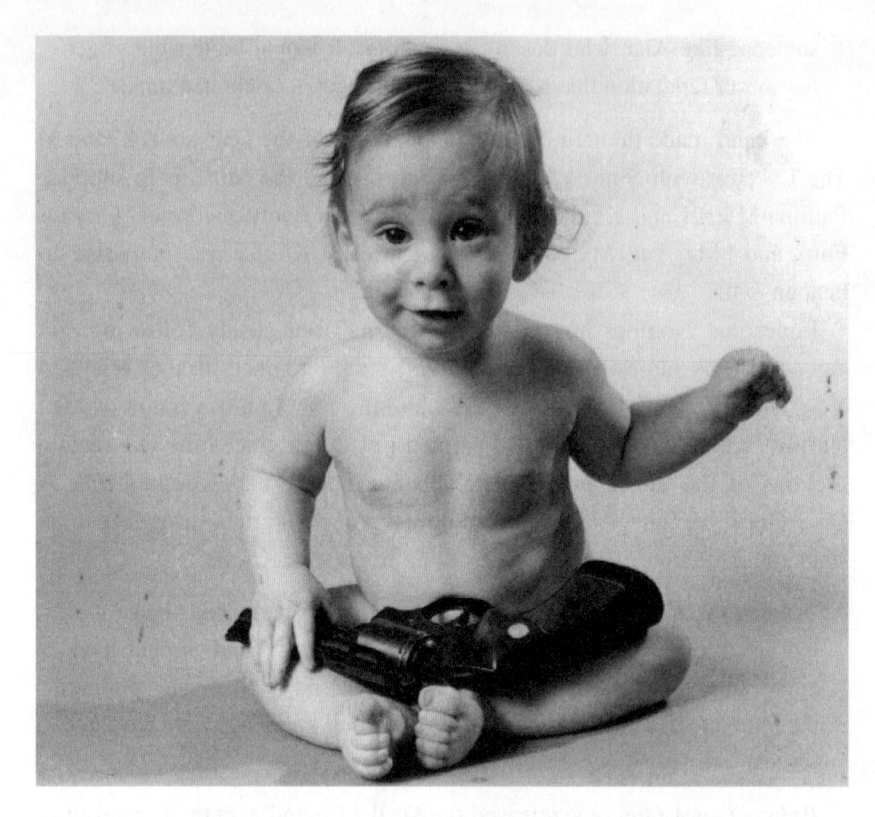

Above: Is that a gun in your nappy or are you just pleased to see me?

Of more immediate concern to the band was the fresh crop of journalists manning the review sections of the music papers. Most of the original supporters of The Only Ones had moved on and the new critics were eager to forge their identities by assassinating their predecessors' star choice. The band's rich concoction of seduction, destruction and addiction was too jaded a stance for the ambitious, health conscious '80s. Perrett was decried as, 'The last survivor of the make-up and fake leopardskin wars', and Ian Penman in the same issue of the *NME* gave *Baby's Got A Gun* the kind of thumbs down that introduced Christians to the lions:

> "Today it's not enough to be bizarre or vague or ambiguous or lost. It's maybe good enough to be lost for words or to shut up or to be quiet. But not those others: they're lies. What it is with The Only Ones — more specifically Peter Perrett because he's the one with all the words — is

that they have nothing new to give us in the way of reproducing their radical passivity. They are awful. They are awful liars."

After such a fine send off, The Only Ones began their 23-date *Baby's Got a Gun* tour in Newcastle on April 17th. In tow as their support act was Wasted Youth. Pete Makowski caught up with Perrett and company when they hit London on May 9th for a gig at the Electric Ballroom:

> "It was the last time I saw The Only Ones play. The Electric Ballroom was a miserable, seedy place. It felt like the gig from hell. Wasted Youth were on stage doing a Doors medley. Backstage it was really miserable. I think because of the drugs, communication had broken down, it had with me, with the band, with Peter. They seemed fucked, basically. Kellie looked so sad, I think he'd had enough. The ironic thing is that the venue was packed. They'd picked up a real following but they were disheartened."

Seedy venues and clouded atmospheres never did the band's playing much harm though, as a line recording made on Revox straight from the desk demonstrates. Widely bootlegged, this show is often reckoned to be the actual source of the Demon live CD issued in 1990.

In spite of the tour, which concluded on May 18th in Brighton, the release of a single "Fools" b/w "Castle Built On Sand" seemed merely incidental, although Radio 2 did briefly pick up on it. At the end of the month, The Only Ones recorded "The Happy Pilgrim", "The Big Sleep", "Oh Lucinda" and "Why Don't You Kill Yourself?" for what would be their last Peel session.

The band had reached an impasse in their career. *Baby's Got A Gun* had been as accessible an offering as they could muster, but it still hit a blue note when it came to ringing up the sales. However, it appeared as though a reversal of fortune was on the cards, when via Kellie's connections The Only Ones were offered the job of opening up for The Who on their summer 1980 American tour. Kellie:

> "I pulled a couple of strings to get us the tour. They weren't necessarily the definitive strings, but Pete (Townshend) wanted us on because of our friendship and because he believed in the band and liked where we were coming from."

Alan Mair had been on the verge of quitting when news of The Who tour was relayed to him:

"I phoned up Kellie and told him I was leaving and he said that Pete Townshend wanted us to tour with them. Then Zena phoned and said we were going to California. I'd always wanted to go to California, so I thought, 'Great, at least I'm going to get to tour that bit of the States'."

Something approaching optimism surged through The Only Ones' camp like an unusual virus. Kellie took immediate action and began to get in shape for the event:

"I started getting really fit for that last American tour. I remember jogging around Forest Hill at 7 o'clock in the morning in a track suit. I used to get truck drivers whistling because I had long hair. Then I'd come back and soak in a bath that was full of salt and lemon, then I'd have fresh spinach, two poached eggs and a pot of coffee."

The Only Ones pulled out of a booking at the Loch Lomond Festival and arrived in the States to play their first date with The Who at the Sports Arena in San Diego on June 18th. John Perry:

"Exposure. The whole point of doing a support slot at that stage of the band's career was wider exposure. At those Who gigs we'd play 12,000 seaters, go down really well, and there'd be people shouting up from the front rows, 'What's the group called?'. Somebody had omitted to see that our name went on the posters."

The Only Ones played two further dates at The Forum in Los Angeles, followed by five nights at the LA Sports Arena before being asked to leave the tour. John Perry:

"Evidently, Roger Daltrey didn't take to us and effectively we were thrown off the tour, mainly I believe, because Daltrey was making such a fuss. In retrospect, I think we were expected to socialise more with them — do a bit of good natured drinking and backslapping, but we were quite reticent. In my case, the reticence was based on respect. It seems that Daltrey interpreted it as us being some stuck up punk band who thought we were better than them. Townshend and Entwhistle were the ones I really respected, but Pete wasn't easy to communicate with

Above: Portrait of a doomed pout. Peter backstage at the Whiskey-A-Go-Go.

anyway, he was drunk or coked or whatever. I thought we were getting on great, but we were asked to leave after the LA dates."

The Only Ones decided to stay on in LA and Zena began organising some gigs. With next to no money, the band were stuck in a motel in West Hollywood. In an area criss-crossed with derelict rail tracks, the Tropicana Motel neither prospered nor floundered, rather it existed in a seedy continuum that drew passing bands year after year. The main motel squatted in a large double court arrangement around the pool area, beyond which there was a collection of private bungalows where The Only Ones had taken up residence. John Perry:

"We were stuck in the Tropicana with very little money in that fucking Los Angeles weather where it's the same everyday, no seasons, nothing changes, it was pretty nightmarish. I started making plans, phoning England, getting people to send me money to get away."

The shades were drawn in the Perretts' bungalow, blotting out the searing light. With one ear to the receiver, Zena jotted down a couple of bookings, while she rocked the baby to sleep. So far she had managed to secure gigs at the Whiskey, Madame Wongs West in Santa Monica, the Cuckoo's Nest in Long Beach and the Old Waldorf in San Francisco. Peter lolled on the bed, mesmerised by the TV, exhausted by the heat and the smack. In the motel complex itself, Kellie was sitting in the coffee shop, making the best of the unexpected turn of events by falling in love with the girl at his side. Alan Mair, meanwhile, was out on the town with his latest conquest. Alan Mair:

"Quite a few of our fans had started to gather around the pool area of the motel. Only Ones' fans were slightly offbeat and they usually wore black. I'd met this Californian girl who looked like Olivia Newton John. I had a suntan, I love the sun and I was dressed like John Travolta, in a nice light blue jacket. I went off to meet Olivia and later on I brought her back to the motel. As I was walking towards the Tropicana, I caught sight of the fans. There was this sea of black clothes, black eyes, black make-up, everyone was stoned. I got the girl through the black sea and into my room when John walked past with some girl with a needle in her arm. I just thought enough is enough. It had all got way too drug-induced."

Mourning Glory

Above: The band nearing the end of the road.

Right: John Perry backstage at the Whiskey-A-Go-Go.

Adding to the general weirdness, local 'scenester' Kim Fowley dropped by to make The Only Ones an offer. With his penchant for novelty acts, the eccentric entrepreneur had been responsible for managing jailbait rock-babes The Runaways. John Perry:

"Kim Fowley knew a studio that would charge $20 an hour but bill CBS $50 an hour — then Peter, Zena and him would split the difference. I think Peter realised that even if the scam was attractive, making a record with Kim Fowley wasn't the brightest idea. We did have *some* notion of ourselves as a serious band."

John, like a bored emperor in exile, arranged his own amusements:

"I'd met a local girl and then my wife and my mistress flew over from England with lots of dope. It was a pretty disastrous situation for the band, but we had fun running around Los Angeles, doing radio interviews, watching the sun come up in the desert."

The real carnage began when The Only Ones went up to San Francisco. *Record Mirror*'s US correspondent Mark Cooper witnessed the band at the Old Waldorf:

"Alan Mair stares into space, lost in his private world, while John Perry fails to play up to the guitar dazzle. He just wanders about a bit, eyes half-closed, lost in a deadly nightshade, so cool he's almost bored. As a result it's left to Perrett to take care of the action, which he does by looking alternatively frenzied and lost, flicking his hair from his eyes, sunk deep in Keith Richards' mirror..."

In San Francisco, the mirror slipped from his grasp, breaking up in infinitesimal shards of bad luck. John Perry caught the sharp end of the first malediction when he flew back to LA:

"I had some business to attend to in LA, so while the band flew on from San Francisco to New York, Suze and I flew back down. We'd finished what we were doing, and on our way to the airport, we stopped off to say goodbye to some people. They were serving tea when Bang! — down comes the door and in come the West Hollywood Sheriff's department. So we got roped into their bust. Suze got slammed in jail, I was let out after a couple of hours. I made whatever arrangements I could, got a lawyer for Suze, then I had to fly to New York where the rest of the band had already gone for another gig. When I got to New York, I heard the story of Peter and the crushed car park attendant and how the band had been advised to flee San Francisco."

John had been dealing with his own dilemmas when the tour reached its legendary watershed in the rather dull setting of a car park. When Peter gunned into the entrance of the multi-storey, he had more on his mind than the petty codes of parking. Unfortunately, the resident attendant had little time for an effete Englishman who refused to toe the line. Suddenly two very different worlds collided. Peter:

"I'd parked the car and everyone else got out and went to the coffee shop. I was the last one to get out of the car when the attendant came up, grabbed me and pushed me up against the wall and told me to move it. I got back into the car, he was standing there with a smirk on his face. I reversed and drove fast towards him. It was like slow motion, his face changed from a smile to sheer horror the closer I got to him. To begin with, he thought I was just going to drive fast and stop at the last moment, but I didn't. I hit him with the front of the car, he flew back over the dustbins in a kind of backwards somersault. The last thing I remember was his feet going up in the air."

Alan was already safely ensconced in the coffee shop when the incident happened, but Kellie caught the entire screeching spectacle:

"That tour was getting so silly. Peter was driving the car in his usual non-love, peace and Woodstock state, when he just lost his temper and aimed the car at the attendant. I've heard so many stories about the stupid event. The police in America treat a car as a handgun in the wrong hands, and that's the way they approached Peter. He was just a spoilt little kid, out of control with nobody to stop him. The Only Ones had the best of everything except management and self-discipline. We started off at 150 mph and ground to a halt. As for Peter, he just got too stoned and nobody slapped him."

A witness jotted down the licence plate of Perrett's vehicle, which was traced back to the Hertz rental company by the police. The last contact Peter had with CBS America was when they called him up in New York to ask him to return to San Francisco where he was facing charges of

"Attempted Murder" and "Assault with a Deadly Weapon". Needless to say, Perrett wasn't about to turn himself in. Instead, the band spent a week on a losing streak in New York. Their only amnesty came at a gig in Manhattan at Trax, where a fervent crowd called them back for three encores. Even so, the band realised they were facing the final curtain. Misfortune rained down on them. Both Alan and Peter's hotel rooms were ransacked for valuables. Two days later, Perrett narrowly escaped getting caught in the crossfire of a double drive-by shoot-out. John Perry:

> "Zena was doing the best she could, trying to raise the money to get us home. I realised it was all at an end when she started talking about a series of dates in Canada. When I heard that, I thought, 'Well I'm not going'. There was no point. We could have done 200 gigs but it wouldn't have made any difference, or got us any further forward. If somebody had advanced us $500,000 and a new deal, it wouldn't have addressed the real problem. People's fundamental natures don't change. Above a certain level of disorganisation there really is no cure. Nothing was going to change; by common consent everything had deteriorated too far and the energy was all dissipated."

While John waited for a friend to wire him some money to secure Suze's freedom and cover the tickets home, Alan was also planning to check out:

> "We were in the Gramercy Park Hotel and I went down to Kellie's room and said, 'I'm finished, I'm leaving the band'. Then I went to Pete and Zena's room and said to Peter, 'I'm out, enough's enough'. He said, 'If you're going to leave the band, I'd like to break it up. I wanted to leave as well but I thought you would all think I was doing the star bit'. Peter had obviously been thinking about leaving in the same way that I had. I don't think he thought that The Only Ones were a good vehicle for him any more. By my saying I was going to leave, it made it easier for him to call it a day."

Mair packed his suitcase and returned to California to top up his tan. Kellie, meanwhile, had friends with a farm in Toronto, who were waiting for him. One by one the touring party dispersed. There was no sharing of yellow cabs to the airport or plans to regroup in England, just some vague farewells with no promises attached. Kellie:

Mourning Glory

Above: Father and son deep in conversation.

THE ONE AND ONLY: Peter Perrett - Homme Fatale

"I really felt bad for the roadies; Chris (Reynolds), Barrie (Evans) and Digby (Cleever). They knew what a good rock and roll machine was and you can't be stoned going around the world. I got a flash of their disappointment — their boys had really let them down, and they'd been through so much for us."

Peter, Zena, Kathy Barrett and the baby left for home within a hair's breadth of Perrett being issued with a warrant. The ensuing legal proceedings had been delayed by a clemency manoeuvre concerning the onset of a liver condition which had begun to afflict Peter. In all certainty, he contracted Hepatitis B on the second American tour, after finding love in Atlanta with Miss Georgia Peach and her needle. The symptoms of the virus can range from mild to debilitating. Perrett eventually succumbed to the extreme end of the scale.

Now that The Only Ones were recent history, Peter was ready to pursue a solo career. However, nobody in the band had considered their contractual obligations to CBS. They were still tied to the corporation. Chrissie Hynde had just asked Alan Mair to join The Pretenders when Zena broke the news to him. Alan Mair:

"I think the most frustrating period was after we broke up for the first time and I was asked to play with Chrissie Hynde, but I couldn't because if I'd have started playing gigs, it would have looked as if The Only Ones had split up. We had to sit it out, waiting to see if CBS would drop us. We hadn't recouped the advance and if we announced that the band had broken up we were facing a debt of a quarter of a million."

CBS had paid for, and were expecting, a fourth album from the band. In a ruse straight out of the film *The Producers* — where the two main characters played by Zero Mostel and Gene Wilder deliberately set about putting on a totally uncommercial play as part of a financial scam, only to be thwarted by success in the final reel — The Only Ones informed CBS that their next record would be an album of covers. At the time it was almost unheard of for a rock band to do a covers album. CBS were delighted by the ingenious idea and the band were forced to think a little more seriously about the project. Peter:

"We went into CBS studios in Whitfield Street and did a couple of songs; The Small Faces' "My Way Of Giving" and Bob Dylan's "Mamma You've Been On My Mind". And we gave them a list of other songs we were going to do, including "Distant Drums" and "Guantanamera"."

Aside from Jim Reeves' 1966 hit single and The Sandpipers' adaptation of a Latin American folk song, The Supremes' "You Can't Hurry Love" and Antonio Carlos Jobim's bossa nova breakthrough "The Girl From Ipanema" were under consideration. John Perry also fancied doing a ten minute half-tempo version of The Archies' "Sugar Sugar".

Rumours of The Only Ones' demise peppered the music papers but on November 3rd they made their first live appearance in four months at the Hope & Anchor. Billed as 'Blanket Coverage', a dozen acts including The Specials and Madness played free gigs to provide heating costs and blankets for the elderly. The Only Ones' set was attended by *Sounds*' Robbi Millar:

> "The Only Ones haven't played together for months. Indeed as they shuffled on stage avoiding electric shocks and debating which number to kick off with, you'd be forgiven for thinking that they hadn't even had a chance to shake hands and exchange pleasantries before picking up their instruments. However, they don't play gigs by the normal code. When they are bad, they are very good, and when they are good, they are ordinary. This was one of the most shambolic and also one of the most enjoyable gigs that I've witnessed in ages..."

If the Hope & Anchor had provided a public rehearsal space for the band, then they were back on form for a Christmas gig at Dingwalls, despite a sly editorial from the *NME* suggesting that the band had fallen on hard times. Financially, The Only Ones may have been heading for a pauper's grave but they trod the boards at Dingwalls with their usual aristocratic assurance, much to the delight of *Melody Maker*'s Steve Sutherland:

> "With backs to the wall and a blood red bank balance, they came blasting in from the cold Camden night, intent on slaying a few fans, slaughtering the snides and proving, once and for all, who's boss around here..."

THE ONE AND ONLY: Peter Perrett - Homme Fatale

Above: Rubble in the world. The band in the luxurious setting of the Tropicana Motel.

The farewell dates culminated in the new year with a gig on March 7th at Leeds University, before they bowed out for good the following evening at the Lyceum Ballroom.

A new genre of bands who had been influenced by The Only Ones, including The Psychedelic Furs, Echo and The Bunnymen and The Teardrop Explodes, rose up and eventually conquered the charts, but it was too late. Time and turmoil had overtaken them even as they were giving the Lyceum a magnificent parting shot. Kellie:

"That Lyceum show was just brilliant. Everything was right. It was probably one of the best shows we ever did. My daughter Janine was there, bless her. She had a box to herself."

Steve Sutherland cried all the way to *Melody Maker*'s live review section:

"Peter Perrett seemed chuffed, overwhelmed and a little embarrassed, asked us to look upon it as a new beginning rather than the end, and dispatched all the classics — "Another Girl, Another Planet", " The Big Sleep" and "Lovers Of Today" were standouts. In his usual charismatic, offhand manner John Perry showed why he's the only man still treading the boards whose guitar solos can make direct cardiac contact. And both Kellie and Mair were as unfussy and solid as ever. I could go on, but I won't. Suffice to say that anyone out there who never bought an Only Ones record is directly responsible for the death of one of Britain's best ever bands and, personally I'll never forgive you."

The gravity of the moment passed Peter by, but perhaps the years that followed endowed the gig with poignant hindsight:

"I really did believe that I'd be back on stage in a few months. I felt a lot of sadness coming from the audience but the enormity of it didn't hit me at all. I saw an article that Steve Sutherland wrote at the time and the final line was something like, 'I hate everyone that didn't buy their records and made them go away'. Which was really sweet."

CBS ended the contract and washed their hands of The Only Ones, covers album and all. For many years at their business seminars, representatives of CBS told the story of The Only Ones as an example of

THE ONE AND ONLY: Peter Perrett - Homme Fatale

how not to make it in the music industry. Today, the band's back catalogue with the company is still thriving.

In the immediate aftermath, Alan Mair went into production work. Kellie left for Toronto and didn't come back for five years. John Perry formed Decline and Fall and began writing a regular column for *International Musician*. Peter meanwhile, was poised on the brink of a solo career. Following the Lyceum gig, *Sounds* reported that Perrett had hooked up with Harry Kakoulli again and was contemplating recording a couple of singles. Both CBS and RSO showed an initial interest at the opening stages of Peter's solo venture.

Happy endings or joyful beginnings, however, were not for Peter.

CHAPTER 13 – The Fall Of The House Of Perrett

For almost a decade Peter Perrett withdrew from public life. These were the missing years when it was assumed that Perrett was simply holed up in a decaying mansion with his family. Between the press and pining fans, comparisons were made with the reclusive, spaced-out Syd Barrett and with the Turner character in *Performance*. The truth was spiralling drug use and related activity. When The Only Ones split up, Peter had every intention of continuing with his music but the full onslaught of Hepatitis B tripped him at the starting post. Zena:

> "For about six months he was really ill. When he got better, he wasn't strong enough to carry on. He fell into a depression and got more and more into drugs to the point where he would hardly get out of bed. He wouldn't want to go out or do anything. The music had kept him going, as soon as it was gone, it was like his reason for living had gone. I found myself becoming depressed, I was looking after his drugs, trying to keep some control and one day I ended up using and finding it an escape. I don't know how it happened actually, it was very gradual. Instead of me getting him out of it, we both got pulled into this twilight world. I didn't really see it happening, it overtook us."

Peter gradually relinquished the desire to write songs and wandered deeper into addiction, becoming a tattered if much romanticised ghost of rumour while the music of The Only Ones endured, as did Perrett's influence on the more discerning quarters of the music scene.

Throughout the '80s an erratic selection of Perrett-related material was released, including "Baby's Got A Gun" b/w "Silent Night" (Vengeance, 1983), *Remains* (Closer, 1984), *England's Glory — Legendary Lost Recording* (5 Hours Back, 1987) and *Alone In The Night* (Dojo, 1986) plus a steady trickle of bootlegs. However, little from the outside world — save for regular police shakedowns — intruded on the Perretts' seclusion. Albert and Amelia passed away before they could hold their second grandson, Jamie, who was born in July '83. Peter missed the chance for emotional reconciliation with his parents as he sat hunched over a

Above: A family visit to the grandparents' flat.

Below: Blonde on Blonde. Jamie and Peter Junior.

The Fall Of The House Of Perrett

rectangle of tin foil, heating up an unending puddle of heroin, drawing deep on the fumes. Smack residue stuck to his teeth like burnt treacle and the bones beneath his face protruded as though they were suddenly going to split the translucent skin that barely contained them. Aside from their user clientele, one of the Perretts' few remaining visitors was John Perry:

"I saw Peter through the '80s. I rarely saw him anywhere but at his house, they didn't go out much. I would go down there from time to time to see how he was getting on. There were two visits about six weeks apart and I noticed when I got there the second time that he hadn't actually shifted from the part of the floor he was sitting on, or changed his clothes, or apparently moved in the six weeks. The pile of tin foil around him had grown, but otherwise he hadn't moved or changed or shaved."

A decade was lost making sacrifices to the dragon — time and money and health were but a few of the things that went up in smoke. The Perretts' fine house fell into neglect. The weeds in the garden rioted, invading the rusty carcasses of two cars long abandoned by Peter and Zena. The building itself had begun to flake and crumble, bringing to mind Edgar Allan Poe's mansion of gloom in *The Fall Of The House Of Usher*. Peter:

"Just after our farewell gigs, the Sussex Regional Crime Squad came round and took us away. They took us to Brighton Police station. They arrested loads of people, forty or fifty maybe, everybody to do with the organisation and anybody that the organisation had any contact with. The history of the raid dates back to 1978 when some of the original people got busted in Brussels after they were caught with 36 kilos of coke in a safety deposit box. The Italians and The Australians went to prison so the organisation was carried on by Alexi Sorvino* and his wife, Mariella*. They were meant to take over running the business but then this Moroccan guy Samir* came into the organisation. He was an associate of Lou Barker*, who was my main distributor.

Eventually Alexi Sorvino got put in prison and Mariella started going out with Samir, he was a really calculating guy, he got Mariella to draw all of the money out of Alexi's bank account and used her to get to know all the contacts in Bolivia, so he was more or less running the organisation. They started to bring in really insane amounts of stuff, which led to Billy going to prison after our Christmas bust. I'm telling you this so you'll know how it led to '81. While Billy was in prison, the police started asking him questions about Lou Barker. We let Lou know that the police had been enquiring about him. Anyone thinking straight would have taken notice, but everything had become so big, there was loads of money involved and Lou was taking so much coke, he and the other people involved had started to lose it. When I was a part of it, the organisation was really together, we were really professional and minimised all the risks.

In 1980, we told Lou that they were being watched, but it didn't have any effect, he didn't curtail his operations. So a week after the Lyceum show we were taken to Brighton. By '81 I had quite a bad habit. I was throwing up all the time and I had bad stomach cramps before they even put me in the cells. Then they stripped me naked and locked the door. I was sweating and the blankets were really rough from moving round. You can't sleep at all, your muscles are tense, you're totally restless. When you're having withdrawals, you lay down but you can't stay comfortable for more than a minute at a time. I've got very sensitive skin, my body was completely raw. They interviewed us every couple of hours, they take you out of the cell and into the interview room.

I was shuffling along with a blanket wrapped around me and one of the police men said, 'The bells, the bells'. With Zena, they'd let her fall asleep and then wake her up and interview her throughout the night. There were two police operations going on — but we didn't say anything in the interviews. After three days, a doctor gave me four or five physeptone (methadone) tablets. It was the most I've ever enjoyed anything 'cos when you're that ill, you enjoy something that brings you back to normality. In the end, the police let us go, they didn't have enough evidence to bring charges. Later on we saw Lou Barker's statement, he was in such a crazy state of mind that he more or less told them his life story.

In the end, Samir got 12 years and Mariella got 8. The least anybody involved got was four or five years. We were lucky that we got out of the organisation when we did, in '78, otherwise we'd have definitely ended up with 12 year prison sentences. After the raid, we stayed in hotels for two or three months. Normally if the police came to a place, I didn't like going back there. We stayed in a hotel in Crystal Palace for a month then we stayed at the Portobello Hotel, where we had the round room with a four poster bed. While we were staying at the Portobello,

The Fall Of The House Of Perrett

we found a house in Fulham. We lived there for about one and a half years. Mick Taylor came round a couple of times. We'd known him since '75, so we'd go up to the top of the house where I had a music room and play for five or ten minutes and then I'd say, 'Shall we have a smoke?' I was never in a state to do anything constructive. I was more interested in getting stoned and as he had that same weakness, we did nothing. There was one week when Martin Hannett came to London to work with me, but all we did was get stoned.

In '83, we moved into Number 3. Little Peter was four and Zena was pregnant. Whenever Johnny (Thunders) came into town, he'd call me. He was doing a gig at The Lyceum and I did the encore with him, I can't remember what I sung, I think it was "Memory". Normally we would just get stoned, we'd score, then go back to the flat or the Big House. The main impressions I have are of him spending hours fixing. He seemed to have trouble finding veins. Once he was in the kitchen and he was just sitting there stabbing at his arm! There was a gig when he made me play acoustically with him. I must have realised it was going to be bad 'cos I turned up late, I was meant to be playing with him at Dingwalls. The only reason he was doing it acoustically was to have more money to spend on drugs, he didn't have to hire equipment or pay musicians.

Later that same evening, he was supposed to play a set at Gossips and as I was there, I had to go on with him. I agreed to do it even though everything told me not to, but he had this way of acting so hurt. I was given an acoustic guitar, it didn't even have a strap on it. There was one mike between us and the audience were two feet away. I don't mind the audience being close when I'm confident and enjoying it, but when you're feeling like, 'What am I doing here?' It was the only time I've been embarrassed on stage.

Johnny used to always say how lucky I was having Zena. He gave me the impression that he was really lonely. I felt that he'd never been close to anyone, that he didn't know how to get close to people. Throughout the eighties, whenever he saw me, he kept saying that I had to get playing again, that it was a real waste of talent. The last time I saw him, was maybe '86, I was really ill, I could hardly move. He came into the bedroom, I probably looked like Jesus Christ, I hadn't shaved for ages, my hair was tangled. He gave me a real lecture about how I couldn't go on like this. He could be really touching sometimes.

THE ONE AND ONLY: Peter Perrett - Homme Fatale

Jamie was born on July 19th, 1983 but he was taken away from us until the November. We turned up at the hospital, we were visiting him to feed him 'cos Zena had come out of hospital but he was still in the premature baby unit. We turned up and he wasn't there, the hospital staff wouldn't tell us where Jamie was, they told us to go and see this horrible woman doctor who tried to convince us that he was suffering from drug withdrawals. They were so ignorant, I've seen kids suffering from withdrawals, it's not something that is debatable, it's pretty obvious that they are suffering. Jamie didn't have anything, he just acted like a normal premature baby. Occasionally premature babies get this thing where they shake for ten seconds but a baby that's having withdrawals cries all the time 'cos it knows it wants something and they shake and sweat a lot. The ignorance of the medical profession really annoyed me. I don't know whether the police had told them that we were involved in drugs. I went crazy, I lost my temper with the people from Social Services.

Eventually we came to this thing where they'd let us visit Jamie at his foster mother's. It's difficult to tell whether people have actual nervous breakdowns or not, but it affected Zena a lot. She'd burst out crying for no reason all the time. I was finding out the addresses of the principal people involved in taking Jamie away. The doctor, the social worker and the head of Social Services – their names were all listed in the telephone directory. If we hadn't got him back, I'd have definitely done something drastic 'cos until you've experienced it, there's nothing that can upset you more. I was close to finding the address of a particular social worker. I knew that she had a ten year old daughter and that she lived between Lewisham and Blackheath. If things had gone wrong, I don't know what I would have done, I don't know if I was planning on kidnapping her daughter or doing something crazy.

The situation completely destroyed Zena's confidence 'cos before that she was really together. It was a kick in the teeth, she'd actually stopped using by the time she had him. She was using at the time she got pregnant — I wanted her to have an abortion but she promised that she'd stop using. She gradually got it together and for about two months before she went in, she didn't have anything at all. The plan was that I was going to get off when she was in hospital, but she'd only just got out when the police came and arrested me for some really stupid thing relating to '82, when they'd come round and found one physeptone tablet on the floor. When I went back to the police station to answer bail, the person I was meant to see wasn't there, so I left a message saying that I'd turned up and answered bail, but somehow he never got the message, so they came round again and arrested me just after Zena had Jamie. I think that's how Social Services might have got to know about it. In November '83 we convinced the high court that we weren't that bad. We were in the Big House, we still had money for nannies. Peter and Jamie were both put on the "at risk" register. It meant lots of trouble throughout out the '80s. They were finally taken off the register in '92.

This was the time when I was using lots of drugs and people who use that much tend to deal. I just mixed with real scum. The intelligent part of you isn't thinking, it's the part of you that's a junkie that is thinking. I kept telling myself it wouldn't last very long, that I'd get it together soon. It destroys your willpower totally, you literally live from day to day. We got arrested again in '84. The police had been watching this Turkish guy, Ali* and they followed him to our place — just as he was leaving, they came in. I was in bed asleep at the time so I couldn't be done for possession of anything, so they charged me with an unknown amount at an unknown date. 'Cos I had a habit, the fact that I had withdrawals meant I must have been in possession. Zena got done for possession because someone in the house dropped a quarter gram on the floor, rather than have it found on themselves.

What we didn't know at the time was that Ali had made some sort of deal with the police. He told them that Zena had given him a line of coke, which meant she got done for supplying. Ali got a two year suspended sentence and we got a two year suspended sentence plus an eleven and half thousand pound fine. Before the court case, which was at Reading Crown Court, the solicitor said, if you say you're going to get treatment it will look better for you. When it came to the court case, I said I was going to go for in-patient treatment. Most people, after the case is over, they forget about it but I started thinking about it. I wanted to get out of the rut 'cos I didn't like life being the same every single day. I wasn't enjoying anything at all. We went ahead with going in.

We went into The Royal Bethlem in May '85. The first time we had a date to go in, we tried to smoke as much as possible before arriving. We were an hour late and they wouldn't let us in 'cos they were really strict about things. A month or two later they gave us another chance. You get the origins of the word bedlam from the Bethlem — it was one of the very first mental asylums. At least it had been modernised when we got there. We stayed for about a month, the idea was to stay longer, but a lot of people left after a month once the medicine finished. They reduced you so drastically that at the end you started feeling really uncomfortable. At the beginning of each day you used to have to give a urine sample. Everyday was organised. They had occupational therapy, so all the weekdays you'd go to classes. There was pottery, art, gym. I did art and tried to go to as many of the gym classes as possible 'cos I enjoyed that. The more physical exercise you did, the better you felt. There was a music session where they gave everybody a turn to play something. I can't remember what I put on, but all the mental patients left the room. The rules were very strict, you're not allowed any visitors for the first three weeks. The mental patients were allowed out into the grounds but the people on the drug wards weren't, and if you had to go anywhere a nurse had to walk with you. Although it was like prison, it was like a holiday camp as well. Zena got back into cooking and needlework, all the things she was good at doing.

It was hard being away from the kids. After the first three weeks, we arranged for them to come and visit. It was Peter's birthday. When they arrived, the nanny had only brought Peter, she hadn't let Jamie come. Although it was a really nice day walking around the grounds with Peter, I was really annoyed that Jamie hadn't come. The nanny had got very maternal towards Jamie and he'd started to call her mum. At that age, being apart for four weeks is a long time for a little baby. We discharged ourselves after a month and arranged to go to Portmeirion.

In the past, we used to go to Portmeirion on holiday with the idea of stopping using. Back in '82 I had booked Government House, which had six bedrooms and four bathrooms, for the whole summer, but every time we ran out of drugs we'd go back to London. When we came out of the Bethlem, it was the first time we'd been to Portmeirion without any drugs. There was a group of us, the nanny and her son — 'cos Peter was best friends with him — Zena, me and Jamie. *Infidels* had just come out, it was the best album Dylan had done for years. My enjoyment of music had been reawakened in the hospital, just listening to things on the radio.

I realised I was happy for the first time in years. I was feeling all my emotions and laughing and crying a lot. I was living again. It reminded me that life straight was worth aiming for. That week in Portmeirion, the weather was really beautiful, I was listening to music all the time and really being happy. When we arrived back in London there was a letter saying we had a month to pay the eleven and a half thousand pound fine or else I'd have to do two years in prison. That option wasn't an option. All the people that I'd ever known who had gone to prison had come out different people.

Ali said he'd lend us the money if we helped get rid of his latest batch. It was painful taking a great big bag of money to Greenwich Magistrate's Court and handing over eleven and a half thousand pounds. Gradually we started using again, then we had a close shave with the police. One of Ali's associates came over to us to collect some money and there was just something about the cab he arrived in. After an hour, I phoned his place and the phone was off the hook. Immediately, I thought he'd been busted.

I started looking out of the side window of the house. By that time we'd got into smoking coke as well. It's very obsessive and all you concentrate on is smoking. We had a couple of friends around as well, so every five or ten minutes I was going to look out of the window. It was pitch black outside and I heard this sound and I called out, 'Who's there?' It just went quiet. I shouted again, 'Who's there, if you don't answer, I'm going to call the police'. These two youngish guys in leather bomber jackets appeared at the side of the house and walked off. They'd been trying to climb up the side of the house to get in on the stairs, so they'd get past the big door. I knew they were police as soon as I heard them, but I didn't want them to know that I realised. I said to Zena, 'They are definitely police', and she was like, 'Oh sure'. When you are taking drugs you don't want anything to disturb you. I dragged her away, she was trying to finish the coke. I said, 'Look, we've got to move very quickly'. We got one of our friends who had a car downstairs to drive me and Zena out of Forest Hill.

We left another person inside the house to open the door for the police and as we pulled out of the drive to go and pick up the kids who were at a friend's house, I saw three marked police cars and four or five unmarked ones. We ducked down and the first of the police cars couldn't get started to follow us. We picked up the kids and got dropped off in Elephant and Castle and booked into a hotel there. Meanwhile, the police had got into the Big House and were searching it. They couldn't believe I wasn't there. They took the guy that let them in into custody and arrested the guy that drove us to Elephant and Castle. We didn't go back to the house for months. To begin with, we stayed in different hotels, but we were running out of money so we stayed with friends.

Every time Ali appeared in court, the police would say, 'We're not ready to bring the case yet, we're pursuing further enquiries and there are still people we are waiting to arrest'. This went on for ages. We contacted a solicitor who told the police that if they wanted to interview me and Zena, he had to be present. They obviously thought it would be a waste of time to interview us with the solicitor present 'cos they wouldn't be able to put any pressure on us. They went ahead with the court case and after about three or four months, we thought it would be safe to go back to the house.

After we moved into the Big House, I didn't touch the guitar. It got to the point where I'd forgotten that I'd ever played music. I didn't used to listen to my records, but after that last scrape with the police I thought it was time to get off again. We started having out-patient treatment. Over the next few years, I got off about three times. Each time it was totally painless. We had a good doctor and in the end the reduction was very small. I was still taking liquid (methadone) but there was nothing left in it. It made me feel secure thinking I could get off without any pain.

The following year we had a really close shave with the police. It was the closest we ever got to really going away for a long time. We were getting the stuff from these Iranian people. It should have been quite a secure little thing 'cos the person we were dealing with was taking it all, he was taking 8 ounces at a time. He was a pretty cool person, living in Shepherd's Bush. Zena had this friend, this girl who used to get her to do little bits for her and her friend. She got Zena to get her an ounce. I used to tell Zena that it was these people who were going to get her into trouble. It's silly jeopardising a business that's on a higher level. The girl sold it to somebody in Folkestone who got busted. The police started following her and she used to come round to our house. As soon as they found out our names and history they moved into some offices just over the road. This local secretary who worked in one of the offices used to buy food at the same delicatessen as our nanny. The secretary mentioned about the police to the people in the delicatessen, who happened to tell the nanny.

We decided to go away to Portmeirion for a couple of weeks, came back and although I wanted to stop doing everything, it's hard because you make good money so we carried on. We didn't have anybody coming to the house but we used to go and meet this Iranian guy near Shepherd's Bush, do the transaction and drop it off to the person we used to sell it to that lived in Shepherd's Bush. The police must have followed us a few times, just to see what the deal was, see the way we did everything and work out the best time to pounce. Because the house was so difficult to get into, they were obviously trying to get us outside, doing a deal.

Every time we went up to Shepherd's Bush, I used to look in the mirror, go through red lights to see if anybody followed. I was pretty sure that no one was following us, but it turned out that they were using a number of different vehicles and motor bikes. One car would follow us for a mile and then turn off, then they'd radio for more people who were waiting for us. I didn't think they'd followed me, so we parked in the main road in Shepherd's Bush and our Iranian friend passed by. We saw him and he turned off. Zena got out of the car and into his car and I followed. We were driving round in circles and I noticed this motor bike was doing the same and when it drove off, I noticed a car driving round in circles as well. I obviously had reason to be suspicious and this convinced me that we were definitely being followed.

When the Iranian stopped the car to let Zena out, I flashed at him to give him a signal. He drove off one way, and when Zena got back into our car, we drove off another way, really fast. We had the BMW at the time. Zena didn't believe that we were being followed. We drove to a friend's house to see if we could stash the stuff. Originally, I had wanted Zena to dump it somewhere but she didn't want to do that. We left after warning the person to stash the stuff. We came out and started driving back to Forest Hill. The police roughly knew the route we took back.

We were coming up to the traffic lights in Earl's Court and the car in front of us stopped and people jumped out, then more people started to jump out of the cars behind us. They dragged me and Zena out and put us in separate cars. Then they searched the car. We were handcuffed and taken to Swanleigh Police station. They searched us and the car over and over again. They couldn't find anything. They arrested our Iranian friend on the way to Milton Keynes.

We'd given him this stash which which was one of those Saxa salt containers, which had a false bottom which he'd put the money in. They didn't find the money. Then they went round to the guy in Shepherd's Bush, but they didn't find anything there either. They kept us in for one night and the next evening we were released. Before we left, they came in and said to me, 'We found a considerable sum of money in your house, I hope you've got an explanation for that'. I said 'Yes, sure'. It was that money that got us into trouble with the fucking house [see

THE ONE AND ONLY: Peter Perrett - Homme Fatale

chapter 14]. Because I thought I might need an explanation for the money, this friend said that we could pretend he was going to buy the house and that he'd given us the money as a deposit. That's how the fucking court case over the house started, which is a real fucking drag.

In '88 we stopped our activities. I just lost the bottle for doing it, my family was more important to me than taking those sorts of risks. It just wasn't worth it. There had been times when Zena had gone out and not come back, she'd been arrested. All the people we knew, that we were associating with, were involved in drugs, so even if we weren't actually doing anything, just visiting them was dangerous. There were quite a few times when Zena didn't come back home at night. Just having to explain to the kids when they'd say, 'Where's Mum? When is she coming home?' I'd say, 'Oh don't worry, she's all right, she'll be home in the morning'. But not being sure whether she's ever going to be home. It was a horrible position to be in, that's what I hated most about it, me and the kids being alone and the possibility of one day having to say to them, 'Mum's not coming home for a couple of years'. That really frightened me. When you've got kids, you're vulnerable 'cos all of a sudden you've got something that's more important than anything else in your life.

When we stopped, I had a considerable sum in cash. That lasted about five months 'cos we carried on using. It's quite easy to spend a large amount of money when you're using smack and coke, we carried on until the money ran out. I said to Zena that I'd rather have no money and be in the gutter than carry on.

Okay, we'd been well off financially. We could do what we wanted to do, but we never did anything positive with the money apart from have holidays. We started having out-patient treatment again. I got off after the first course of methadone which must have been the beginning of '89. I started writing again, I started playing the guitar. The first song I wrote was "Baby Don't Talk". Just writing that song gave me a buzz for a year. I didn't write another song for a year after that."

Chapter 14 - Orpheus Ascending

Peter emerged from the underworld like a part-time Orpheus, with one scruffy, sneaker-clad foot still in the shadow of Hades. The myth of Orpheus, the Greek poet and musician who was allowed to go down to Hades to bring his wife, Eurydice, up to the land of the living, contains parallels to the Perretts. Orpheus blew his deal with the Gods after he turned to look back at Eurydice who was promptly returned to the underworld. The musician was then torn to pieces by the Maenad women of Thrace.

The Perretts were simply unable to distance themselves from their problems at will. The past had left its mark both mentally and physically. Although weak and acutely socially withdrawn, Peter was the first to raise his head to see what lay beyond their old life. Zena:

> "In the relationship, I had always been the stronger person. I used to keep things together, pay the bills. When I went under, that was it, everything fell apart. I think he was expecting me to surface first and he was surprised that he was the one that did. Maybe that's what I wanted. Maybe that's why I let myself go that way. I wanted somebody to look after me. It was funny how Peter had to take the lead. When he started getting well, he could see the state that I was in, and kept saying things like, 'Can't you see that nothing's going to get better because it isn't the right path, we're never going to be able to handle things in this state'.
>
> If you have some control, even when bad things happen, you can deal with them, but when you have no control, it gets even worse. You also become very vulnerable. It was almost like being a tramp in the gutter and people kicking you when you're down. It seemed that when we were successful, we had all these people around who wanted to be friends but they'd all gone. We didn't see anybody. People took advantage of our state. Our home was nearly taken from us. We did become very vulnerable."

The Big House became a manifestation of its inhabitants' baleful existence. Peter, Zena and the children dwelled in the highest point of the house, barricaded from life and all but the faintest of natural light. A spate of burglaries, which began after Peter's parents died, added to the air of despondency. Peter:

> "We had the first burglary in '83. I thought it was bailiffs 'cos we'd had a letter saying they'd be calling around. When I saw these men taking things out, there was loads of people lying around stoned. I started trying to wake them up to see if they had a couple of hundred quid on them that I could give to the bailiffs to make them go away. By the time I went downstairs, Zena had come back up the the road from shopping. She said, 'What the fuck's going on?' and I said, 'Oh, it's the bailiffs'. Zena said 'They're not fucking bailiffs!' They didn't get away with that much because we caught we them in the middle. The next burglary was '85, when we were in hospital. Then the main ones were in '89 and '90. Once one burglar had been in and seen all the antiques, all the other burglars in South London got to know about it."

In spite of the neglect, Number 3 was a salvageable, spacious property with large surroundings. In the terminology of the late '80s property boom, the Big House had potential. After discovering a secluded mansion in Wales for £65,000, with its own beach, spring water well and swimming pool, the Perretts decided to sell up. The rest of their plan included building a 24-track studio in the Welsh mansion. However, a simple premise rapidly developed spiralling complications. Peter:

> "When we decided to sell the house in September '88, we had offers of £225,000 for it, in writing, from two different people. We accepted one of them, then when the buyer wanted to go through with the contracts, we found a notice had been put on the house. These people that I'd met through associates [see previous chapter] had taken me to court, saying that I'd agreed to sell it to them for a £150,000. I then had discussions with them, they made me an out-of-court offer for £185,000. They knew I wanted to sell up quickly and they said they'd drag it on and on. My solicitor told me it would only take a year to get to court. It ended up taking three. By that time the housing market had collapsed, so even though we won the case, we couldn't sell the house for what they'd offered us out of court. We got into a lot of debt. We borrowed the

money off the bank to fight the case because we thought we'd be able to sell it in a year's time and pay the bank back."

The medium who helped draw Peter back from half-life was a pleasant, rather delicate chap called Henry Williams. Having dabbled in photography and journalism with some degree of success, Henry became haunted by thoughts of, 'Whatever happened to Peter Perrett?' He began a personal quest to divine Perrett's whereabouts and eventually connected with Jon Newey. Adding a dash of further mystery to the plot, Newey refused to divulge the Perretts' phone number but described the exterior of the Big House and gave a rough approximation of its location. Eventually Williams found Number 3 and left a note for Peter with a neighbour, who confirmed that the Perretts were still in residence but rarely went out. Henry bade farewell to Forest Hill, only for Zena to ring him the next morning, heralding a series of phone calls back and forth. After several months Henry Williams took to acting as the Perretts' eyes and ears, summarising the current state of the music business for them. Gradually a slender degree of trust came to exist between Peter and Zena and the young journalist, who observed at close quarters the full extent of the ongoing domestic turmoil. Henry Williams:

"The circumstances of their old house were extremely unusual. It was out of a Dickens' plot — shades of Miss Haversham. The house was completely full of antiques. There were these beautiful old French chairs that they were sitting on upstairs, but because they were in everyday use, they had become badly damaged. What intrigued me as a fan, was all these clothes that I recognised from pictures taken of Peter in The Only Ones which were hanging up on pegs, mouldering away.

A lot of their things had been stolen and the rest they had to sell. Once I had to help them clear the house out after I had a call from Zena, who said, 'You're going to have to come over because we don't trust anyone and these antique dealers are going to arrive'. I got there and there was two different firms, a snotty West End dealer and someone from Crystal Palace. They started arguing over the Perretts' things and Peter ran off in fright. Zena was deeply worried as to what had become of him because he just couldn't take it. He disappeared into the betting shop, while the dealers carried their possessions off to auction.

> But, it has to be said, that without that sort of doomed romanticism he probably wouldn't go on writing songs or have written the songs that he did. The whole set up at the house was so poignant. It still had his father's name on the doorbell. I took a friend of mine over there, an estate agent, when they were trying to sell the place and Peter was saying, 'Well, my father kept this place so tidy, there used to be flowers growing over here'. And all that was left was desolation."

In the Summer of '89, as the hot weather began to dry out the Perretts' remaining possessions, producing the curious ancient apple scent of heat and mildew, Peter donned his sunglasses, laced up his ratty sneakers and nervously set out to meet the press. While scouting for the Perretts, Henry reported on a new crop of bands including The Church, Ultra Vivid Scene and The House Of Love, who all possessed distinct Only Ones overtones and were prepared to pay them lip service. In the meantime, John Perry had tracked down the original master tape and was overseeing the release of *The Only Ones Live* (Mau Mau through Demon Records). Critical response to The Only Ones had turned full circle and the press embraced *Live* as if it was a long lost love just walked back through the door. In keeping with tradition, Peter showed up at the *Melody Maker*'s office three hours late, but John held the fort, while Steve Sutherland's tape recorder rolled. On arrival, Peter broke the silence of the missing years with his usual unguarded candour, speaking out on an angina attack, drugs, detox, love and poverty. The interview drew to a conclusion with Perrett's financial frustration blocking his creative path:

> "I'd got to the point where music meant nothing to me, all my senses were so numb. I couldn't get a tingle down my spine when I listened to music. I thought that getting that back again would be the only barrier I had to cross. I don't wanna form a band and start gigging, the most important thing to me is making good records. I haven't got the strength to stand up to a tour now, so I just want to get into a situation where I've got enough decent equipment at home to be able to do some decent demos... all I want is for someone to lend me £250,000..."

Peter's winsome return to print ended with a plea for patronage from a wealthy fan. John Perry perceived Perrett's comments as a low self-estimation of potential worth. John Perry:

"I personally didn't think that applying for charitable status was a good move. It seemed that Peter was unaware of the commercial potential, if the project was organised. He seemed to overlook the fact that he could *earn* the money."

Rumours ran rife in the music press that Peter would be making a guest appearance at The House Of Love's six-date run at the ICA in June but he kept his distance. Peter:

"They contacted me about doing a guest appearance with them, but I'd never heard of them. I said to them that maybe I'd do it if they arranged a rehearsal. I didn't want to do anything without seeing how well they played and I didn't want to just turn up and jam it. If it was going to be done, I wanted to do it right. I've since been told that they were untogether at the time 'cos their guitarist was just going to leave."

The other Perrett-connected hearsay that circulated through the second half of the year contained a great deal more in its favour — Peter and John Perry were reported to be playing together again. While it was too premature for any official announcements, the two former Only Ones were hanging out a little, making Portastudio tapes in High Wycombe and picking up acoustic guitars at John's house in Colnbrook.

Although Peter returned to his lofty, crumbling tower, the vow of silence had been broken and he maintained certain links with the outside world. Because both Perrett and John Perry had become visible on the music scene once again, the Strange Fruit label were able to contact them concerning the release of The Only Ones' Peel Sessions. When the Peel Sessions series was being planned, The Only Ones had been the first choice made, but the company had been unable to locate anyone from the band. When released *The Peel Sessions* cut a brilliant swathe through the years of darkness surrounding the band.

Despite a renewed interest in Peter and his projects, the Perretts' home life remained as fraught as ever. At the beginning of 1990, the family moved back down the road to the basement flat, which had been kept on as an emergency bolt hole. Forced to abandon their eyrie in the sky, they settled into the subterranean lair. Zena's original stylish decor was now peppered with the black sooty stains of perpetual damp. Their belongings were shoved into an avalanche of carrier bags which filled the flat's one bedroom. Little Peter moved into Koulla's former cupboard and a bed was made up for Jamie in the narrow hallway. The skylight in the shower/toilet had become home to a family of snails, and tendrils of weeds pressed down against the glass, giving the claustrophobic impression of a premature burial suite. Peter and Zena dealt with the situation as best as they could and the front room still bore the remnants of their former wealth. A fine oriental cabinet, an intricately carved table and a delicately woven carpet with an edging of miniature pagodas had been salvaged, along with a grand white sofa and Peter's French chairs. Occasional guests could still sit pretty in the parlour. Zena:

> "Everything up the road collapsed, the stairs fell down, the electricity got cut off. There was nowhere else to go so that was it. In a way it was good, there were too many reminders. It was like being in a big tower with loads of doors protecting us. Being here made us more vulnerable, there is just one door, then you're out on the street. The only trouble was that Social Services didn't know where the kids were. The police came to take them away when they followed the kids home from school. Because the kids were wards of court, Social Services have to know what address you're living at, but because we didn't inform them, they were going to take the children into care. We got a solicitor and after about a year they took the wardship off the children. We used to have to see a social worker every week. It was like being under a microscope all the time."

It was no wonder then, that the songs Peter had been writing were inlaid with pain. Between mid-February through to March 12th, Peter and John began weekly recording sessions at a studio in Ruxley Manor on the Kent borders. Using the in-house tape operator, John Bowden, and a drum machine, Perrett and Perry swiftly resumed their partnership. Although Peter would later comment that he was unsure of himself upon returning to a studio after so long a gap, his voice had actually improved. It wasn't as if Peter's ordeals had left him raw and bleeding, as with Marianne Faithfull's vocal maturity, rather his usual lost soul singing had grown less brash and found its pitch, which was further highlighted by John's deliberately minimalist backing. John Perry:

"His voice was recording beautifully. It had deepened and got richer, less edgy. The sparseness of the instrumentation really featured it. Just a plain drum loop and Peter's guitar, then I'd add bass and guitar, and Peter dubbed a vocal, maybe a tambourine. It was easily the best work we did. There was nothing between the listener and his voice."

Peter and John put down four tracks. The lead-in number "Wildlife Park" a plea for harmony from predatory forces is shadowed by Perry's keening guitar. "Twilight World" is a poison paean directed at Zena's former "friend" who indirectly initiated the Perretts' last major bust:

All the dreams in this town baby
Are horror films, without any score
Last time I saw her
She was just about ready
To audition for a part in a George Romero movie
Down on my knees,
I'm pleading with you to get her out of our lives
She's clinging to you
She's scared you'll leave her behind
In her twilight world.

Despite the zombie film reference, John's accompaniment is a sprightly affair. "Baby Don't Talk", the song that reunited Peter with his muse after the missing years, is full of fragile hope, with a message to Zena: '*You used to sparkle like a jewel, the pride of the collection*'. Perry gives the number a charming, melancholy appeal. "That's The Way It Always Goes" is a revision of an old England's Glory number entitled "Shattered Illusions", and probably works the least well out of the four songs. In April, John took a tape of the songs to Ivo Watts-Russell at 4AD Records. John Perry:

"Ivo stuck the tape on and work in the office more or less halted. Somehow, almost by accident, on these plain un-eq'd monitor mixes we'd got this wonderful, rich vocal sound. Ivo asked what we needed to finish the tapes, and in an extraordinary gesture, put up a couple of thousand pounds seed money without any strings. Just said he'd like to hear the results."

John and Peter then went their separate ways for several months. The guitarist left for Denmark where he was scheduled to play with the Sisters Of Mercy on their *Vision Thing* album. The Sisters' project added yet another name to Perry's impressive CV, which already included work with Marianne Faithfull, Robert Palmer, Michael Nyman, Patti Palladin and Johnny Thunders, amongst others. Meanwhile, Peter began sifting through various offers which were mainly relayed to him by Henry Williams. Primal Scream's Bobbie Gillespie wrote to Peter in praise of his craft, while both Ride and the Stone Roses sent copies of their latest material.

Peter might have become more visible but he was still vulnerable. Returning to his music and playing with John had been momentous but there was also a certain security in reuniting. Perrett and Perry knew each other well. Taking up a proposal from a complete outsider carried the risk of the unknown to someone as unused to social interaction as Peter.

The seeds of the *Faster Than Lightning* video compilation began with good intentions after one of the managing directors of Rhythm King Records contacted Henry and mentioned that a pop-video company, Popata, were interested in making a visual history of The Only Ones. Popata was run by Fiona Styllianou who dated a Perrett-obsessive musician, Tommy. Together, the young couple honed in on Peter and Zena. To complicate the Perretts' already disordered home life, Peter's step-sister Edith had sent her daughter Orrit over from Israel to stay with them. Uncle Peter, with the best will in the world, had offered to help his niece kick a vicious smack habit. Unfortunately all concerned ended up stubbing their toes on the problem.

When Fiona made her opening pitch, the creaky doors of the Big House were thrown wide open. Tucked away in the recesses of Number 3, gathering dust, lay a treasure trove of Only Ones footage. Ms Styllianou began a painstaking salvage operation that culminated in the *Faster Than Lightning* video. If nothing else, Peter wanted to show his sons that he'd once fronted a well known band. The boys had scant knowledge of their old man's starry past and the proof lay in the disintegrating reels.

Another counter-plot concerned Fiona's boyfriend's group, Love's Young Nightmare. Unsigned but unbowed, they had managed to secure a publishing deal with Warner Chappell. Tommy sent Peter a tape of the band's proposed single "Dream On" with a view to involving him in the production.

After much persuasion Peter agreed to produce "Dream On" and a cover of The Beatles' "It's All Too Much" for them. Five days were booked then cancelled, after Peter delayed the session for a week. Self-conscious of the gothic ruin that passed for his teeth, Perrett put off making any appearances until some emergency dental renovation work was carried out. Once Peter regained his ring of confidence, the sessions went ahead at Warner Chappell in Marble Arch.

Love's Young Nightmare got a considerable amount of press coverage out of the Perrett production sessions. Once again there was a rash of Peter Perrett-related ephemera splashed across the music papers. The Only Ones' first single "Lovers Of Today" was to be included on a US indie sampler on Rhino (Connoisseur in the UK) while the English band Breathless released a single on their own Tenor Vossa label. "Always" had a cover of "Flowers Die" on the B-side featuring John Perry.

In the meantime, *Faster Than Lightning* was coming together. Popata in association with Virgin Vision, had agreed to pay Peter £45,000 for his co-operation. On one muggy late summer afternoon, the bedroom in the basement flat was turned into a makeshift studio. Specks of dust singed in a blaze of arc lights that faced Peter. Even though he was wearing an outsize pair of midnight black shades, the glare scorched like radiated neon as he waited for the cameras to roll. Clips of Peter talking about The Only Ones were going to be spliced between the live material. Originally Steve Sutherland was supposed to be conducting the interview but a bout of food poisoning had laid him low, so Henry Williams had to cover:

> "There was a kind of jinx about the Perretts. Steve Sutherland was violently sick the night before and then my car broke down on the way to their house. In the end I had to do the interview. I tried to get the information out of Peter — all the interesting stories, but he clammed up a bit. I wasn't that great at interviewing people, I never used to ask questions, I just used to talk randomly. There's so many interesting things about The Only Ones but I didn't manage to get any of them out."

Eventually, Fiona's efforts paid off and for the most part *Faster Than Lightning* works well as a much needed visual record of The Only Ones, but any triumph was marred by gathering mistrust and ill-fortune. Peter:

> "Basically, Fiona was the production company who were meant to be getting the video together, putting it in order and Virgin were going to give me £45,000. We trusted her. She said that the most her budget would come to would be £10,000. The only thing that was expensive was getting two tracks from the BBC, at a £1,000 each. I insisted that I get £15,000 up front out of the thirty that was left, then she was going to take £10,000. I was going to get a further £20,000 later on, when she got the cheque. More or less the same day that she received the cheque, her company went into liquidation. I was ripped off for twenty grand. It would have got me out of all my financial trouble. I would have been able to pay off what I owed the bank but because I wasn't able to, with interest it has gone back up again."

Using the money Ivo Watts-Russell more-or-less donated, Peter and John Perry returned to Ruxley Manor to produce a further four songs — the desolation of Peter's personal life often distilled in the lyrics. "Place Of Safety" is practically a straight autobiographical account of The Perretts' battle with Social Services over the care of the boys. The wonderful "Happy Families" is suffused with all the bitter-sweet sentimentality of one of Dion's rock 'n' roll valentines and Perry dresses it in swathes of angel hair fretwork and strings. "Dead Man Walking" is a sinister, rocked-up affair as Peter's voice swirls like cyanide around the condemned man. The final track "World In Chains" hides its tears under a deceptively gentle pop covering.

The hitherto controlled tension that existed in Peter and John's relationship began to resurface when Peter went back into Ruxley alone, to fill up the tape with synthesizers and female vocals provided by Koulla. Peter thought John had become a touch artistically jaded, while the guitarist favoured a stripped down approach to the new batch of songs. Peter:

> "I felt that the constructive thing to do was learn about new technology. Learn what synthesizers, samplers and sequencers did. I was like a little kid with a new toy. I'm easily impressed by clever gadgets. It seemed

quite amazing that you could press a button and all these weird different things would happen. It gave me time to sit back and listen to the sounds they make and decide what I did and didn't like. Also, it was fun putting my songs down on tape again and imagine how they could sound but I never thought of them for public consumption."

The release of a series of high quality products that began with *Live* and continued with *The Peel Sessions* and *Faster Than Lightning* generated a great deal of sustained interest in Peter. While he was excited by the possibilities it could open up in terms of furthering his music, he was unprepared to deal with it alone. Zena was in too weakened a condition to be able to act on her husband's behalf, so Henry Williams, whose life had started to take him in other directions, endeavoured to find Peter a suitable manager. Henry Williams:

"At the time all the major rock writers were my contemporaries. They had all been 18 or 19 when The Only Ones had been going, and for Peter to come back from the depths had got them all hugely excited. In a way it was a bit unfortunate because it may have made it seem easier to Peter than it was actually going to be. He suddenly found that all sorts of people were really interested in him, whereas no one had been asking any questions five years earlier. He may not have realised how fickle these things can be.

There where loads of people interested in the video — old fans, new fans. American bands were coming along trying to get hold of Peter's number. There was one band called Come who were on Sub Pop, Nirvana's old label. There was another band, Dinosaur Jr, that reviewers started noting were reminiscent of The Only Ones. There was even a band purporting to be The Only Ones, booking themselves pub gigs. I couldn't deal with all of it, I wasn't cut out for that sort of thing.

At one point, I thought John Perry could manage it. He might have been really good because he handled the *Live* album and *The Peel Sessions* really well, but there was a degree of tension between them. The only thing that I thought I could do was suggest this friend of mine, Adrian Maddox, who was managing a group called The Cranes. He'd started off this PR company with another guy, Tony Beard, who now manages The Auteurs, who have an Only Ones touch to them. I wanted Adrian to act as a buffer between Peter and the music business."

Up until this point in his tidy career, Adrian Maddox had navigated his way around the music business with relative ease. He was young, ambitious and shrewd enough to be able to obtain most goals but, once he became involved with Peter Perrett, he got himself a free ticket to the Bermuda Triangle of rock 'n' roll. Adrian Maddox:

"Henry suggested that Perrett should meet me about management. I think at some point, Perrett checked me out and was told I was kosher. It took ages and ages to set a meeting up. It was a series of stops and starts, cloaked in complete secrecy. Henry was to pick me up in Brixton and take me down there, then on the way through Dulwich, we had to stop and make a phone call to ensure everything was all right and it wasn't going to be cancelled at the last minute. Henry was all for blindfolding me on the way there so I didn't know where the place was and he made me swear that I wouldn't tell anybody. We arrived at the "molehole", the basement flat. The place looked devastated from the outside and is devastated on the inside. It's incredible, all the electrics have gone and the Electricity Board won't fix them. There is a whole section in the bedroom, where the wall is collapsing. I've personally never experienced living conditions quite as bad as that."

Sinking into the vast, white sofa in the front room, Adrian saw Peter in the flesh for the first time and wondered if Anne Rice could be coerced into writing a publicity sheet. Adrian Maddox:

"He'd completely collapsed in on himself, was extremely skeletal and mummified, but he was still able to talk and was enthusiastic. I had expected him to be lolling around a lot more. It was a paradox where he seemed very animated but his body looked completely decayed, worn away by junk. He's very vampire-like and as in the case of the vampire, there is something deep and tortured yet fundamentally decent, but he's led by some sort of curse."

After several more meetings, both parties verbally agreed to work together and Adrian attempted to put some order into the chaos that held sway over Peter. Press releases and a photo session followed. To further the campaign, Adrian wanted to duplicate a few copies of the Perrett mixed Ruxley demos so interested record companies could listen to the

Orpheus Ascending

new material. From Maddox's perspective it was a logical progression but Peter was reluctant to let the tape go. Peter:

> "I hadn't been into a studio for thirteen or fourteen years They were the first eight songs I'd written, it was meant to be a private thing, I'd wanted to get all the rustiness and cobwebs out in private. It's important for people not to hear anything until it's ready. People weren't just going to say, 'Great, he's writing again' and have blind faith. From a critical point of view, they might be thinking that I've lost it and anything substandard would have only confirmed those fears. But Ivo had liked the demos, so I thought even in their rough state, maybe, just maybe, there are people who are such fans, they could imagine how good they could be. I gave one copy to Adrian. He then prepared a press pack to go with the tape, and began to tout the demos around."

Along with all the bills and bank reminders that hit the mat in the basement after Christmas, one letter dated January 16th '91, from Deutsch Inc New York, promised to give rather than take away. Deutsch Inc, an advertising company, were seeking Peter's permission to use "Another Girl, Another Planet" in a prime-time IKEA television commercial. The song would be heard playing in the background, through a radio, while a young man got ready for a date with a new girlfriend. Unfortunately, Peter could not agree without negotiating through CBS or re-recording the song, and the moment was lost, but how sweet the irony might have been if the design-conscious, consumer-friendly IKEA company had used such a flagrantly decadent number to sell furniture.

A second, unconnected, dispatch from the States reached Peter two months later. Bad news travels fast and the lonesome death of Johnny Thunders hit Peter like a stray bullet. His old friend had arrived in New Orleans hoping to set up a new career angle but met with a host of angels, instead. Johnny made his final exit amongst a growing speculation that has swung between murder and misadventure. Peter:

> "Obviously I was very shocked, but my overriding emotion was anger that I wasn't going to be able to see him again. I felt that there was loads of things left unsaid 'cos I'd kept him at arms length over a period of time. Now I felt strong enough to give him a good talking to, like he'd tried to do with me when he saw me down. I was really upset because I

felt I could have helped him and we could have worked on an album together that was worthy of him. Before, when I'd worked with him, I'd been busy with The Only Ones, so I didn't have the time to put everything of me into it.

Also, you want to know why, how did it happen? You hear all these different stories and you don't know exactly what the truth was. I don't think there is any glamour in dying young. It's just sad, Maybe if I believed in an afterlife, I wouldn't be so scared of death. It just seems that we have such a short time. I want to live to 120 if possible, but I don't want to get to the point where smack doesn't keep away the pain 'cos I think that's one of the great benefits. I can't wait to get old and close to death's door, then I can really get out of it."

Mercifully, the Hampshire Drugs Squad treated Peter with a great deal more care than the New Orleans Police Department when they initially recorded Thuders as being just another junkie John Doe. In February, the Hampshire Drugs Squad were looking into the amount of heroin and cocaine coming in to the Portsmouth area from London. As a result, a team of officers were appointed to bust a number of London addresses. One of the officers, John Roberts got word through the squad about a musician known as 'Peter the Parrot' who had a habit. John Roberts:

"One of the lads mentioned it to me purely because he knew I was a bit of a music freak, but he didn't believe that the name could be kosher. It suddenly clicked that it had to be Peter Perrett. If anyone was going to pay him a visit, it was going to be me. "Another Girl, Another Planet" was one of the greatest singles of the era and reading as much of the music press as I do, I knew Peter Perrett was a great Dylan fan. Now, I've been a Dylan fan since the mid '60s and I've also produced a number of privately published Dylan books.

Early one morning, I found myself knocking on Peter Perrett's door, armed with a warrant. Peter and Zena were both at home and I explained what it was about. Everything was ever so laid back. We searched the place because we had to, but we were very apologetic. I take no great pleasure going through people's lives, and we got on very well. I was ever so pleased, as Peter and Zena were, that we didn't find anything. It quickly became clear that we were on the wrong track and I was very pleased about that. We had a great chat about everything except drugs.

During the search I found a copy of Dylan's *Real Live* album. I remember saying, 'Well Pete, you might be a musician but I'm on this album, you can hear me in the crowd cheering, if you listen really hard'. I got the absolute knock-back, when he said, 'Oh right, well you see that guitar over there, that's the guitar I lent to Mick Taylor to play at the concert'. I thought, 'Jesus, that's really put me in my place'.

I did get upset with Peter once during the search. Dylan had just finished a week's residency at Hammersmith Odeon, what did I find? — a backstage pass, gold dust! I said to him, 'Wow, you got to meet Dylan then?' He said, 'No, I chickened out at the last minute'. Naturally we got into a long chat about Dylan, and he mentioned that he'd always wanted to see a decent copy of *Eat The Document,* which is a film of Dylan's 1966 tour that never got released, but there were a few copies of it around on video. He mentioned that he'd got a copy but the quality was dire.

A couple of weeks later, I was back in London again on a totally different enquiry, so I rang Peter and Zena to check if it was okay for me to drop in and possibly have a coffee. When I got there, Peter said that he was delighted that someone had sent him this superb quality recording of the *Eat The Document* video, but naturally I didn't know anything about that! I left clutching a copy of The Only Ones' *Faster Than Lightning* video. What really got to me was the inlay card included a bit about the trouble Peter had gone through with the police and it did make me smile because Peter had written on the inlay card, 'To John Roberts with love from Peter Perrett'.

I would just like to reiterate that there was no evidence at all that Peter was involved in anything that we were looking into."

Adrian Maddox was still working away in the background, attempting to raise Peter's profile and secure him a deal. Whichever way Adrian tried to disperse the spectres of misfortune that loomed over Peter, they came back threefold. Another meeting with Ivo Watts-Russell at 4AD came to nothing. Adrian then contacted the former Rough Trade supremo Geoff Travis who was working in A&R for Blanco Y Negro. Perrett broke out in an allergy rash and his car died in the middle of Gray's Inn Road, en-route to the appointment. Travis met the frantic Maddox and an itchy Perrett in a café that overlooked Peter's smouldering vehicle. Even though Geoff

Travis was enthusiastic, Blanco Y Negro cut any possible deals off at the pass. At Dedicated Records, Peter confessed to being financially irresponsible, while Maddox kicked him under the table for his indiscretion:

> "I was trying to convince everybody that I rang that Perrett was on form, he'll be clean, be very business-like and professional, but then everything mitigated against it, when they saw and had to deal with him. I was very anxious that the first meeting I set up with people was done very professionally."

Maddox did manage to secure Peter a publishing deal for The Only Ones' back catalogue with Complete Music, but his most crucial manoeuvre came when he suggested that Perrett should make an exclusive guest appearance with The Heart Throbs at the Camden Underworld.

Unlike Orpheus, when Peter came out on stage at The Underworld on October 25th, he never looked back.

Epilogue - Sticky Endings

All it had taken to jam up the pavements outside the Camden Underworld was a tiny notice in one of the music papers headlined, "Perrett in live comeback shock". Inside the venue, dressed in a transparent black shroud, Zena reassured her husband and pencilled kohl around his eyes. The previous afternoon, Peter had met up with The Heart Throbs for the first time, to run through a brief rehearsal at Terminal Studios. By October '91, The Heart Throbs position on the indie ladder was somewhat precarious and The Underworld gig was part of a plan to rejuvenate their career. Steven Ward, their keyboard player:

> "It was quite extraordinary when he walked in. He is such a remarkable looking guy, with this translucent skin. He was very shy, very reserved. We didn't have very much time to rehearse, he wanted to do some of his new material but we only had two or three hours booked. We eventually decided that the easiest thing for us to do was a cover of Patti Smith's "Pumping My Heart" and "Lovers Of Today" for the encore."

At the Underworld The Heart Throbs ran through their set with good-natured resignation, aware that the audience was predominantly Perrett's. When the fans first caught sight of the diminutive singer/songwriter, they surged towards the stage. Peter luxuriated in the response as he struck the first chord and faced the crowd. Peter:

> "I got such a buzz out of it. When I went on everybody started shouting and screaming. It just felt so great. After the gig I couldn't sleep for nights from the excitement. Zena said to me, 'You've got to get a band together and start playing live'."

Amongst the many people who came forward to congratulate Perrett after the gig, was an old friend called Steve Brickle, who runs a merchandising business. He suggested that Peter should come over to his house and try jamming with his wife, Miyuki, a classically trained pianist and talented keyboard player. While Peter accepted Steve's social invitation, he logged the musical proposal at the back of his mind.

THE ONE AND ONLY: Peter Perrett - Homme Fatale

The year drew to a close with nothing of any particular substance tied up in a bundle of vague prospects. One further gig of such a low key nature came and went without barely anyone hearing of it. On December 20th, Peter and John Perry ducked into a basement club on Oxford street, for a guest spot with an outfit known as The Pleasure Victims. John Perry:

> "They were some grubby semi-glam outfit — Peter was appalled — but the point was to play to some management people we were talking to who, to be blunt, wanted to see for themselves if Peter was physically up to playing live."

The new year saw yet another resurrection of "Another Girl, Another Planet" only this time it went out with The Psychedelic Furs' "Pretty In Pink" on the flip side. The single, which reached number 41 in the network charts, was released to promote the new wave compilation *Sound Of The Suburbs* (CBS), but the album that really made an impression was the definitive, 21-track, Only Ones collection *The Immortal Story* (CBS). Compiled by Peter with backline support from Adrian Maddox and Henry Williams, it received a standing ovation in critical terms. David Hepworth in *Q* magazine:

> "The Only Ones' noise hasn't dated, which is one of the few advantages of being an anachronism. Were they to be starting out in 1992, they would spark a bitter bidding war between Creation and Heavenly and probably go straight into the top 5. And Mike Kellie would be allowed to boast about having been in Spooky Tooth."

Following the release of *The Immortal Story*, Adrian Maddox sought the faintly glowing neon exit sign that was barely visible in the fog of confusion that perpetually surrounded the Perretts. Adrian Maddox:

> "It's hard to describe how two and a half years can drag by with almost nothing happening, punctuated by outbursts of panic. Although it could be construed as negative in a professional sense, I do feel that during the time I was with him, even though he refused to sign a management contract, that I advanced his career in a series of stages. It's just that in between, there were these huge pauses with the two of them pulling away from everything, when you couldn't even make contact with Peter. That's why it couldn't go ahead, pure self-destructiveness. There were

too many crises and catastrophes. It was almost supernatural. I couldn't deal with it any more. It was like having a poltergeist in the house."

In mid-May, Peter and John Perry spent three days in a studio located in Euston, called The Beat Factory, where they put down four songs "Land Of The Free", "She Dreamt She Could Fly", "Love At All Costs" and "Black From Red". John Perry:

> "The basic tracks went down beautifully but I have to say that Peter was all over the place during the overdubs. In the middle of some prosaic operation — say comping vocal parts — a detail would catch his ear and without being able to clearly express what he wanted he'd set the engineer to chase the idea. The poor engineer would consequently spend thirty minutes completely resetting the board when a new, unrelated, but even *more* exciting idea would flash across Peter's brain, and countermanding the original order he'd lurch off on an entirely new tangent. Adding reverb to echoes of echoes. I'm all for inspiration but you have to have a sense of process. Those sessions turned out OK, but it looked to me as though it'd just get worse as we got into better equipped studios. More toys, less focus. Sad, 'cos the songs were sounding powerful."

The Beat Factory sessions came towards the end of a sporadic yet intense period of Perrett and Perry related activity. John had attempted to co-ordinate a series of meetings with potential management and producers as well as working on percentages and a plan of action to launch their partnership into full flight. Eventually, the scheme fell apart as John began to realise that the pitfalls that had engulfed The Only Ones were reappearing, while Peter in turn had become convinced that the only way forward lay in getting a completely new band together. John Perry:

> "Clearly Peter had been proceeding on two fronts, trying to play all ends against the middle. The work I did with him in the studio was done from the start on the basis of a partnership, with percentages and divisions of revenues defined. It was a new way of working for Peter and one that he didn't entirely care for. He put up with it because it was the only way I was going to work, but at the same time he was using the Henry's and the Maddox's to see if he could pull in a solo offer.

THE ONE AND ONLY: Peter Perrett - Homme Fatale

The business side of The Only Ones was always conducted in a sort of fog, a cloud which grew more nebulous the closer you approached any specific detail — subsequently it emerged that no accounts were ever kept — and by about May '92 the same sort of confusion was starting to grow up around the new venture. Time to go. In one of Peter's more candid actions, he later placed an ad in the *Melody Maker* saying Peter Perrett seeks *backing* musicians, and what became The One were recruited. I stopped working with Peter and resumed my friendship with him."

Following Zena's perseverance and Steve Brickle's oft-repeated invitations, Peter finally checked out Miyuki's musical abilities in April '93. The prelude to the formation of The One began. Peter:

"All the time Zena had been saying, 'You've got to get a band together', but since she got involved with drugs, I suppose I respected her opinion less, but because she'd been going on about it, and then Steve started hassling me to go and play with Miyuki, I was talked into going around to Steve's with my acoustic guitar. I hadn't done anything about it for ages 'cos I thought, 'Oh she's just Steve's wife, it's not likely that she's going to be a great keyboard player', but she was brilliant. Miyuki has a great feel and technique. It was then, that Steve said, 'If you want to look for other musicians, I'll pay for it'."

In classic fashion, for the first two weeks of the *Melody Maker* ad's run, the wrong number was printed. Once the misprint was corrected, the auditions went ahead at Terminal rehearsal studios in August. Everyone from Perrett freaks who couldn't play a note but just wanted to catch a glimpse of the pale poet, to established musicians who brought their own roadies, came down for the occasion. All of the serious contenders had been briefed in advance to learn "Another Girl, Another Planet" and "The Big Sleep". As Miyuki was already established as a member of Perrett's new band, she shared in the decision of the final vote on the musicians who made it on to the short-list. Miyuki:

"Richard Vernon was an easy choice, he is a very good bass player. We had some powerful drummers but Steve Hands was the most musical."

Above: The One (l-r); Richard Vernon, Jay Price, Steve Hands, Miyuki, Peter Perrett, outside the basement flat.

The choice of guitarist was a little less immediate. For a while a Dutch musician called Robin from The Fatal Flowers was favoured, but ultimately it was the languidly pretty 24-year-old Jay Price, with his deft touch in melodic pop psychedelia, who got the part.

The rest of the year was spent in becoming acclimatised to one another and rehearsing in the downstairs area of the Big House. Even though Peter made himself relatively accessible to the members of The One, he is rarely communicative outside of making music, and still remains something of an enigma to the band. Jay Price:

"He's not the easiest of people to get to know. I've never really thought Peter's ever taken in anything I said. At first I found it really off-putting, but then you realise he's actually taken it all in, which is a credit to him. Peter is a really intelligent person, but I think that sometimes his intelligence doesn't come across because he's so introverted. He says that words are precious. I think he's a bit barmy as well. Whether he lost the plot before — I mean that in a nice way — he's just got a weird angle on life."

In January '94, Peter and The One made their debut at The Milky Way in Amsterdam. Steve Hands:

"We were all in the dressing room, nervous as hell and Pete turned to us just before we went on and told us we were like a little team going out to play a game. He's really sweet in ways like that, he said, 'Go out there and do it, none of you have anything to prove'. It was a brilliant show. The first English gig was different again, at the Underworld on January 25th, I was really nervous. It was packed to the rafters and quite emotional."

The gentle devotion that the audience bestowed upon Peter at the Underworld seemed to have more to do with love than rock 'n' roll. For Perrett, it wasn't just a one way affair. Peter:

"My desire to get love from people is almost obscene. Before, with The Only Ones, in a way I resented having to be that public. Although I obviously enjoyed the audience reaction, I didn't really appreciate them. Now, I get a lot of pleasure from being able to put smiles on people's faces. I think it's like when you're young, you want the girl to come 'cos it's good for your ego but when you're old, you want a girl to come because you love her and want to please her. That's the difference between how I think of audiences, it's just growing up."

Further gigs around London showcased Peter's newer material, such as the enchanting "Daughter" (released on a CD sampler in Volume Ten magazine, '94), "Wildlife", "Twilight World" and the wrenching "You Gave Birth" as well as a selection of Only Ones' classics. In April, recording began at The Gallery, financed by Steve Brickle, where they put down four tracks — "Baby Don't Talk", "Twilight World", the melancholy "Made To Fall Apart" and "The Company Of Strangers". The songs were originally intended for demo use only, but were later released as the *Cultured Palate* EP (Dwarf Records - Oct '94). That these were early days in The One's development is apparent. The mix is not the most complementary but it's a committed effort and Peter's gift for delivering tragedy in exquisite disguise makes Edith Piaf sound almost jovial.

After a brief recess, the band prepared for a short tour of Japan — three nights at The Loft in Tokyo and one at the Osaka Music Hall. A couple of days into the trip, Zena had to fly home leaving Peter to fend for himself. Without Zena by his side, Perrett became in turn, ill-tempered and overly vulnerable. He found solace in the tranquillity of a temple in the city. Steve Hands:

"Tokyo is like New York, a high rise, crazy city. In the middle of all this chaos, there was a beautiful little temple. Peter said he loved the ritual and asked if I would like to come and join him. Before you pray in the Buddhist way, you wash in some water, throw in coins and then ring a bell. He asked me if there was anything I wanted to pray about. He told me to pray for three things that I really wanted to happen."

Two years later, it seems as if Peter's prayers fell short of heaven. The One are still together but they have become increasingly disengaged from Perrett. After the initial burst of activity in '94 which culminated in a short British tour, their live appearances are now few and far between. In Autumn '95, Peter and The One signed to Demon Records, and this year saw the release of the *Woke Up Sticky* EP and an album of the same title. Producer Marc Waterman applied a firm hand to the album's proceedings. While this freed Perrett to concentrate solely on his music, Waterman's crisp technique banishes any fanciful or romantically dishevelled moments that have their place in Peter's spectrum. The band are compressed and curtailed and the nervous energy they exuded live, is dismissed in favour of a single emotional plane. Nevertheless, Perrett's songs can still be sublime. Each nightmare crawls out from under the bed, every sorrow is pinned up against the wall like a tormented butterfly.

Woke Up Sticky received mixed but generally favourable reactions. Inevitable and often unfair comparisons were drawn with The Only Ones. Peter views his work with The One as his expression of the present and therefore his most vital statement but such an influential, gilded musical history will not disappear into the great goodnight of former glories. As Peter puts it, "It's difficult writing about The One because it's still an unfinished story".

Compounding The Only Ones' ongoing posthumous career, *Live At The BBC* (BBC Worldwide/Windsong) was released in the spring and the Lightning Seeds covered "Another Girl, Another Planet" for the flip-side of their *Ready Or Not* EP (Epic).

Naturally, Peter has grand ambitions for The One and wants to go on and make more albums and acquire some financial security, but he is wary of embracing the kind of fragile dreams that vanish with the first, cold light of morning, just as he is retiring to bed. Peter:

> "I believe that if you start thinking about the good times, they won't happen. You have to concentrate on now. It's terrible isn't it? As you get older you're beaten down, but when you're young, you're optimistic about everything. I feel like two different people. As far as my songs are going, I'm still untouchable, but anything that doesn't have to do with my music, I feel very vulnerable."

The future of the Big House still hangs in the balance. The council have agreed to give the Perretts a restoration grant but their bank is still piling up exorbitant interest on Number 3, leaving Peter and Zena in considerable debt. The grim possibility of repossession still looms, if the Perretts cannot come up with a regular repayment scheme. Zena remains damaged by the past and their seemingly unending problems, but as a couple who have recently celebrated 25 years together, they are inseparable. Zena:

Above: The One play the Splash Club in Kings Cross, Jay Price and Peter.

Below: Peter joins Therapy? on stage at the Shepherd's Bush Empire.

> "When he got the group together, I thought things were changing. I expected things to be a lot better than they are. I just feel that a lot has to come from us before things happen, maybe a lot has to come from me, I don't know. When I see Peter up on stage, I realise how happy he is. He's doing something fresh and he's excited by it — I didn't think that anything could touch me again. After the last ten years I feel a bit dead inside. I suppose I'd like to be more in control of my life."

Despite all the difficulties, the basement flat is nearly always filled with live music, and the front room has become Peter junior and Jamie's cramped rehearsal space. At 17 and 13 respectively, the boys have formed a band, The Cunts — "'Cos that's what our dad used to call us!"

Jamie is every inch his father's son, from the way that he moves, to the manner is which he picks up his Gibson semi-acoustic 345. Peter Junior has inherited his mother's serious streak, and is a less flashy performer than his little brother, but the differences in style and personality enhance their joint effort. The boys have regular guitar lessons with John Perry, who they consider to be a brilliant teacher and receive on-going guidance from their father. Peter:

> "Family life's good 'cos I get a buzz from hearing the kids play. They come out with some great things and at least I know I've given them one positive thing in life, their music. They wouldn't consider being anything else in life but being in a band."

Above: The Big House in Forest Hill.

Leave it all behind
It's up to you
Who wants to be happy forever?
Up to you
You know that fate brought us together
And when time has left you too weak to resist
I hope you will remember this

(From "Someone Who Cares" by Peter Perrett)

Nina Antonia and Peter Perrett in summer 1995.

About the Author

Nina Antonia is a regular contributor to music publications like *Mojo* and *Record Collector*. She is the author of *In Cold Blood*, an authorised Johnny Thunders' biography which was originally published in 1987 and has been updated for re-release soon. Nina ponders deeply over William Blake's notion that "the road of excess leads to the palace of wisdom". Aside from her writing, she is training to be a drug counsellor.

The Cast

Mick Atkins regrets "wasting years and years taking drugs. If I'd have stayed with music, I probably would have got into something more successful, developed a bit of a career, possibly".

Kathy Barrett still lives in South London. She is now married and has another child.

David Clarke thought Peter had died until he heard The One were gigging. He is now a rock 'n' roll dispatch rider.

Giovanni Dadomo says he is, "Trying to stop drinking before it kills me", and that he would prefer it if nobody lived out the examples of those he has loved and lost from Sid (Vicious) to Johnny Thunders.

Koulla Kakoulli married Malcolm Hart in 1981. They had two children, Alf ie and Loulla. She formed High Time with her husband but the band split up, along with their marriage. She has since settled down with the new man in her life, Andy, and had another child in '93 called Nico. She would like to return to the music business.

Mike Kellie. Since returning from Canada after the retirement of The Only Ones, Kellie has been a shepherd in North Wales. He has recently recorded an album with former Spooky Tooth colleague Luther Grosvenor, entitled *Floodgates,* which will be released in August '96. As a practising Christian, Kellie is still writing and recording. He will be performing live with a new band in the near future.

Nick Kent lives in Paris with his partner Laurence Romance, and their young son James. His selected writings on rock music *The Dark Stuff* was published by Penguin in '94. He is currently writing a novel and a Neil Young biography is promised.

Adrian Maddox now works as a television producer and editor.

Alan Mair: "It was only 6 weeks after I joined The Only Ones that we recorded the songs " Breaking Down" and "Out There In The Night". At that point I thought this is a very special band with one of the all time great songwriters. I still think this today, but I knew during the last American tour that we had taken the band as far as it could go, so it was time to move on. After The Only Ones disbanded, I remained in Los Angeles doing production work. I eventually returned to London, to write and record some songs I had been commissioned to write for a film. I have remained in London doing production work and writing. I am currently completing some recording with my new band 4 AM, which will be released in the autumn."

Pete Makowski hitchhiked for the very first time in his life to see Peter and The One play at the Joiner's Arms in Southampton. He is now drug free and works at a needle exchange in Dorset.

Jon Newey subsequently played and recorded with a number of bands including Nick Kent's Subterraneans and Chris Jagger's Atcha, as well as working for *Sounds* from 1977-91. Currently he is publisher of *TOP* magazine and writes for a number of other music publications and books.

David Sandison is trying to make a living as writer "having got real about rock 'n' roll". However, he buys two lottery tickets a week and if he wins he will go back into rock management, despite all the grief he knows it will entail.

Lynne Shillingford is now married with children and lives in Hong Kong. She sends the Perretts cards at Christmas and the boys birthday greetings, every year, without fail.

Henry Williams has vanished.

Other titles from SAF Publishing

Cabaret Voltaire - The Art Of The Sixth Sense by Mick Fish & Dave Hallbery (2nd edition) — currently out of print.

Tape Delay by Charles Neal (2nd edition) — £11.95. Features: Nick Cave, New Order, The Fall, Lydia Lunch, E. Neubauten, Psychic TV, Swans and many more.

The Can Book by Pascal Bussy & Andy Hall — £8.95.

Wire... Everybody Loves A History by Kevin Eden — £9.95.

Kraftwerk: Man, Machine and Music by Pascal Bussy — £11.95

Meet The Residents by Ian Shirley — currently out of print

Wrong Movements - A Robert Wyatt History by Mike King — £14.95.

Dark Entries: Bauhaus & Beyond by Ian Shirley — £11.95.

Plunderphonics, 'Pataphysics & Pop Mechanics by Andrew Jones — £12.95. Features: Chris Cutler, Fred Frith, Henry Threadgill, The Residents and many more

Forthcoming

No More Mr Nice Guy - The Inside Story of the Alice Cooper Group by Michael Bruce (original guitarist with the group) — Due autumn 1996.

Digital Gothic - A critical discography of Tangerine Dream by Paul Stump — Due spring 1997

Necessity Is.... (featuring original memebers of the Mothers of Invention). Coming soon

BOOK TRADE DISTRIBUTION

UK & Europe: Airlift Book Co, 8 The Arena, Mollison Ave, Enfield, Middx. UK.
Tel: 0l81-804 0400 Fax: 0l81-804 0044

USA: Last Gasp, 777 Florida Street, San Francisco, CA94110.
Tel:415 824 6636 Fax: 415 824 1836

Canada: Marginal Distribution, Unit 102, 277 George St North, Peterborough, Ontario, Canada K9J 3G9. Tel/Fax: 705 745 2326

Also : Cargo, Caroline Export, Firebird (USA), Impetus, Lasgo Export, ReR, See Hear (USA), These, Tower, Touch, Virgin, Wayside Music (USA), and all good bookshops.

Mail order: Direct from SAF Publishing at address below. Payment can be made by cheque or Mastercard/Visa/cheques. (All foreign cheques must be in pounds sterling and drawn on a British bank.)

Postage per book: UK Free — Europe £2 — Rest of the World £4 (air mail).

If you require further information, details about foreign rights, or book proposals contact:
**SAF Publishing Ltd, 12 Conway Gardens, Wembley, Mid dx. HA9 8TR, England.
Tel: +44 (0)181 904 6263 — Fax: +44 (0)181 930 8765**